Lost Worlds

STUDIES IN EARLY MODERN GERMAN HISTORY

H. C. Eric Midelfort, Editor

Lost Worlds

How Our European
Ancestors Coped with
Everyday Life and Why
Life Is So Hard Today

*(Die verlorenen Welten. Alltagsbewältigung durch unsere
Vorfahren—und weshalb wir uns heute so schwer damit tun)*

Arthur E. Imhof

Translated by
Thomas Robisheaux

University Press
of Virginia

*Charlottesville
and London*

Publication of this translation was assisted
by a grant from Inter Nationes.

Originally published in German as
Die verlorenen Welten. Alltagsbewältigung durch unsere
Vorfahren—und weshalb wir uns heute so schwer damit tun
by C. H. Beck'sche Verlagsbuchhandlung
(Oscar Beck), München, 1984.

THE UNIVERSITY PRESS OF VIRGINIA
Translation and preface © 1996 by the
Rector and Visitors of the University of Virginia

First published 1996

⊗ The paper used in this publication meets the minimum
requirements of the American National Standard for Information
Sciences—Permanence of Paper for Printed Library
Materials, ANSI Z39.48-1984.

Library of Congress Cataloging-in-Publication Data

Imhof, Arthur Erwin.
    [Verlorenen Welten.   English]
    Lost worlds : how our European ancestors coped with everyday life and why
life is so hard today / Arthur E. Imhof ; translated by Thomas Robisheaux.
        p.   cm.—(Studies in early modern German history)
    Includes bibliographical references and index.
    ISBN 0-8139-1659-3. —ISBN 0-8139-1666-6 (pbk. : alk. paper)
    1. Social history.   2. Germany—Social conditions.   I. Title.
II. Series.
HN13.I4713   1996
306'.0943—dc20   96-6721
                                                                     CIP

0-8139-1659-3 (cloth)
0-8139-1666-6 (paper)

Printed in the United States of America

Dedicated to the memory of
Erwin, 1943–1982, and
Robert M. Netting, 1934–1995

Contents

Illustrations

Translator's Introduction

THIS LIVELY LITTLE BOOK is a rarity of modern academic literature: an original and scholarly history written in an accessible and engaging style. The title conveys the author's belief that knowledge about the past should not be the private and esoteric preserve of academic historians. Indeed knowledge about the worlds that immediately preceded our own may help anyone trying to come to terms with the meaning of life, death, and dying today.

This little volume is about daily life in the not so distant past, the age before industrialized urban life, modern science, and technology. Over the last thirty years everyday life has become one of the most discussed topics among historians of premodern Europe. In the past historians generally paid scant attention to the mundane events of everyday life. Great events and great leaders were thought to be the only subjects worthy of the historian's attention. The reader may be familiar with the work of Fernand Braudel, the great French historian who, as one of the first to call our attention to the neglected world of the everyday, showed us, and showed us brilliantly, why we should care about population, diet, housing, money, and transport in the preindustrial world.

Since Braudel's time this new kind of history has become well established across the Western world. In Germany it is often known as *Alltagsgeschichte,* or "everyday history." In fact, the German title of Imhof's work, *Die verlorenen Welten,* cleverly evokes the spirit of one of the classics in modern social history, Peter Laslett's *The World We Have Lost.* Imhof freely acknowledges his debt to Laslett, calling Laslett's book the "godfather" of his own. Like Laslett, Imhof was trained in demography and family history. They share an interest in the family and the household and the raw statistical facts of life—birth rates, death rates, age at marriage—that made life so different in the preindustrial world. But Imhof sees the past differently from Laslett. "I do not think that just *one* world has been lost to us, but many little worlds," Imhof writes. For him people in the past lived in countless little worlds, worlds that were unique, localized, and highly individualistic. We should be careful not to make them seem drab, colorless, and uniform. Indeed it is we, not our ancestors, who have created the standardized life cycle most of us today experience.

Perhaps one reason for this caution about life in the past is Imhof's perspective as a historian of Central Europe. Some historians like to think of the German past as peculiar and different and implicitly assume that the histories of England and France were more normative for Europe as a whole. This is a deceptive notion. These countries evolved under unified monarchies, and their histories may give the misleading impression that the premodern past was more uniform than it in fact was. The pattern Imhof identifies for people in German-speaking Central Europe was actually more common for Europeans. Most people identified themselves first with the family and household, a village or small town. They spoke a local dialect, shared in a regional culture, and were only vaguely aware of the affairs of the kingdom. The main character of this book, a peasant by the name of Johannes Hooss, is a classic example of this traditional way of life. Johannes Hooss may have lived in a remote village in Hesse, a small and fragmented principality in the Holy Roman Empire, but many aspects of his life were shared by millions of Europeans in the early modern era.

Imhof is one of the most original minds writing history in Germany today. He was born in Switzerland in 1939, studied in Belgium, Italy, and Germany, and is currently Professor of History at the Free University of Berlin. His earlier work focused on the population history of the region around Giessen, Germany. The reader will notice that his interest in historical demography provides him with the starting point for this book as well. In this case, however, he leaves the narrow world of historical demography and branches out into folklore, religion, anthropology, psychology, art history, and other disciplines.

His eclecticism and his boldness in addressing modern problems has naturally drawn the criticism of specialists. These features of his work are what give it charm and a broad and interdisciplinary appeal. Imhof himself shrugs off such criticisms. He believes that academic historians have a role to play in addressing the issues of our day, that they should not remain isolated in their ivory towers. He is well known to the German public. Since this book was first published, in 1985, he has published a number of equally engaging books, including *In the Gallery of History, or A Historian Looks at Pictures; The Art of Living;* and, most recently, *The Art of Dying.* The titles of these books suggest why his lectures and workshops are as well attended by demographers, art historians, physicians, counselors, and other health care professionals as by historians.

The reader should not be surprised that this book addresses major and troubling problems familiar to all of us today: the search for meaningful values in life, the ethical problems created by long life expectancies, the meaning of death. Some readers may find their cherished notions about the superiority of our modern culture and technology challenged. But Imhof does not call for a return to the "good old days." He is not a romantic. He does want us to respect the lives of people who lived in the past, however, and to learn, where we can, that the answers to modern problems require the wisdom of the humanist as much as the knowledge of the scientist.

Preface

THIS BOOK TOOK SHAPE while I was traveling. A research leave, combined with a leave of absence during the 1982–83 academic year, had made it possible for me to participate in several exchange programs and to give a number of guest lectures. In my suitcase I carried only the figures, graphs, and illustrations that would serve as teaching aids at various universities as far away as Cape Town, Jerusalem, Kyoto, Bloomington, and San Francisco.

One of the consequences of writing without the help of books and journals from my institute and the libraries at home is a book almost completely lacking in scholarly footnotes and having only a short general bibliography at the end. All of the comments accompanying the illustrations, however, refer to the precise sources I consulted at the time I was working on them.

One can reflect about history without relying on specialized books and journals. It often seems to me, in fact, that the more distance you have from them the better it becomes. If you are interested in the history of common people and everyday life, as in this case, you can start anywhere and anytime. The drama of human life unfolds in every corner of the world. The facts of life—birth, growing up, maturing, marriage, having children, getting sick, growing old, and dying—are experiences familiar enough to everyone. But instead of reading about them you observe them firsthand, talk about them, experience them, and then stand back and reflect on it all.

You quickly discover, however, that the same biological events that everyone experiences—birth, growing up, maturing, growing frail, death and dying—do not have the same meaning for everyone and for every group in the world. But however stimulating and eye-opening cross-cultural comparisons may be, they are not the subject of this work, nor do I have the qualifications to discuss them. What I have been asked to do, what is the exclusive goal of this book, is to discuss aspects of everyday life in Central Europe over the last three to five hundred years as exactly as possible, showing the sources and methods with which this kind of history can be done and sharing my thoughts about it. These are the only goals of the chapters that follow.

Everywhere I went the starting points of my discussions were the same: the figures, graphs, and illustrations that appear in this book. Each discussion, however, took a different turn depending on where I was and what the disciplinary interests of the audience were. Even though we generally agreed that similar findings here and there could have completely different causes and that we should not make comparisons without considering time and place, comparisons almost always came up. And why not make comparisons? What was the harm in South African colleagues, after listening to a presentation of material from chapter 5, openly wondering whether the "cultural improvement" of the black population, a process carried out according to Christian precepts and still undertaken there with missionary zeal, was not leading to the opposite of what was intended? The entire cosmologies of African tribes were attacked until they disintegrated. Only then was it discovered that the Christian worldview offered in their place was out of keeping with the realities of everyday life. South Africa's black people were therefore robbed of their old values while the new eternity that was promised them was already obsolete. A void was opening up for them, but it could not be filled by a world materially better off but strictly this-worldly in its orientation. A fair trade-off? I doubt it.

In other places the concepts I brought with me were developed and elaborated in new ways. During a stay in Jerusalem, for example, I was reminded of how the ideas and aspirations of people continually threatened with survival revolve around stabilizing principles over generations and how they provide an anchor that transcends the individual even in the most difficult times. To so many Jews, scattered to the winds for many centuries, no other place on the globe united them spiritually as did Jerusalem, the center of their world and worldview, an idea uniquely summed up in Henricus Bünting's map of the world, published in Helmstedt in 1585 (fig. 1).

Despite all of the stimulating ideas and discussions of this sort, this book is based strictly on the material I know well from my own work and research on Central Europe. Here, and here only, can I make well-founded arguments and stand by them. In doing so I would not claim that these materials and the examples I have chosen and worked on have any greater weight than others do. The case study I have chosen—Johannes Hooss, his everyday world, and the Vältes Farm which was the center of his and some of our forbears' world and worldview—is not what is important here. What are important are the fundamental questions and general problems that arise from such a case study: people's need for stability and for a meaningful worldview, for example, values around which life can revolve that transcend the individual and which last for generations. That the reader should be

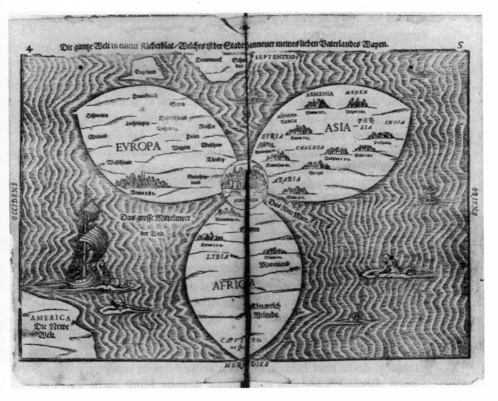

1.   Map of the world as a clover leaf with Jerusalem in the center. From Henricus Bünting (1545–1606), *Itinerarium Sacrae Scripturae: Das ist, Ein Reisebuch, über die gantze heilige Schrifft* (Helmstedt: Lucius, 1585), 4–5. *Source:* Herzog August Bibliothek, Wolfenbüttel, sig. Jb 4° 11. The idea of Jerusalem as the center of the world was hardly alien to Christianity. Here Christ suffered and died on the cross. Henricus Bünting was born in Hannover and educated in Württemberg as a Protestant minister. His travel book was published in numerous editions and translated into several European languages.

moved to reflect about his or her own world and worldview at the end is inherent in the nature of writing such a book. The more this happens with this book, the more successfully I have achieved my goal.

Without the help of others this book would never have been written. I would like to thank the following institutions for their generous material support: the German Academic Exchange Service in Bonn-Bad Godesberg; the Union Internationale pour l'Etude Scientifique de la Population, with headquarters in Liège; the Goethe Institutes in Munich and Kyoto; the National Science Foundation in Washington, D.C.; the American Association for the History of Medicine (especially Professor Toby Gelfand in Ottawa, Canada); the University of Pretoria (Professor F. A. van Jaarsvel); the Hebrew University in Jerusalem (Professor U. O. Schmelz); and the Volkswagenwerk Foundation, Hannover, for years of generous research support. For a sabbatical leave I want to thank the Free University of Berlin and colleagues in the History Department who showed understanding for this project. Not least of all I thank my own research group at the Friedrich Meinecke-Institute, especially Joachim Allmann for a great deal of critical advice, and Gert Schulze and Gabriele Giesecke, who transformed the results of the research into graphic form. These days it does not strike me as superfluous to thank Beck Publishers for their willingness to publish this book, and Dr. Ernst-Peter Wieckenberg in particular for very much appreciated editorial help.

Lost Worlds

Introduction

WHEN COMPUTERS WERE introduced into the discipline of history several years ago, a number of things suddenly seemed much easier to historians. The computer relieved us of time-consuming and tedious work, especially when dealing with long series of numbers. If data about prices, wages, numbers of cattle, crop yields, temperatures, rainfall, state and church taxes, age at marriage or death, family size, and the frequency of remarriage over dozens of years or decades were fed into a computer for a particular region, for example, within seconds it provided printouts about long-term climatic change. Even more, if we wanted, it would also tell us what effect these changes had on crop yields and cattle herds, and how these, in turn, affected prices and wages, increases and decreases in the age of marriage, the numbers of infant births and deaths per family, and the average life expectancy in a particular year.

In the beginning we were like blind people looking at all of these new statistics that poured out. We were literally blind, since for a long time we could not see that we had programmed the computers as "modern people" with a modern perspective on the past. From the computers we actually only wanted to know about things that interested us today.

This is of course not the fault of the computer. One cannot blame the computer for its lack of intelligence, that it is only capable of carrying out commands, even if it often does so with incredible, even blinding efficiency. The fact that it could easily calculate statistics to the tenth decimal point without a single pause led us into a false sense of security; it led us to believe that we could now know exactly how things were in the past. I don't object to this kind of historical research in itself. As is well known, every generation rewrites the past. As new sources and technical aids become available, they will understandably be put to use, naturally to answer questions that seem important at the time.

My unease actually stemmed from the fact that in the midst of all of this, one thing was missing: how our forebears viewed the past through their own eyes. Their concerns were often entirely different from our own, and it occurred to me more and more that we were approaching many problems improperly. Often we even asked the wrong questions. We were interested, for example, in knowing about the increase in life expectancy over the last several generations and, pointing proudly to our computer printouts, could boast about how life expectancy doubled and even tripled from about thirty years to sixty or seventy or more years today.

But this reflected our own concerns. What our ancestors would have thought about it is an entirely different matter. Even if they would have understood the issue and would not have stood around shaking their heads about it, the question itself would probably have seemed strange to them. Terms like *life, lifespan,* and *life expectancy* had completely different meanings to them. For them life consisted of two parts. The first part, a person's earthly existence, was more or less important and was filled with activity. The second part, the eternal part, was longer, incomparably more significant, and involved salvation in the afterlife. What difference then does it make whether one dies at age ten, twenty, fifty, sixty, eighty, or even a hundred? How naive it is to ask about increasing life expectancy! What does one mean by *increasing* life expectancy? While we were apparently increasing life expectancy in a dramatic way, were we not simultaneously disconnecting ourselves from the eternal part of life as a result of de-Christianizing our worldview? What difference does it make to double or triple the only part of life that is left to us, our earthly lifespan, when we have lost eternity! Increasing it five- or tenfold would still not amount to anything!

I have therefore attempted in this book to look at the world of our forebears through their own eyes. If it did not sound so grandiose, one could also say that I want to do them justice. I wanted to know what they thought their own problems were, what those problems looked like, and how they came to terms with them. There was therefore nothing else for me to do than to reconstruct their world from the ground up and to bring to life, as precisely as possible, the living conditions for this or that group. I therefore stepped back from the computer and all of the magnetic tapes and looked individually at these ancestors of ours before they disappeared by the thousands into the computer, only to appear anonymously again at the end as statistical averages. From my sources—the church books, tax lists, court records, cadastres, inheritance contracts, wills, and protocols—I knew each one by name. I knew when they were born, whom they grew up with, when and whom they married, and how many children they had. I also knew how many horses, sheep, oxen, and cows they had, as well as how many meadows, pastures, fields, vegetable gardens, barns, and stalls. I even knew what services and dues they owed their lords, what offices they held, and more.

In the end my choice fell on Johannes Hooss, a peasant who lived on the Vältes Farm in the north Hessian village of Laimbach from 1670 to 1755. If I were asked how typical he and his everyday problems were for the seventeenth and eighteenth centuries, I would respond immediately with the disappointing answer, "Not at all!" I would also point out, however, that this is the wrong question to ask. There are representative life courses only when people live roughly the same length of time, and such has been the case for only a few generations. Back then one person died in infancy, another in old age, and yet another died sometime in between. One mother died while giving birth to her first child, but another died long after she had buried every single one of her children. What does a statistical "average age" of thirty possibly tell us about this period? It actually confuses us about the realities of the time more than it explains them.

Nonetheless I devote the entire first chapter, "The Little World of Johannes Hooss," to this single person. The one that follows it is called "A Multitude of Little Worlds." What I am initially interested in showing is how the world of just one of our ancestors may have looked. How did he create a network of people during his life? Which social ties were the strongest ones and which the weakest? How far did his network extend, and at what point was he drawn into other people's networks? How was he influenced by space and time, by collective memories about his parents' farm, the village, and the region? Johannes Hooss is not the one who was typical in this case. What was typical was the smallness of the world our ancestors lived in. Johannes simply illustrates in a concrete way one of the many possibilities of the time.

There were a multitude of these little worlds in the past. In the second chapter there follow some reflections on the forces that shaped them: geographic location, the distribution of land between arable and woods, urban and rural settlement patterns, farm size, land use, property relationships, political power, religious confession, and much more. It should be obvious at this point that there was no typical single farm or community. In the same way that every life course was unique and colorful, different from any other at the time in ways that are not the case today, so it was with every piece of property, every farm, and every community. What was typical was the colorful mosaic-like quality of life: the richness and multiplicity of possibilities, the lack of uniformity.

As I reconstructed these worlds I often felt that the typical sources of the historian mentioned above were inadequate to the task. Here and there I added to them ones less commonly used: from paintings in art museums and stone images carved on public buildings to literary works and fairy tales. The historian has to be cautious in using this evidence, since paintings, fairy tales, and symbols are not reflections of a single reality from the past. As a result, they cannot be used uncritically. But within the context of our questions they give rise to reflection, especially when discussions with colleagues from other disciplines make their interpretation more certain. What I often discovered was that other scholars had asked these same questions in their own way long before the historians did. As a result, I have learned a great deal from folklorists about pre-Reformation remnants in the religion of the common people in Protestant regions, and from other scholars I learned about the development, purpose, and usefulness of the concept of cultural regions and their traditions.

However colorful and different from each other these little worlds may have been two to four hundred years ago, they all shared one feature in common: their very existence was constantly threatened. Since time immemorial our ancestors have prayed, "Protect us, oh Lord, from plague, famine, and war!" Chapter 3 shows, however, that between 1550 and 1700 they had more reason for this desperate plea than did many generations before or since. The extent of the devastation from these three scourges peaked at the same time during this period. They spread like wildfire through the human and animal populations and laid waste entire stretches of countryside. Those parts of the population ravaged repeatedly and severely by these scourges were gradually traumatized and showed lasting consequences in their collective attitudes toward life.

By their nature human beings have neither succumbed willingly and permanently to adverse conditions nor stood idly by and accepted life-threatening conditions, whether in these regions or in others that were less seriously afflicted. People have always protected themselves, creating some grip on life that could support them through it all. They have sought long-term stability. Chapter 4 examines this struggle. What especially impressed me were the ways in which our forebears achieved a kind of stability that endured for generations. Experience taught them that they had only a limited chance of survival against plague, famine, and war once these broke out in their little worlds. The plague did not spare the wealthiest among them. Crop failures struck even the largest of farms, and war made no distinctions between wealthy and poor.

These experiences led to the wise realization that a stable world was not to be built upon the life of the individual. On the contrary, in an age in which every individual life was constantly threatened and insecure, such a pursuit would have led to extreme instability. Only in modern times can one count on the individual in the long run, since all of us live relatively long lives of sixty, seventy, or eighty years. It is sensible and worthwhile today to invest in an individual human life. In the past other values necessarily predominated, values that outlived the uncertain lives of individuals. What was of decisive importance at any single moment was not the individual farmholder and his personal well-being, for example, but the welfare and the reputation of the farm itself. What mattered was not the family living there at the moment, but the family succession, the family line. Generation after generation, and property holder after property holder—less as individuals than as people filling a role—revolved around this idea. An idea, a social norm, and not the individual, was at the center of the world. Our own highly developed sense of individualism and egocentrism seems to be only one of the many consequences of our having a more secure and longer life span.

Once you look for the things that made life stable in the past, you can find them everywhere. They often had to do with deliberate and systematic practices, such as refusing to split up the sizable Vältes Farm for more than four hundred years, passing it instead intact to the next generation. This custom not only guaranteed a certain prosperity to the family living there at the time, it also enabled the family to pursue the goal that was in the end more important for the farm: a subtly thought out strategy of marriage alliances. For generations the property kept its attractiveness on the marriage market because of the wealth and prestige associated with it, and this secured the farm as an integral part of an extensive and carefully developed social and economic network of farms of comparable standing. Children not inheriting the Vältes Farm did not go away empty-handed when they married. They profited from this system as much as the heirs did and therefore supported it without protest over the centuries.

Other families may not have had such opportunities, but they still achieved stability in their own way. They emphasized the role of the head of the family, for example, by giving two, three, or four children the same name. What was important was not the individual who carried a particular personal and family name but that a role be permanently filled by someone who always carried this name. Despite the high infant and childhood mortality of the time, one child always survived with this name and could slip into the role sometime during his life. Even the tiniest house might remain for centuries in the hands of individuals with the same name. What was stable and survived was the name; what changed was the person who assumed the role.

Just as often, countless manifestations of the collective unconscious also provided stability in life. Since these elements endured over long periods of time, they established everywhere for our ancestors a mental framework for everyday life. As traditional values they no longer had to be continuously reflected upon, thus leading perhaps to more free time to think about more important things. The young people of a particular locale can therefore be observed as always getting married on Mondays and Tuesdays, and in other places on Saturdays or Sundays. Even though any day of the week could have been chosen for a wedding given the actual rhythm of work in the countryside, in places where weddings took place on Mondays the custom endured for centuries.

Today we have largely done away with such customs and like to make fun of what seem to us to be pointless traditions. But the question is whether instead of the supposed freedom we have gained (in this case, the choice of wedding days), we have lost in the bargain a framework for life that these customs provided. At the very least we have created more problems for ourselves.

We would not do justice to the world and worldview of our forebears were we only to discuss the threats to their physical existence that plague, famine, and war brought. The most important part of life, as I mentioned above, was the afterlife. Belief in the afterlife naturally affected people's lives in this world. What interests me are not so much the official teachings of the Christian churches as figuring out what our ancestors adopted from these teachings in dealing with their everyday lives, that is, how official ideas, often in different forms, were incorporated into their own worldview.

The Catholic Church taught that without baptism there was no hope for resurrection from the dead, for example, no possible entry into the eternal kingdom of God. The parents of many stillborn children or parents whose children died soon after birth adapted this teaching to their own circumstances in a custom never fully recognized by the church. In their despair they looked for some faint sign of life in the body, the so-called "children's life signs," to help them meet their responsibility to baptize the child and save its soul from wandering about eternally in darkness. They carried the tiny bodies to specific pilgrimage sites and waited there, praying fervently until the dead child showed signs of life—the cheeks becoming rosy, for example, from the reflection of the candles. They were baptized in this condition and then, as soon as death came again, were buried in consecrated ground. In this way the children's souls were rescued for salvation. At the same time, something was also done for the parents in return, since the "pretty little angels" that had just gone to heaven would surely, for their part, put in a good word for their fathers and mothers.

All of these examples explain not simply how our ancestors created physical stability in a threatened world, but also how they relieved themselves of the psychological strain associated with the staggering infant mortality rates of that time. From the church's teaching on baptism they took the unconditional promise of redemption and applied it, in the form of the "children's life sign," to infants who died before they received the sacrament of baptism. Despair was transformed into the certainty of salvation, and this in turn contributed to psychological stability.

Here again we find ourselves examining aspects of life that would otherwise easily escape our modern way of seeing things. By committing themselves to Christian beliefs, even unofficial ones, our ancestors also brought all of their little worlds, their microcosms, into harmony with the larger world, the macrocosm. Since God had created the bigger world, the cosmos—and the stars, heavens, earth, plants, animals, and people of which it consisted—as well as all of the smaller worlds of the same material, the macrocosm and the microcosm therefore formed a unity in which everything was related to and influenced by everything else. In our prayers today, in fact, we still say "on earth as it is in heaven." What this actually means no one any longer knows. Our horoscopes today serve as faint reminders of what was once thought to be the great influence of the stars and constellations on our well-being. Even superstitious people today no longer believe that the sun "rules" Sunday, and the moon Monday, even though everyone uses these ancient names for the days of the week.

From this idea of the harmony between microcosm and macrocosm—the way that thousands of smaller worlds were given dignity as part of a single larger world—followed the idea that even the smallest persons were never lost or left entirely to their own devices. Such a worldview, which accorded with the Christian idea that we all rest in the all-embracing arms of God, must also have contributed to a spiritual stability that was difficult to upset even during the worst outbreaks of plague, famine, and war. Chapter 4 of this book is about the broader world and the smaller worlds of our forebears and my effort to look at them through their eyes.

Chapter 5, the final chapter, on the other hand, deals with our own time and why we have such a difficult time with so many things. I did not set out to learn about the people who came before us, their problems, and how they dealt with them simply for their own sake. Not did I do so out of curiosity about their everyday troubles. And I certainly do not have a nostalgic longing for the so-called good old days. Their constant pleas for mercy before the recurrent scourges of plague, famine, and war are not so easily forgotten. I don't want to invoke here the grand notion of "learning from the past," since every part of the past is so unique that deriving lessons from it to apply to contemporary or future problems is hardly possible. Still, I believe that thinking about the world of our ancestors, and how they dealt with their challenges, is relevant to our own time. We need first to understand the trade-offs we have actually made in the making of the modern world before we can successfully approach the problems they have brought with them.

At first sight it seems that plague, famine, and war, the ancient scourges of humankind, have been tamed, if not brought under complete control, over the course of a few generations. In an earlier age these threats to human existence repeatedly led to conditions dominated by real fears. These fears have been removed today through the development of effective medicine, an abundance of food in the supermarkets, and a functional balance of nuclear terror now in existence for several decades. But the question is whether we have traded once-tangible fears for a vague and growing anxiety that is much more difficult to come to terms with. The reason for this, it seems to me, lies in the fact that the old scourges of plague, famine, and war have been removed only from the foreground of events. In reality they continue to threaten us in changed but no less unsettling forms. Instead of dying a swift death from the plague or other infectious diseases as in the past, today we die a slow and, in many cases, lingering death. We have to deal with incurable suffering, not only physically, but also psychologically. We damage our health through excessive eating and an imbalanced diet, shortening life just as famine once did in its own way. The notion that a balance of nuclear terror guarantees eternal peace is also difficult to believe.

These thoughts should make us look back with less arrogance on the world of our ancestors, plagued as it was by epidemics, malnourishment, and war. Are we really better off in this regard today? Even if this were the case, we still have more difficulty dealing with these same old problems of disease, hunger, and war in the new forms than did people in the past, since what really separates us from them is the fact that we have lost the worldview that sustained them and have not as yet replaced it. Television, telephones, travel, and satellites may have made our world much larger, but it is no longer a part of a larger whole that rests in the all-embracing arms of God. Our lives have doubled and tripled in length and have become more secure for many more years, at least in a biological sense. At the same time, however, we have lost eternity; all that is left is our physical existence. Death and dying are terminal points rather than passages to another life. A healthy body has become the sole guarantee of our lives to such an extent that we have made a fetish and an idol out of it. When one's body gives out one's entire being also fades. Suffering and death no longer have meaning.

Carelessly we have abandoned the stabilizing values of our forebears, from the simplest traditions and values to the most complex strategies that survive over generations, since we believe we no longer need them. Enduring values that transcend the individual have been set aside, and at the center of the world we have placed the individual, around whom everything revolves and with whom everything ends. By giving the appearance of pushing back disease, famine, and war and leading longer lives in general, we believe in our own immortality during the best years of life. But that isn't true, no matter how much we gloss over the decline of the body and banish the process of dying from our everyday lives and consciousness. The cathedrals of faith and prayer have been replaced with clinics of health and science. But clinics are not cathedrals. They can only treat physical ailments. We have replaced the spires of churches with towers of books in university libraries. But all this rational knowledge is not the same as wisdom.

If we were to draw up a balance sheet, it would seem that our ancestors had much more difficulty with the "simpler" things in life, especially those associated with physical survival, than we do today. Yet without envying them or advocating a return to their worldview—something impossible to do anyway—there is no harm admitting that death and dying, the "harder" things in life, were easier for them. Their worlds may have been physically smaller than ours, but their worldview extended infinitely further. As I have said, one cannot go back. Our world now has satellites and telescopes, towers of knowledge instead of towers of faith. But we should not harden in our contemporary emptiness and purposelessness, rushing frantically through the best years of our longer lives only to let ourselves confront the nothingness one day when our bodies begin to fail. We have brought about these changes, and most of us also accept them, at least for the moment. Why not take the next step now with equal decisiveness and try to create once again a functioning and integrated worldview that deals with the hardest things in life?

It is my task as a historian to point out what has come about with these changes and where we are currently. But I am no psychologist, philosopher, sociologist, or theologian. I am no expert saying how this goal can best be achieved. But it is nonetheless true that this task must be undertaken. It is difficult to live without a worldview, and more difficult still to die without one. As long as we do not have one we will have trouble with both life and death. The need for a worldview is all the more pressing the longer we live, the earlier we retire, the less we must worry about everyday life, and the younger our children are when they grow up and leave home.

This slim book will have achieved its goal were it to stimulate all of us, specialists and nonspecialists alike, to reflect on these issues.

CHAPTER I

The Little World of Johannes Hooss

HIS STORY BEGINS three hundred years ago in a small peasant village in the northern part of Hesse known as the Schwalm. The village was called Leimbach and consisted of only six peasant farms. A traveler who set off north on the road from Frankfurt am Main through the Wetterau region would see on the other side of Alsfeld, and about two-thirds of the way to Kassel, the four lower farms on the right side of the road, and, on the left, the two upper farms. All of them were called by simple numbers, or, as was often the case in the countryside, by the names of current or past tenants. Upper Farms 1 and 2 were known as the Grebe Farm and the Hans-Curts Farm. Lower Farms 3, 4, 5, and 6 were called the Baste, Vältes, George-Hinrichs, and Konrads Farms, respectively. One would have looked around in vain for a church. Leimbach, along with the two neighboring villages to the east, Loshausen and Zella, was part of the parish of Zella. It was there that the Leimbachers were baptized.

The six peasant farms of Leimbach were properties of considerable size. Each one had a number of buildings, most of which formed a square around an inner courtyard. The head of the household, along with his family, lived in the main building facing the street. People therefore called this part of the farm the "young house." The "elders' house" stood across from it all by itself with its own living accommodations. When his strength declined and he wanted to leave the fate of the farm in the hands of someone from the next generation, the elderly peasant retired to this house. The square was completed by the stalls on one side and barns on the other.

None of these farms comprised less than 74 acres of good land. The largest was the Vältes Farm, with 106 acres; the smallest, the Hans-Curts, had 84. On each of them lived farm laborers and servant girls who helped out with the work, and each had stalls for at least four horses. Tax records provide us with a more precise picture of these farms for the first time in 1746. At that time fifty-five people lived in the village, including nine farmhands and twelve servant girls. Thirty-eight horses, 28 cows, and 360 sheep were distributed among the six farms. Since no one had divided up the farms' lands in Leimbach since the middle of the sixteenth century, they had remained theoretically the same size over the last two centuries. This has remained unchanged down to the present day.[1]

The two villages just north and south of Leimbach also had farms that were quite impressive in size. Six farms in Ransbach and five in Gungelshausen comprised over fifty acres of land each. But these were the only communities one can find in this entire area with farms of such considerable size, farms that held out the prospect of a certain level of prosperity to each of their tenants. Only two of the forty-two farms in Loshausen, for example, comprised cultivated lands of a comparable size, and this was the case only because Loshausen was one of the villages in which two large estates remained in the possession of nobles. More than half of all other tenants had to make do with less than twelve acres of land each, hardly enough to support a single family.

Not all of the region's villagers were therefore peasants like those from Leimbach, Gungelshausen, or Ransbach. On the contrary, many of them are best described as peasants with side occupations. "Peasant day laborers," for example, earned extra money during the harvest or threshing season by working on the nobles' estates or on the large peasant farms. Others worked primarily as rural craftsmen. In any event, these villagers, their wives, and their children constantly looked around for supplemental income. They scratched out a living as so-called cotters or as the poorest of peasants who resided in the village but who did not have full village rights. Contemporary statistics capture them in a colorless way, however, and hide from us their misery.

The peasant holding the Vältes Farm three hundred years ago was Vält (Valentin) Hooss. The Vältes (or Valentin's) Farm has carried his name for centuries since that time down to the present. He was certainly not the first Hooss to have been the farm's proprietor, but his name was honored in particular, perhaps because he had taken over the farm at a very tough time and kept it from ruin and disgrace in the face of adversity. Vält was born in the middle of the Thirty Years' War (in 1626), and between 1618 and 1648 the war repeatedly ravaged the villages of the Schwalm region. In 1635 he lost his father to the ravages of the plague. The next year his twelve-year-old brother, Johannes, his one-and-a-half-year-old sister, Guda, and his mother all died. Three half-grown orphan boys of ten, five, and four were all who remained on the farm. An uncle from the nearby village of Ascherode and a peasant from the Hans-Curts Farm stepped in as joint trustees of the farm and looked after it for ten years. In 1646, when he was twenty years old, Vält took over the farm himself. Yet it took more than a decade after the return of peace in 1648 before the house and farm were in good enough shape that he could consider getting married, and in 1659 he started his own family with twenty-three-year-old Elisabeth Kauffmann.

Our story really begins here with the parents of Johannes Hooss. Even though Johannes was born in 1670 on a relatively wealthy peasant farm as the fourth child of Vält and Elisabeth, he could always hear a song sung around the house about the precariousness of even this modest prosperity. Much as his own parents repeatedly learned through immediate and personal experience during the second half of the Thirty Years' War, this modest affluence was continually at risk through plague, famine, and war.

In 1677 Johannes Hooss was seven years old. Along with his ten-year-old brother, Hans Class, he could already help out his father and the farmhands in the fields. Perhaps he led the horses around by the reins or even drove the wagon and the horses a distance down the road. When the fields were prepared for plowing, he may have sat on the harrow and learned how the added weight of his body helped the implement work more effectively. When everyone had to get to work bringing in the harvest in the summer and fall, his two sisters, Anna Catharina and Anna, may also have been out in the fields with him on occasion. But the girls, who were sixteen and twelve at the time, otherwise stayed around the house with their mother and the servant girls or helped take care of the small farm animals.

Once Johannes had reached this age he no longer simply played around his parents' farm and the family's lands. On the two farms next door there were also two boys who were almost as old as he was. Both of them were named Johannes as well. The Johannes at the Konrads Farm was only a week younger than he was, while the other Johannes, from the George-Hinrichs Farm, was almost a year younger. Our Johannes may have played with them often. In fact, he could have played with any of the children in Leimbach. They may have played together with wooden horses, hitching them up as they did at home, since all of the farms here were roughly equal in everyone's eyes and all of the children had horses at home, just as peasants like these were supposed to.

Little Johannes grew up this way from the time he was a little boy, with everything fitting together "just so." Not until the early nineteenth century and the so-called Dissolution Laws of 1832 and 1848 (in electoral Hesse) could even big Leimbach peasants operate their farms and manage their lands as they wanted to. While they had been able to acquire their farms through inheritance, these peasants, in addition, worked a complex patchwork of lands, each parcel of which carried entirely different obligations. Whether to divide the farm among the children or pass it down intact to a single heir, whether to keep horses or not, and how many—they could not make any of these decisions on their own.

About half of the cultivated land within the boundaries of Leimbach was made up of seigneurial land. This land may have been distributed as heritable leaseholds attached to the six farmholds, but the Count of Ziegenhain actually owned the land, and he resided in Ziegenhain, a fortress town about an hour's march by foot on the other side of Ascherode. Since the county had passed into the possession of Hesse in 1450 and after that the two titles were united in the Landgraviate of Hesse, their landlord actually lived in Kassel. The peasants of Leimbach owed him carefully prescribed dues, as well as carting services, for the use of these lands. They were therefore required to maintain a certain number of horses to work their lord's estate in Ziegenhain for a prescribed number of days during the year. Other parcels of land were held as leaseholds from among the freeholdings of the nobility. These were either inherited or rented out for a limited period of time. But the owners of these lands lived farther away still, in the communities of Kirchheim or Ballnhausen, and imposed still different levies on the Leimbachers. To all of these lands were added a few cleared fields, some patrimonial properties, and, finally, individual parcels that actually belonged to their neighbors in Ransbach or which lay within the boundaries of Ransbach, Zella, or Ziegenhain.

It would never have occurred to the horse-owning Leimbacher peasants to work their fields with draft oxen or bulls. Small holders from Loshausen did exactly that, but they owed their lords only labor services and not carting services. They could not have even afforded to buy horses. The Leimbachers therefore looked down on them with contempt. Children took on this contemptuous attitude almost instinctively in their play. How could the children from Loshausen know how to hitch up horses when they did not even have them at home? Children just couldn't play with their social inferiors.

On the whole, the peasants of Leimbach were grain farmers, not cattle farmers. The middle of the Schwalm lowlands, where the village was situated, encompassed rich soils and enjoyed a favorable climate. Fine crops of rye and wheat grew there. Out of a total of 593 acres of land in 1750, three-quarters were in arable and only one-quarter in pasture. The peasants had few cows as a result: only twenty-eight head. In nearby Loshausen the situation was completely different. About half of the 969 acres of land were turned over to meadows and pastures. The village had 114 cows and 20 oxen. In Leimbach, on the other hand, not a single cow was to be found.

The problem for Johannes in growing up in Leimbach, however, had more to do with the fact that the circle of his peers was so tiny. With the exception of the two Johanneses from the Konrads and George-Hinrichs Farms, there were hardly any children his age. Little Elisabeth lived at the Baste Farm in the last house on the same side of the street, but she was just a year old. On the other side of the street, at the Grebe Farm, the Ritter family had only two small children, and both of them were infants. Curt Riebling lived at the Hans-Curts Farm, but he was twenty-two and lived as a young bachelor alone with his mother, the sixty-three-year-old widow Elsabeth.

Nonetheless, little Johannes crossed the road all of the time since people lived on the other side who were different from anyone else in the village. These were people so old that they remembered the times long ago, and they also had time to tell stories about these times at length, and could tell their stories over and over again. At the Grebe Farm lived Grandmother Catharina, and she was three years older than the widow Elsabeth who lived next door. She must have been an iron-willed woman. After the death of her husband in 1662 she managed the Grebe Farm as a widow for a dozen years all by herself. Only in 1673 did her son, Johannes, take over the farm. He was twenty-four at the time. The Grebe Farm was the only one where three generations lived together under the same roof. All of the other farms had only parents and children. There were also no aunts and uncles in the village in 1677. Everywhere there were nuclear families, much as we have today.

What the other side of the street offered little Johannes, and what may have unconsciously fascinated him, was a completely new dimension to his life. Just as by crossing the road his world grew physically, so it extended in time as well. In this way he gradually became aware of the village, its immediate surroundings, and its past at the same time. He developed a solid understanding of both its physical and its temporal dimensions. The line that divided the world on the other side of the street from the world of events of his grandparents' generation blurred. His horizons expanded in both directions.

Figure 2 may help us in better understanding this tiny and yet complicated world of Johannes Hooss. At the lower left of the figure one can see the heart of the village. Lower Farms 3, 4, 5, and 6 are on the right side of the road. Above them and to the left are Upper Farms 1 and 2. The designations *central, middle,* and *outer* mark Johannes's slowly expanding horizons as he grew up within the village. They begin with the narrow bounds of his parents' house, the Vältes Farm, then extend to the Baste, Konrads, and George-Hinrichs Farms, and finally reach beyond this circle to the other side of the street, to the Hans-Curts and Grebe Farms.

The development of each family on these six farms is reproduced in the tables for the years between 1670 and 1689, that is, from Johannes's birth to the time of his marriage. These family tables make it easy to figure out who might have been a playmate, a confidante, or a friend, where he or she lived, and who

2.   World of Johannes Hooss during his childhood and youth, 1670–89. Johannes Hooss was born on August 17, 1670, on the Vältes Farm (Farm 4) in Leimbach as the fourth child of Vält (Valentin) and Elisabeth. He inherited the farm and married on October 10, 1689. *Inner circle:* members of the family from the Vältes Farm (Hooss's parents' house). *Middle circle:* family members from the parents' house and the three neighboring farms on his side of the road: Farms 3 (Baste Farm), 5 (George-Hinrichs Farm), and 6 (Konrads Farm). *Outside circle:* family members from the parents' house, the three neighboring farms on his side of the road, and the two farms on the other side of the road: Farms 1 (Grebe Farm) and 2 (Hans-Curts Farm). Farms 1 and 2 were also called the Upper Farms; 3, 4, 5, and 6 were called the Lower Farms. *Sources:* Gottfried Ruetz, ed., *Hessisches Geschlechterbuch,* vols. 18, 19, and 21, Schwalm vols. 1, 2, and 3, *Deutsches Geschlechterbuch,* vols. 157, 159, and 176 (Limburg an der Lahn: C. A. Starke, 1971–77); Schwälmer Stammtafel-Material und Datenbank, Friedrich-Meinecke-Institut of the Free University Berlin. I am thankful to pastor Gottfried Ruetz for a great deal of personal information, and especially for the temporary loan of a complete copy of handwritten Hooss family letters from the papers of Pastor Giebel of Treysa, vols. 1–5, nos. 1–14 (Bonn, November 1937–Christmas 1941) (no longer published).

Leimbach 1670-1689: Composition of the 6 Farmsteads
(Underlining indicates the person in charge of a given farmstead)

Farmstead 1: Grebe Farmstead

Generation/ Position	Age in 1670	Presence in Leimbach 1670-1689
Grandmother (f)	59	1670-1689, <u>1670-1673</u>
Father (m)	21	1670-1689, <u>1673-1689</u>
Mother (f)	18	1673-1689
Aunt (f)	18	1670-married out in 1676
Children		
Johannes (m)	-4	1674-1675
Maria Leiss (f)	-6	1676-1689
Elisabeth (f)	-7	1677-1689
Catharina (f)	-9	1679-1689
Johann Henr. (m)	-13	1683-1689
Caspar (m)	-15	1685-1689
Johannes (m)	-17	1687-1689
Henrich (m)	-19	1689

Farmstead 2: Hans-Curt Farmstead

Generation/ Position	Age in 1670	Presence in Leimbach 1670-1689
Grandfather (m)	63	<u>1670-1676</u>
Grandmother (f)	56	1670-1689
Father (m)	15	1670-1689, <u>1676-1689</u>
Mother (f)	9	1678-1689
Uncle (m)	27	1670-1689
Aunt (f)	18	1670-married out in 1672
Children		
Elisabeth (f)	-11	1681-1689
(2nd wife)		
Catharina (f)	-15	1685-1689

Farmstead 5: George Hinrichs Farmstead

Generation/ Position	Age in 1670	Presence in Leimbach 1670-1689
Father (m)	42	1670-1689, <u>1670-1682</u>
Mother (f)	41	1670-1689
Children		
Johannes (m)	17	1670-1689, <u>1682-1689</u>
(his wife) (f)	6	married in in 1682
(childless marriage)		
Hans Class (m)	15	1670-married out in 1682
Johannes (m)	12	1670-married out in 1685
Hans Heinrich (m)	4	1670-1689
Johannes (m)	-1	1671-1689

Farmstead 3: Bastes Farmstead

Generation/ Position	Age in 1670	Presence in Leimbach 1670-1689
Father (m)	22	<u>1670-689</u>
Mother (f)	13	married in in 1673-1689
Children		
Johannes (m)	-4	1674-1675
Elisabeth (f)	-6	1676-1689
Catharina (f)	-8	1678-1689
Anna Marga. (f)	-11	1681-1689
Gelasia (f)	-15	1685-1689
Catharina Elis. (f)	-18	1688

Farmstead 6: Konrads Farmstead

Generation/ Position	Age in 1670	Presence in Leimbach 1670-1689
Father (m)	29	<u>1670-1689</u>
Mother (f)	21	1670-1689
Children		
Catharina (f)	3	1670-1678
Johannes (m)	0	1670-1689
Helwig (m)	-3	1673-1689
Elisabeth (f)	-5	1675-1689
Anna (f)	-8	1678-1689
Anna Cath. (f)	-12	1682-1689
Johann Jost (m)	-17	1687-1689

Farmstead 4: Vältes Farmstead

Generation/ Position	Age in 1670	Presence in Leimbach 1670-1689
Father (m)	44	<u>1670-1686</u>
Mother (f)	34	1670-1677
Stepmother (f)	20	1678-1689
Siblings		
Anna Cathar. (f)	9	1670-married out in 1681
Anna (f)	5	1670-married out in 1688
Hans Class (m)	3	1670-1680
EGO Johannes	0	1670-1689, <u>1686-1689</u>
Johann Jacob (m)	-3	1673
Johann Jost (m)	-4	1674
Johann Hen. (m)	-5	1675
Martha Elis. (f)	-6	1676
Stepsiblings		
Johann Val. (m)	-9	1679-1689
Hans Henrich (m)	-10	1680-1689
Johannes (m)	-11	1681-1689
Johann Adam (m)	-13	1683-1688
Catharina (f)	-15	1685-1689

was too young or too old to be one. It also shows where grandparents still lived and how individual families expanded and then later contracted.

The new window on the past that Johannes discovered by listening to stories at the Grebe and Hans-Curts Farms involved, above all, the story about the Great War. Both of the old women remembered it well. Indeed they remembered the entire war, since both of them, in contrast to his parents, were born before it broke out: Elsabeth in 1614 in Gungelshausen and Catharina in 1611 in Mönch-Leusel, north of Alsfeld. These communities lay not more than a dozen kilometers from each other and were located on the same route the armies marched over. They were often also on the battle lines drawn between the two towns of Alsfeld and Ziegenhain. Catharina and Elsabeth therefore had personally experienced the chaos of the war repeatedly. These shocking experiences affected them profoundly, and they carried the memories of them all of their lives. Before they died, however, the women told stories about the events so often that they went over into the collective memory of all of the Leimbachers. Some parts of the story, in the meantime, were embellished, while others were left aside or exaggerated. The general result was that for everyone in Leimbach two and three generations after the actual events, the word "war" meant fear, terror, dread, suffering, famine, burned farms, fields that were laid waste, rape, and flight to the safety of the fortified town of Ziegenhain. The memory of the war survived as a scourge that threatened life, limb, and property.

Such side effects aside, the war was devastating enough for the lowland communities of the Schwalm. From the winter of 1622–23, when General Tilly's troops took up quarters in Hesse, the people suffered under its chaos almost without interruption right to the end of the war. For them it was, if not a Thirty Years' War, then at least a Twenty-Five Years' War. Children, youths, and young adults eventually knew nothing but war except from hearsay. The enemy's troops came down the strategic highways, and behind them came their own from Hesse-Kassel, foraging in the villages along both sides of the roads and then fighting several bloody battles in front of the Ziegenhain Fortress. Their own soldiers may have had some considerations for the people of the land, but they all still requisitioned supplies and took up quarters in exactly the same way. Friend and foe alike took horses and oxen as draft animals for the artillery or for other transport, seized sheep and cattle from barns to be slaughtered, and plundered barns for grain, even removing the seed grain for next year's planting. Regular work in the fields had long since stopped under such conditions. Crop failures resulted and famine began.

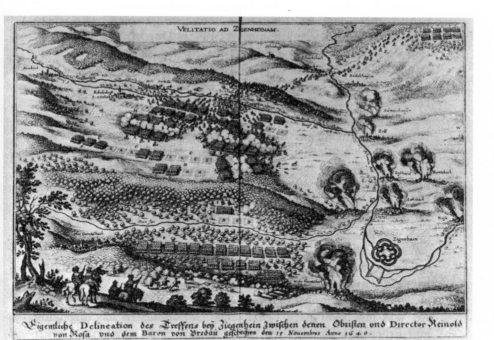

VELITATIO AD ZIEGENHEINAM.

Eigentliche Delineation des Treffens bey Ziegenhein zwischen denen Obristen vnd Director Reinold von Rosa vnd dem Baron von Bredau geschehen den 15 Nouembris Anno 1640.

3.   The march to battle at Ziegenhain Fortress (lower right in the picture) between the imperial troops under Field Marshal Lieutenant Baron Johann Ludolf von Bredow and the Hessian, Weimar, and French under Cavalry Colonel Reinhold von Rosen on November 15, 1640. The battle has gone down in history as the Battle of Riebelsdorf (back left). The villages of the Schwalm lowlands are burning. *Source: Theatrum Europaeum,* pt. 4 (Frankfurt am Main: Matthäus Merian, 1643). On this subject see Hans Freiherr von Rosen, "Das Treffen von Riebelsdorf," in "Der Reiteroberst Reinhold von Rosen," *Schwälmer Jahrbuch* 1971: 106–9; and Eduard Braun, "Das Gefecht bei Riebelsdorf im Jahre 1640 und Valentin Muhly," ibid., 1984: 95–104.

The worst years came in the late 1630s and early 1640s. In a 1643 survey of the Ziegenhain district, to which the Schwalm villages belonged, nine of the thirteen localities listed at least half of the inhabited buildings as burned down, destroyed, or abandoned. In 1636–37 alone no fewer than twenty-six of the thirty-six dwellings in Loshausen went up in flames. In Gungelshausen only three of the seven buildings were still standing.

On November 15, 1640, when yet another battle commenced at Ziegenhain between the two opposing armies, practically all of the defenseless villages of the Schwalm lowlands, as Matthäus Merian records it, were in flames (see fig. 3). Looking at this picture three hundred years later, we become witnesses as Loshausen, Ransbach, Zella, Salmshausen, Steina, Treysa, and Niedergrenzebach are reduced to flames and ashes. Leimbach had suffered the same fate a few days before, on November 11, 1640. In the battle known as the Skirmish at Riebelsdorf (upper left in the picture) an imperial army of about 3,000 cavalry and 1,800 infantry under Field Marshal Lieutenant Baron Johann Ludolf von Bredow met a Hessian-French-Weimar allied force totaling 2,400 infantry and cavalry under Colonel Reinhold von Rosen. The battle ended in the defeat of the imperial forces. Even if we treat the recorded number of casualties with caution and assume that the reported losses of 1,400 horses and 600 soldiers were an exaggeration, that only a half or a quarter of that number were actually lost, replacements still had to be found quickly. Wherever horses, draft animals, or livestock were to be found in the area, they were immediately seized by the troops. The peasants were left to fend for themselves in plowing their fields, bringing in the harvests, or finding something to eat.

Even before this happened the Schwalm villagers looked around to see how many people were left living. Many had not survived, not only because the soldiers inflicted suffering through fire, plunder, and theft, but also because death went everywhere with them, even to places where not a single blow was struck or a person killed. The troops spread plague everywhere, and, as a result, one of the most destructive epidemics of plague in modern German history ravaged the population in 1635–36. That frightful combination of plague, famine, and war known to all ages as the "angels of death" was now complete. As we already know, Johannes's grandfather and grandmother, and two of their children as well, died from the plague on the Vältes Farm at that time.

One naturally wonders whether social relationships played a much more significant or more fundamental role as safety nets in these insecure times than they do today. The modern institutionalization of social welfare often creates an environment rendering social relationships more or less superficial and contrived. Weren't relatives always the real safety net in the past, as when Johannes Hooss's uncle and neighbor took over the stewardship of the farm, the ten-year-old orphan, Johannes, and his two younger brothers for no apparent personal gain? Or didn't the general insecurity of life pull survivors together to protect each other in the face of the daily spectacle of death? We easily lose sight of this context. Behavior that is self-evident when people are mutually dependent is hastily and cynically interpreted as an expression of self-interest or is elevated as an expression of Christian love. Because of our well-developed social systems, we are the first people in history to be able to indulge in egotism, to think and care only for ourselves, assuming that some agency or other will take care of our neighbors when they get sick.

It is precisely this amazement with the behavior and attitudes of our ancestors that lies behind my desire to find out what people were like only a few generations ago. Why did they act this way? Whom did they grow up and associate with? What was their little world like when everything was so unstable and they were so obviously determined, despite it all, to survive? Let's pursue this a little further and get a closer look at the life of our Johannes and his little world.

Let's look at Johannes Hooss in 1684, when he was twice as old, that is, when he was fourteen. He still lived on his parents' farm, but he now associated with different people from the ones he knew when he was seven. This had happened not only because the others had grown older and had changed physically and psychologically in the intervening time, but especially because of the basic events of everyday life. Birth, death, and marriage had all come to the Vältes Farm. Only his father, Vält, and his second-oldest sister, Anna, still lived there. At least the names in the register suggest that it was they. They were now fifty-eight and nineteen years old, respectively.

In 1677 the death of his mother left Johannes partially orphaned. This was certainly not the first time he had experienced death in his parents' house, but it was perhaps the first time it had affected him in such a direct and devastating way. Death had already come to the Vältes Farm in 1673, 1674, 1675, and 1676, but that had been when Johannes was three, four, five, and six years old, and it had always involved brothers and sisters younger than himself. No sooner had they come into the world than they left it: the first at seven weeks, the second at eleven days, the third after eight weeks, and the fourth after ten days. Johannes had not even been able to get accustomed to them. His mother's death, however, must have been quite a different experience for the seven-year-old boy because with her went one of the most important people in his young life, if not the person at the center of his whole circle of personal relationships. His father, after remaining a widower for fifteen months, may have partly mended the family by marrying twenty-eight-year-old Elisabeth Stumpf from Wasenberg, a neighboring village to the west. Johannes's world was then outwardly whole again. But even at that there was probably still a powerful difference between his new stepmother, a stranger, and the mother he had grown up with and knew well.

There was something else that was strange to the boy, something he had to deal with for the rest of his life. Where had his mother really gone? In 1681 his older sister, Anna Catharina, also left home when she married someone in Ransbach. But she always returned home for visits, or he traveled the short distance to see her there. His mother did not come back, though, and yet to Johannes she remained very much alive in his memory. Was there another world not visible from Ransbach, Wasenberg, or any other place he had been to? How was he supposed to understand that?

We also don't know what became of his older brother, Hans Class. We see him for the last time at his confirmation in 1680, when he was fourteen. After that he disappears from our view. Even back then the world apparently didn't end at Ransbach or Wasenberg for some people. A search through all of the church registers in the whole Schwalm region and other neighboring parishes would not turn up a notice of his funeral. Was he a dropout from a world that seemed too small to him? Didn't Hans Class live in an age when entirely new parts of the globe, and not just the world beyond the next forest or hill, had long since been discovered and were still being discovered? Wasn't this the age when flat landscapes had become part of the repertoire of Dutch paintings of daily life, paintings so expansive and full of light, air, and space that one loses oneself in the distance? What a dramatic contrast with Merian's picture of the Schwalm! Look at the pictures of Philip Koninck (1619–88), Merian's contemporary, or Hercules Seghers (1589/90–1633/38) before him! Like the thought of the age, the perspective in their paintings opens up into the distance completely differently from the way it does in the picture of the Schwalm. In Merian's picture the perspective stays fixed on the next hill (see once again the piece by Merian in fig. 3).

Moreover, one should not overlook the fact that in this same period the Schwalm region also formed part of a regional thoroughfare, and this led to both good and bad consequences. During a war the roads brought fear, terror, misery, suffering, plague, and famine to the region. At other times the roads brought brides for young farmers, good news, and fantastic tales suggesting undreamed-of possibilities. Frightening rumors also spread up and down the roads, rumors about the distant and terrible Turks, a horrible plague that had broken out somewhere, or a cattle disease that was approaching and emptying out the pastures and barns, sparing neither sheep nor horses. Novel ideas were constantly reported that gave wings to the imagination. Did one of them seize hold of Hans Class? Or did he simply take advantage of the opportunity afforded young Hessians to enroll in the army, even in peacetime, and set off to see the bigger world? Did this perhaps appeal to him more than the prospect of taking over the Vältes Farm? He was still the eldest son, even though according to Leimbach custom his seniority did not necessarily guarantee that he would inherit the farm intact. His enrolling in the army was not unlikely either. Since 1677 treaties had existed in which Hesse-Kassel "leased out" troops to other foreign powers, first to Denmark, then to Venice, England, and Holland. The landgraves were not the only rulers who tried to improve their inadequate finances in this manner. But they still did it on such a scale and with such determination that the label "soldier merchants" stuck to them and has gone down in history. Generally speaking, however, the world into which a peasant with such a small plot of land was born into in those days remained the only world he knew his entire life.

Despite all of the deaths, marriages, and departures, the Vältes Farm filled up once again with people. The twenty-five-year difference in age that separated Johannes's father from his youthful bride did not harm the fertility of their marriage, which had been sealed in 1678. After that another child was born into the world almost every year. By 1684 Johannes had no fewer than four stepbrothers: five-year-old Johann Valentin, four-year-old Hans Heinrich, three-year-old Johannes, and one-year-old Johann Adam. Another baby was on the way. She would be born on February 9, 1685, a girl, and would be called Catharina.

For fourteen-year-old Johannes, now the oldest son at the Vältes Farm, all of these babies and small children were hardly the best companions. His stepmother may not have been either. Even his nineteen-year-old sister, Anna, who still lived at home, may have had other things on her mind than her half-grown brother.

As his social ties within his father's house loosened, they became tighter with boys his own age who were growing up on the neighboring farms. There were five of them now who banded together. Besides our own Johannes there were still the two other boys from the George-Hinrichs and Konrads Farms, now thirteen and fourteen years old. In addition, they had brothers: eighteen-year-old Hans Henrich at the George-Hinrichs Farm and eleven-year-old Helwig at the Konrads Farm. The contacts that Johannes made, cultivated, and even jealously guarded within this network may have been among the closest and most formative during his eighty-five-year life span. He grew up into the adult world gradually as a member of a well-defined group of young men, his personality uncertain and immature at first but receiving strength or at least protection within this community. As boys pretending to be older than they actually were, they respected the rules of adults, often paying more attention to them than the adults did themselves. For they were the ones who, with the adults' silent consent, mercilessly exposed those adults who violated social norms with their raucous customs and charivaris. They reminded others of what was seemly and proper in Leimbach, and did so roughly if they had to.

Between them a social network developed that lasted a lifetime. These were networks strong enough to survive a war when it came, the burning down of someone's farm, or the loss at a single blow of all of one's horses to disease. Even after marrying, becoming a husband, and fathering his own children, a young man may still have felt close to this older and formative group. Often, in difficult situations and in particularly relaxing moments, he may even have felt closer to this group than to the new family he had begun.

Communities like this, and not the large extended family commonly presumed for this period, tied individuals together and supported them during their lifetimes. Large extended families did not even exist in Leimbach, or anywhere else for that matter. Historians of everyday life therefore have to pay close attention to the origins of these communities, the people they included, the conditions they had to contend with, and how they did so.

In meeting this challenge we immediately run into serious problems, since communities of this kind were never permanent or fixed. They can be studied only with difficulty. Contacts between people are first made, whether loosely or closely, and then they are expanded, deepened, rounded off, loosened, or broken off. Any network of people that we can discern is tied together by a number of individuals, all of whom have their own unique lives. They start out as children, grow up, mature, marry, have their own children or remain childless, move away or stay put, lose children and a spouse, become old and miserable, or die in the fullness of their years.

Before getting into an area of research fast becoming difficult to survey, it is appropriate to consider the circumstances that make contacts between people easy or, on the other hand, difficult. When do they develop relatively naturally? What kinds of social barriers exist, and when does resistance have to be overcome? I have illustrated six different "social barriers" in figure 4. Using the figure, anyone can draw up his or her own list of theoretical possibilities. "Physical barriers" certainly play an important role between any individuals making contact with each other. It is a matter of no small consequence if two people enter a house every day through the same door, sleep

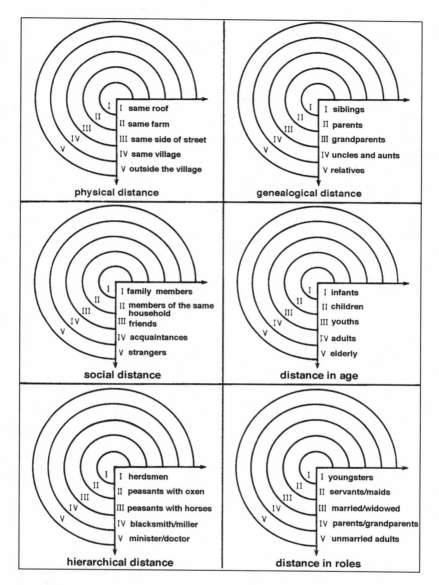

physical distance

I same roof
II same farm
III same side of street
IV same village
V outside the village

genealogical distance

I siblings
II parents
III grandparents
IV uncles and aunts
V relatives

social distance

I family members
II members of the same household
III friends
IV acquaintances
V strangers

distance in age

I infants
II children
III youths
IV adults
V elderly

hierarchical distance

I herdsmen
II peasants with oxen
III peasants with horses
IV blacksmith/miller
V minister/doctor

distance in roles

I youngsters
II servants/maids
III married/widowed
IV parents/grandparents
V unmarried adults

4.   Social distances and barriers in the building of a social network. Social network analysis is central to historical social anthropology. I owe thanks for a number of references and stimulating suggestions to Andrejs Plakans, Professor of Anthropology at Iowa State University of Science and Technology in Ames, with whom I worked for three years on a project supported by the National Science Foundation in Washington, D.C., and the members of the Cambridge Group for the History of Population and Social Structure in Cambridge, England.

under the same roof, or live on the same farm, even if in different buildings. It is significant if their homes are on the same side of the street or are divided by it, whether they live in the same locality or in different ones. "Genealogical barriers" work the same way: contacts among siblings and between parents and children are more likely than with more distant relatives. "Social barriers" make contacts more natural between members of the same family, between dependents of the same household, and between friends than between acquaintances or strangers. "Age barriers" draw people of the same age together more easily than they do young and old people. Regarding "hierarchical barriers" and "role barriers," obstacles are even more pronounced. Swineherds and horse-owning peasants avoided contact with each other in the old days, much as young and single people avoid old aunts. Even where we assume that contact existed between people, however, this tells us little about the relationship's intensity or endurance and the tenor of the feelings it involved.

These ideas may simply result from a commonsense reading of figure 4, but they should help us understand how groups and whole networks of people are put together. Keeping this in mind, let me emphasize what I was saying above: that all three Johanneses were the same age and in the same developmental stage as young adults, that their homes were on the same side of the street, and that all of them were the sons of horse-owning peasants. The barriers for them to overcome in getting together were therefore low. The prospects were favorable for the development of a strong network between them.

These initial considerations seem important not only in explaining the possible development of social networks but also in explaining the boundaries of such groups. We can easily draw a diagram with a particular person in the middle as Ego and then sketch in the lines between him and the others with whom he probably cultivated contacts. As a child Ego may have initially developed close relationships with siblings and parents within the circle of the family, but his world expanded as he grew up. Ego would then develop ties beyond his family, to neighborhood boys his own age, for example, much like the ties we have reconstructed for seven-year-old Johannes in Leimbach.

No one stands alone in the world, however, and these boys from the neighborhood were no exception. Perhaps they had gotten together long before Johannes joined them. All of them had their own siblings and parents, and all of them made their own circle of associates according to age, sex, interests, and social standing, and according to whether they were single, married, or widowed. Ten-year-old Catharina at the Konrads Farm, for example, may have known twelve-year-old Anna on the Vältes Farm, or eleven-year-old Hans Henrich at the George-Hinrichs Farm may have had contact with ten-year-old Hans Class from the Vältes Farm. But the world was even bigger than this. It stretched out beyond the boundaries of the three lower farms where they lived. Whatever their ages, the six Leimbach peasants had to constantly coordinate their joint economic and legal affairs with each other. They may also have protected common interests involving a third agent—their lord's steward from Ziegenhain, for example, concerning carting and carrying services. Every individual within a social network, and not simply the one we place in the center as Ego, develops his own relationships. A friend's friend has his own friends, and all of them have their own as well. All of these people need not know each other. Not every social tie that a person has is of interest to others.

With regard to this circle of people in Leimbach, one must also realize that the six families living here could hardly have composed their own marriage market. By virtual necessity farm holders had to find wives from outside the village. As we noted, Grandmother Catharina moved from Mönch-Leusel as a result of her marriage. The widow Elsabeth married and then left Gungelshausen. The wife of young Ritter at the Grebe Farm came from Arnshain, northwest of Alsfeld, and Nikolaus Süßmann, the farmer of the George-Hinrichs Farm, had a wife from Zella. Both of the peasant women on the Baste and Konrads Farms came from Ransbach. Even the farmer of the Baste Farm came from somewhere else at that time. He had grown up in Ascherode, and he acquired the farm in 1667 by buying it.

All of the places that have been named were not more than a dozen kilometers from Leimbach, the center of our world. A two- or three-hour walk was enough to reach any of them. Leaving in the morning, one could be back in the evening at milking time, even on short winter days, since the agricultural work cycle afforded peasants the time and the leisure for such long visits.

What seems even more significant to me, however, was the fact that neither Mönch-Leusel nor Arnshain was a part of the Schwalm. They did not even lie within the administrative authority of Ziegenhain District. Indeed they were in neither Neukirchen nor Schönstein Districts, two former districts of the old County of Ziegenhain. Instead they were situated in another part of the country, a territory that lay under a foreign ruler. From Leimbach one could not see either of these villages, since they were located, in contrast to other places where brides came from, not in the open, virtually level, and easy to scan lowlands of the Schwalm, but rather on the other side of the ridge that bordered the Schwalm, beyond the Arnshain Heights. Were the Leimbachers to set off on the way there, they could have seen far into the lands on the other side. The horizon opened up. The boundary of their usually small world broadened. And if they were to venture into Mönch-Leusel or Arnshain, the people there would have told them about yet other villages and still other people. But they would have done so in a somewhat different language. They no longer called an eyelid an *Augenlid* but an *Augendeckel*. The new fruit of the earth, the potato, was called a *Katoffel* and not, as in the Ziegennainer region, a *Katüffel*. Everything was simply a bit different from home.[2]

To be sure, the women who married into Leimbach experienced sharp and abrupt changes in their personal ties, just as this was generally the case with the men who came from the area and took over a farm. But marriage presented itself at the same time as an opportunity to extend the boundaries of the little world of Leimbach a bit, to let a steady, fresh breeze into the air that otherwise threatened to become torpid and stale.

In political and religious terms, Mönch-Leusel and Arnshain belonged at that time to another world. In the eyes of the authorities, an unholy boundary ran just south of the Schwalm, one that had opened up like an abyss dividing the House of Hesse in a family dispute over the question of religious faith that lasted for generations. On the one side, the Schwalm side of the line, lay the Calvinist Landgraviate of Hesse-Kassel, and on the other, Lutheran Hesse-Darmstadt. The split became open during the Thirty Years' War when both of the territories made alliances with their enemies and fought bitterly against each other. As a strategically important border region the Schwalm lay once again on the front lines. And yet despite all of this, as we have seen, marriages were continually contracted across this boundary that was so artificial in its origins. What did local people care about the disputes involving the two rulers in Kassel and Darmstadt! What difference did the sophistry of the reformers make to them!

In figure 5 (p. 30) Johannes has doubled in age once again so that now (in 1698) he is twenty-eight. The development of the six families in Leimbach are shown in the same way as they were in figure 2 for his childhood in 1670 and his youth in 1689. In this case they represent the period 1689–1699/1700, that is, the years of his first marriage.

In the meantime Johannes's world had broadened in some ways, while in others his interests and field of vision had contracted. His world expanded in 1696 when his childhood friend Johannes from the Konrads Farm married and moved to Wasenberg. The two friends did not break their ties but kept them up on a restricted basis through visits with each other. In addition, Johannes had taken a bride in 1689 from Ransbach, a neighboring but still foreign village. On the other hand, it had already been necessary for him in 1686 to narrow his horizons to the Vältes Farm. After the death of his sixty-year-old father, the property had passed into his hands. He was only sixteen years old! Three years later, as we have already mentioned, he married and started his own family. Two years after that, in 1691, he became a father for the first time, followed in 1693 by a second child and, in 1696, by a third. They had all been girls, one after the other. The oldest, Anna Catharina, died one year after her birth, and the second, Anna, survived only four weeks. Only the third one, another Anna Catharina, had survived, and she was two years old in 1698. A fourth child, yet another girl, came on December 1, 1698, but she was stillborn, and the difficult delivery cost her mother her life. She died that same day in childbirth.

Johannes now had good reason to take care of the legacy he had received from his father and to concentrate on the interests of the Vältes Farm. With the exception of his three-year-old daughter, only step relations lived with him. All of them were either still marriageable or would soon become so. In any event they would be prepared to take over a farm. They included his forty-nine-year-old stepmother, Elisabeth, a widow; his twenty-year-old stepbrother Johann Valentin; an eighteen-year-old stepbrother Johannes; and his fourteen-year-old stepsister, Catharina. If one keeps in mind that he was surrounded with these step relatives, then it was hardly surprising or unusual that on July 22, 1700, Johannes, a widower, would marry for the second time after only six months of mourning. Such hastiness was not necessarily called for under the circumstances. Little Anna Catharina had started to become self-sufficient, and there were no other infants or small children in immediate need of a substitute mother. Besides, at least two other female dependents lived on the farm who could have looked after a single three-year-old child. Fourteen-year-old Catharina was not too young for the task, nor was the fifty-year-old stepmother too old. But this was precisely the point: they were Johannes's stepmother and stepsister.

What might surprise us even more, at least at first sight, would be what we see upon closer examination of the two marriages that took place in

Leimbach 1689-1700: Composition of the 6 Farmsteads
(Underlining indicates the person in charge of a given farmstead)

Farmstead 1: Grebe Farmstead

Generation/ Position	Age in 1689	Presence in Leimbach 1689-1700
Grandmother (f)	78	1689-1700
Father (m)	40	<u>1689-1700</u>
Mother (f)	37	1689-1700
Children		
Maria Leiss (f)	13	1689-married out in 1694
Elisabeth (f)	12	1689-married out in 1696
Catharina (f)	10	1689-1700
Johann Henr. (m)	6	1689-1700
Caspar (m)	4	1689-1700
Johannes (m)	2	1689-1700
Henrich (m)	0	1689-1700
Niclas Henr. (m)	-2	1691-1700
Margarentha (f)	-4	1693-1700
Catharina (f)	-6	1695-1700
Hans Curt (m)	-8	1697-1700

Farmstead 2: Hans-Curt Farmstead

Generation/ Position	Age in 1689	Presence in Leimbach 1689-1700
Grandfather (m)	75	1689-d.1692
Father (m)	34	<u>1689-1700</u>
Mother (f)	28	1689-1700
Children		
Elisabeth (f)	8	1689-1700 m. Johannes Hooss, 1700
Catharina (f)	4	1689-1700

Farmstead 5: George Hinrichs Farmstead

Generation/ Position	Age in 1689	Presence in Leimbach 1689-1700
Father (m)	61	1689-1700
Mother (f)	60	1689-1700
Children		
Johannes (m)	36	<u>1689-1700</u>
(his wife) (f)	25	married in in 1682
(childless marriage)		
Hans Heinrich (m)	23	1689-married out in 1692
Johannes (m)	18	1689-1700, married out in 1700 to heiress of Farm 3

Farmstead 3: Bastes Farmstead

Generation/ Position	Age in 1689	Presence in Leimbach 1689-1700
Father (m)	41	<u>1689-1699</u>
Mother (f)	32	1689-d. 1696
Children		
Elisabeth (f)	13	1689-1699, married 1700
Catharina (f)	11	1689-1700
Anna Marga. (f)	8	1689-1700
Gelasia (f)	4	1689-1700
Martha Elis. (f)	-1	1690-1700
Johannes (m)	-6	1695-1700

Farmstead 6: Konrads Farmstead

Generation/ Position	Age in 1689	Presence in Leimbach 1689-1700
Father (m)	48	<u>1689-d.1694</u>
Mother (f)	40	1689-1700,<u>1694-1697</u>
Children		
Johannes (m)	19	married out in 1696
Helwig (m)	16	1689-1700,<u>1697-1700</u>
(his wife) (f)	10	married in in 1697
Grandchildren		
Elisabeth (f)	14	1689-married out in1696
Anna (f)	11	1689-married out in1699
Anna Cath. (f)	7	1689-married out in1700
Johann Jost (m)	2	1689-1700
Catharina (f)	-10	1698-1700

Farmstead 4: Vältes Farmstead

Generation/ Position	Age in 1689	Presence in Leimbach 1689-1700
Stepmother (f)	39	1689-1700 d.1723
Stepsiblings		
Johann Val.(m)	10	1689-1700,married out in 1707
Hans Henrich (m)	9	1689-d.1694?
Johannes (m)	8	1689-1700,married out in 1708
Catharina (f)	4	1689-1700,married out in 1706
EGO Johannes (m)	19	<u>1689-1700</u>,married in 1700 daughter of Farm 2
(his first wife)(f)	17	1689-d.1699
Children		
Anna Cathar. (f)	-2	1691-92,d. 4 mos. old
Anna (f)	-4	1693,d. 4 weeks old
Anna Cathar.(f)	-7	1696-1700, married out in 1710
stillbirth (f)	-10	1699

Leimbach in 1700. This time no one came from the outside; the four partners all came from within the village. There could hardly be anything else at work here than a marriage strategy. To get to the point, Johannes, a widower, took as his bride nineteen-year-old Elisabeth Riebling, the oldest daughter from Upper Farm 2 (Hans-Curts), and brought her to his farm. That left no one to inherit the property on the Hans-Curts Farm except Catharina, the fifteen-year-old daughter. What a clever move! Love was not the question. Perhaps for us it is, but it wasn't for Johannes. He may surely have acted out of selfish reasons, but not in the sense that he wanted to gratify any desire to make a love match. Instead he behaved in the selfish manner of an ego who felt himself part of a family line. It was his own family line he was thinking about, to be sure, not that of the step relatives living on his own farm.

The personal relationships we look for in marriage or in the intimacy of the family might have been found elsewhere back then. The other marriage that took place at the time led to Johannes's oldest childhood friend settling back in the village to live. On January 31, 1700, the last Johannes, the one who had grown up on the George-Hinrichs Farm, married the heiress of the Baste Farm. From this time on he was the proprietor of the farm. By means of all of this the two Johanneses became property-holding neighbors and could only have grown closer to each other as a result.

We could spin out the story further and let Johannes age by seven years or even seven more. In so doing, new thoughts come to us about his world

5. World of Johannes Hooss during his first marriage, 1689–1699/1700. Johannes Hooss was born August 17, 1670, and grew up at the Vältes Farm (Farm 4), his parents' farm. He inherited the property after the death of his father, in 1686. On October 10, 1689, he married Catharina Fenner from the neighboring village of Ransbach. This marriage ended with the death of his wife on December 1, 1699, during the birth of her fourth child. Subsequently Johannes married Elisabeth Riebeling on July 22, 1700, the oldest of two daughters from the Hans-Curts Farm (Farm 2). *Inner circle:* Vältes Farm (Farm 4): Johannes Hooss's farm with his stepmother, stepbrothers, stepsisters, and his own children from his first marriage. *Middle circle:* Vältes Farm and the three neighboring farms on the same side of the road (Farms 3, 5, and 6—the Baste Farm, George-Hinrichs Farm, and Konrads Farm). *Outer circle:* Vältes Farm, neighboring Farms 3, 5, and 6, and the two farms on the other side of the highway (Farms 1, the Grebe Farm, and 2, the Hans-Curts Farm). Hooss's second wife, Elisabeth Riebeling, grew up on Upper Farm 2, the Hans-Curts Farm. *Sources:* as for figure 2.

and the circle of people around him up to his death on December 30, 1755. Although his long life came to a peaceful end just before the outbreak of the Seven Years' War—a war that would affect Hesse terribly between 1756 and 1763—he nonetheless suffered some heavy blows in his lifetime. It is worthwhile reflecting on them and trying to imagine oneself in his place. The future turned out differently for him from the way he had planned it, even though it was carefully prepared for in 1700. To be sure, neither his stepmother, who died in 1723 at seventy-three, nor his stepsister would ever take over the Vältes Farm. They contracted marriages in Wasenberg and in Obergrenzebach, a village on the other side of Ziegenhain, and left the farm between 1706 and 1708. Still, he was unable to pass on the farm to a son of his own.

Of the twelve children he had had with his second wife, Elisabeth, only five survived to a marriageable age. The sixth, seventh, eighth, and ninth children were boys, to be sure, and all of them were baptized, amidst great hopes, Johannes, Johann Valentin, and Johann Henrich. But none of them lived more than eight years. Old Johannes appears to have become resigned to his fate when, in 1720 and 1723, two more girls came along. In the meantime his second wife had turned forty-four, and hopes of a future male heir rapidly faded. On November 29, 1724, he therefore bequeathed the farm to his eldest daughter from his second marriage, Catharina, then twenty-one, and her husband, also twenty-one, who was a distant relative from the Gungelshausen branch of the family and was actually named Johannes Hooss! (Anna Catharina, his daughter from his first marriage, had married and moved to Zella in 1716.) According to the transfer contract, also dated November 29, 1724, his son-in-law took over the buildings—along with the fields and pastures, six horses, ten cows, four pigs, eighty sheep, five geese, and twenty-five chickens—and paid the round sum of a thousand shiny Hessian talers.[3]

Now fifty-four years old, Johannes retired along with his wife and set up housekeeping in the elders' house that lay across the way. In order not to become idle, he specified in the contract that the dovecote and the beehive were to remain in his possession and under his care. A horse was also to be kept ready for him to use, "for riding beyond the boundary of the commune." Did he intend to visit the farm of his boyhood friend and namesake Johannes, who had married and moved to Wasenberg in 1696? We assume so.

The decision that he made to retire at fifty-four makes us think about the meaning and purpose behind the idea of dividing life into stages in accordance with one's physical abilities and mental powers. This is not the same thing as what we call "the best years of life," even though we often start with the idea that the years of one's greatest physical strength implicitly coincide with the "best years" mentally. We all know about putting off things to a later stage in life. Why not pass on the farm, like Johannes Hooss did, to a younger, physically stronger generation when one's own powers had begun to wane and then turn more to "riding beyond the bounds of the commune"? This would not have been simply for the sport of it. It was also to seek out other elderly men who were free from their physical work, to talk about the current problems of the community with older companions who were experienced, mature, and wise.

Let us return for a moment to Johannes and Elisabeth in the elders' house of the Vältes Farm. The two of them apparently did not feel uncomfortable there as a retired couple, nor did they feel shunted aside and passed over, for on April 17, 1726, a twelfth child was born: yet another Johannes! Who wouldn't understand the terse comment—"Since they gave over their property to the second daughter of the last marriage almost a year and a half ago, a great joy has come to him"—appended to the usual entry in the baptismal register? One doesn't have to turn many pages in the register, however, to find out how it all ended. The fifth son, the fifth Johannes, was buried that summer, on July 28, 1726. Nothing more is to be found in the church registers about how Johannes and Elisabeth took this event. There is also nothing more about other births that may have followed. It was finally all over.

I will break off the story at this point. However fond I am of the story of Johannes Hooss—and history is very much about telling stories—I am not simply interested, in the end, in the story of one person. I am more interested in the world of Johannes Hooss, and the first chapter says so in the title. As far as I am concerned, it could have been the world of Elsabeth Riebling, born Glintzer from Gungelshausen. We got to know her as widow Elsabeth on the Hans-Curts Farm. It could have been the world of the Grebe Farm's grandmother Catharina, who came from the other side of the Arnshain Heights. It could even have been the world of Matthäus Burkhart from the Swabian village of Gabelbach, or that of Gerdt Peters from the East Frisian village of Hesel.

I would have explained their worlds, and many others, in much the same way. Each of these people was born into a little world at roughly the same time, lived several decades in it, tried to shape it where possible or, when that world proved stronger, to make do with the circumstances. Matthäus Burkhart (1663–1729), the oldest surviving son of the Barthel Farm in Gabelbach, naturally lived under different conditions within his little world than did Christoph Geißler (1663–1714). Burkhart was listed in the first tax register from 1663 as holder of the largest property in the entire village commune, being assessed three gulden and twenty-eight kreutzer. Geißler, on the other hand, grew up in the same place but held a small so-called cottager's place, and was assessed a mere thirty kreutzer and four heller, that is, a seventh of Burkhart's (1 gulden = 60 kreutzer; 1 kreutzer = 8 heller). The peasant at the Barthel Farm possessed at that time, so it is recorded, thirty-one *Jaucherts* of land, six horses, seven cows, an equal number of calves, and two pigs. The cottager, by contrast, had only two *Jaucherts* of land, a single cow, two calves, and a pig. [*Jauchert:* amount of land one team of oxen could work in a day.—Trans.] There is no mention of a horse, let alone an ox.[4]

Gabelbach was at that time a small village like Leimbach. It too had six farms, although next to them were seventeen cottagers' places and seven additional "small houses." Yet the worlds of the boys, Matthäus and Christoph, who were both the same age, would have differed sharply from each other from the time they were born. Did they at one time play together, the one a son of a prosperous peasant who worked his farm with horses, the other a son of a poor peasant who owned only a cow? As adolescents did they belong to the same group of village youths, establishing ties in the same social network so that when they married in 1687 and 1691 they could, when they needed to, help each other out? The thoughts above based on figure 4 lead us to doubt it. The population of a village is not the same thing as a village community. Living roughly at that same time in Hesel we find Gerdt Peters (1670–1739), described in the local church register simply as "a day laborer." He belonged neither to the class of householders nor to that of the more settled workers. Those who had houses in Hesel possessed the proud old peasant farms, while the other workers lived in the smallest rural accommodations and not infrequently, at least for periods of time, worked on the farms of the bigger peasants. Gerdt ranked one step below them. He had to wait until he was thirty-four years old before his living was secure enough for him to find a wife.

After discussing and thinking about all of these little worlds, one point has impressed itself on me, and, in light of what follows, I would like to emphasize it as strongly as possible. Anyone who thinks the phrase "equal opportunity" carries little meaning today should think about the fact that the idea had no relevance whatsoever only a few generations ago at the time of our ancestors. I will make this clear in the next chapter using two examples. First we will look at the completely different life expectancies of the period. Johannes Hooss lived to be eighty-five, but a number of his children never even reached one year. Then we will examine the more complex issue involving the many small worlds themselves. Here there is hardly a trace of equal opportunities.

Looking at these two issues leads to the conclusion at this point that none of the individual life cycles, farms, villages, and regions I mention were ever representative cases. Indeed they could not have been. In a period in which every person had a different life course there were no average ones, that is, there were no typical ones. To calculate a purely statistical "average life expectancy" for a time in which every person reached a different age obscures much more than it says. Who doesn't find it silly to cite the average life expectancy of the father of the Hooss family and his children as fifteen years, and then present this as typical for the seventeenth century?

We have to learn not to ask the wrong questions at the start. In this case we shouldn't look for what was representative when we should be looking to show how this was only one possibility out of a hundred. The answers will still be significant enough. They will only turn out to be different from what was expected at the start. The attraction of doing research, being reflective, and thinking oneself back into these periods in the past lies precisely in this.

The idea that equality was lacking at that time in almost all areas of life, and that this was true to a great degree, naturally has very far-reaching consequences. This will become evident in the following chapters. The fact that each person had a separate life course and life span created a much more colorful situation than the one today, in which all of us live roughly the same number of years under relatively similar conditions. Given the decided uncertainty and variability of those days, planning ahead was extremely difficult. Our ancestors must have been thinking about a lot in order to bring a measure of stability to their lives and their little worlds, to achieve their goals for the future. But they did so with astonishing success! The following chapters turn to precisely this theme.

CHAPTER 2

A Multitude of
Little Worlds

YPICALLY WE SAY, almost as if we need to protect our sense of individuality, that no one is typical or average. And yet, whether we like it or not, all of us today are much more "average" than our ancestors ever were.

Each of us born in a given year becomes part of an age group, a birth cohort. With only a few exceptions, all of those in an age group have much the same life cycle before them, at least in its chronological sense. We all start school at the same time, begin our training or university studies in the same year, enter a career path, and at about the same age marry a partner about as old as ourselves. We have one or two children with him or her, enter the post-childrearing stage at about the same time, and retire and die at the same age, men dying a little earlier than the women. An increase in life expectancy means an increase for all of us. When the working years are shortened they are shortened for everyone. Our life cycles have become more predictable, calculated, and uniform, and, in so doing, they have also become more colorless, more interchangeable, and more monotonous. Every life cycle is more or less the same as the "average life course."

This modern condition in which the data of individual and average lives are practically identical then leads us, applying our experiences backward in time, to ask similar questions for periods in the past. What was the "average age of marriage" in this or that time? How old did people get? The following example should make it evident that, historically speaking, we shouldn't ask such questions. When we do we are asking the wrong question. Only when we are ready to understand that it was precisely the deviations from the norm, and not the averages, that were the rule can we finally see that what made up the many small worlds in the past was the impossibility of their being interchanged, their uniqueness and singularity, not their representativeness.

About fifty kilometers southwest of the Schwalm region in the peasant village of Heuchelheim near Gießen, also in Hesse, a total of 1,104 first marriages were contracted between 1691 and 1900. In all of these cases both the bride and the groom were getting married for the first time. If we think like moderns, asking about the "average" age of the women who were marrying for the first time, we would discover that it was 24.1 for the first decade (1691–1700) and 24.3 for the last decade (1891–1900). At the beginning of our period men married at age 25.8 and at the end at 25.4. Had nothing changed over this long period that stretched over two centuries? Indeed it had, something absolutely essential! What obscures the key change, however, is the misleading notion of uniform "average values," that is to say, it is obscured by the wrong question.

A closer look at the left and right sides of figure 6 immediately reveals something that is much more significant than any of the uniform averages. It leaps right out at you. During these two centuries a decisive development took place in Heuchelheim, one so obvious and clear that discovering it would give any historian joy and satisfaction. This is a real aha experience, an exciting discovery in the midst of what is often tedious research.

The age of every one of the 1,104 women who got married in Heuchelheim is marked year by year with a dot on the left side of the graph. Reading the graph from bottom to top, that is, in the direction of the present, we discover a very broad scattering of dots, that is, individual marriage ages, in the first decades. The more time passes, the tighter the dot clusters become. At the end of the nineteenth century a concentration of dots around a middle value finally becomes evident. The individual age of marriage and the "average age of marriage" have begun to coincide more and more. The origins of this pattern are also easy to understand. Over the course of the nineteenth century, members of the older generation died less often in middle age. Since their deaths were being put off until old age, more of them were able to finish out their careers. This then led increasingly to the practice of passing on the farm at an appropriate age and then retiring to the elders' house. The age of marriage for members of the next generation simply adjusted to this fact.

Since this development naturally affected men who were marrying for the

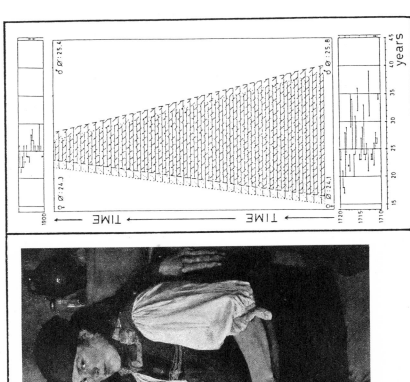

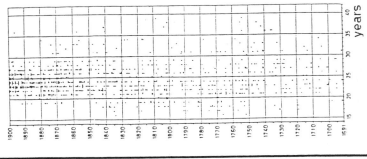

first time, there was an additional consequence. Reading the lower right part of the figure below the pyramid, we discover that at the beginning of the period many marriages showed a substantial difference in age between the two partners. At times the bride was younger, at other times, the groom. At that time one could find a number of unequal partners much like the ones frequently depicted a century ago among the Bavarian rural population by the German painter Wilhelm Leibl (1844–1900) (see the middle portion of fig. 6). Today they are the exception. In his time something so obvious wasn't something to gossip about. There was nothing ominous about it.

If we linger over this picture a bit longer we come across other things that our forebears must have taken for granted. We have lost sight of them since then, and, in discovering them anew, we might be astonished by them. Physical attractiveness, for example, did not play as important or decisive a role in choosing a partner in Leibl's time as it does today with our more standardized age of marriage. In our marital relationships we are drawn much more to people our own age, that is to say, people with young bodies, than was the case with our ancestors. Over a long period of time, closeness in age may stabilize our "intimate marriages" today in a way that it did not earlier. Sexual appeal may therefore play a justifiably greater role for us in our choice of marriage partners. In Leibl's time, however, stability came from other values. In addition, marital relationships were not burdened with the same expectations that we have today, since personal networks functioned differently

6.   Age at marriage from the late seventeenth to the late nineteenth centuries. *Left and right:* the trend in ages at first marriage in the Upper Hessian village of Heuchelheim near Gießen, 1691–1900. *Left:* each dot represents the age at first marriage of 1,104 women. *Right* (above and below the pyramid): age differences in years between partners marrying for the first time in 1710–20 and 1900. Marriages in which the woman was older than the man are identified by a mark with a crossed line and specially noted with a mark at the far right. The pyramid reflects schematically the dramatic trend toward marriage ages clustering around an "average age" over these two centuries. *Source: Historische Demographie als Sozialgeschichte: Gießen und Umgebung vom 17. zum 19. Jahrhundert, pt. 1,* Quellen und Forschungen zur hessischen Geschichte, ed. the Hessische Historische Kommission Darmstadt and the Historische Kommission für Hessen, vol. 31 (Darmstadt and Marburg, 1975), 315–23. *Center:* Wilhelm Leibl (1844–1900), *Old Peasant and Young Girl: The Unequal Couple* (1876–77) (Städelsches Kunstinstitut Frankfurt am Main). An additional painting by Wilhelm Leibl on the same theme (*In the Peasant Sitting Room*) hangs in the Neue Pinakothek in Munich. It was painted in 1890.

at that time, especially when it came to the degree of exclusivity. Men and women weren't so much fixated on their partners as they were oriented outside the relationship toward people who were like them. Today if marriage partners are not well suited for each other it leads either to divorce or to the almost unbearable psychological strain of a love-hate relationship. Such a development was much less likely in the more open marriages of earlier times.

Once again it seems to me that the question of whether people married for love back then is an inappropriate one. What we call with exaggeration "the intimacy revolution"—the term given to describe changes in marital relationships—presupposes another "revolution," that is, people turning increasingly to others at the same age and stage in the life cycle.

I have used this initial example only as an illustration of how different individual worlds were from each other back then simply on the basis of the enormous disparities in the biological life cycle. It also illustrates another reason why all of the "little" people we have studied—Johannes Hooss from Leimbach, Elsabeth Riebling from Gungelshausen, Matthäus Burkhart from Gabelbach, and Gerdt Peters from Hesel—are so important to me. The fact that it is impossible to interchange their lives should help me to avoid asking the wrong questions initially and to understand their life circumstances in an appropriate way. By no means do I want to suggest that I might know their individual stories in detail, including Johannes Hooss's, whose story has been so broadly sketched here. The sources are simply not good enough for that. I have to be satisfied with what has been left to us, and this is, generally speaking, precious little: their names (to talk about our ancestors as anonymous is already a mistake); a thin set of statistics about birth, marriage, and death; perhaps something about their property; and the positions of honor they held. We have a few court records as well, since all of them appear to have had the occasion for disputes, whether with neighbors, other heirs, or a presumed or legitimate claimant, all of which was hardly a wonder given their complex kinship relationships.

These little worlds were anything but perfect, and yet one should not speak of them as evil and corrupt little places either. People in those days mainly lived life not by thinking about it but through their behavior, that is, through what they did and didn't do. The modern "civilized world" has simply reversed the relationship. Most of us think before we act, this having been drilled into our heads through years of mandatory schooling. Plain spontaneity was much less restrained in this earlier time. Unchecked self-expression through word and deed was much more taken for granted back then than it is today.

It is necessary then to use one's imagination to reconstruct what their world might have been like out of these pieces. In addition to the personal data I had already assembled, I also gathered evidence about the outward circumstances of the time, from relationships among kin and neighbors to other relationships in the community, the legal and economic conditions surrounding land use, and the various state and seigneurial burdens and obligations. Moreover, I gathered material about what it meant to be an integral part of an open or forested landscape, the conditions along the roads, relationships with authorities, loyalties among the religious confessions, and the contents of collective memory.

Examining the parts of this mosaic more closely, we turn once again to Johannes Hooss and his world, this time mainly asking how such worlds came to be. What were their boundaries? At what points were they open to the world? Where were the centers around which everything turned? A problem similar to the one we encountered above in delimiting the networks of personal relationships comes up again in this case. How should we reasonably limit such a study? Even when one notes that a given road runs from point A to point B, most of the time it does not stop there. A side road branches off of it, and then there is one after that, and so forth. The world also does not end on the other side of the forest or the hills that act as a boundary, but in the end one cannot include in our considerations the entire planet.

I am not the first person to encounter this problem of setting out to define a "cultural region" with boundaries well enough established that it left a mark on the people living within it. On the contrary, the research on cultural regions, as it is called, has been carried out for a long time, and still is. It is represented by scholars from very different disciplines, including linguists, cultural geographers, geneticists, folklorists, legal historians, and students of religion, to name only some of the most prominent among them. The difficulty for social historians who join them in studying a cultural region lies mainly in the fact that the subjects studied by our colleagues have been narrowly defined by their disciplines—only the language, for example, or the spread of a costume or a particular labor technique, of a specially inherited disease or of the veneration of a particular saint. The result is that these cultural regions hardly coincide with each other.

One need only spread out a few carefully prepared and exceptionally detailed maps showing the main points of this research in order to convince oneself of the colorful variety of cultural boundaries. One map illustrates how the German language was spoken on this or that side of the political boundaries of Germany. Another one shows how the boundary lines crisscross Germany between regions in which inheritances are equally divided among all heirs and those in which the oldest or youngest among them are preferred. Geneticists also identify pockets where certain diseases are inherited due to the incest that results from intermarriage. Finally, the boundaries between religious confessions may or may not coincide with any other type of cultural boundary.

The solution to this puzzle is an obvious one. One simply takes one area as an example and then draws it in on every single one of the region's cultural maps. Quickly one discovers what cultural areas the region belongs to. It was the same way with our ancestors. Not every Catholic spoke German. Hesse was never a priori a territory defined by partible inheritance. Not all Calvinists were townspeople, and vice versa. The individual cultural boundaries, whether they were linguistic, political, confessional, economic, legal, or customary, often coincided with each other. They may even have determined each other. But this was not necessarily the case. To ask what single factor defined any given cultural region is, it seems to me, to once again ask the wrong question. There were cultural areas oriented around the economy, ones determined by religious confession, others defined by topography, and still others shaped by language. And there were other possibilities still.

By extension Johannes Hooss's little world was shaped by cultural regions that differed widely from each other in their significance and their openness to the outside. Each one also had different dimensions, central points, and peripheral areas. Here and there we have already mentioned a few of these cultural boundaries. The political boundary, and the religious boundary that coincided with it, ran immediately to the south of the Schwalm region between Calvinist Hesse-Kassel and Lutheran Hesse-Darmstadt. In times of war—during the Thirty Years' War, for example—the line separating these political foes became battle lines. Yet this line was a hard and fast boundary only to the political and religious leaders. Lower down the social ladder, residents on both sides of the border were in no way hindered from finding marriage partners in the enemy's territory. However deep divisions were between the state authorities and the churches, these people were hardly influenced by them and were not at all frightened of each other. The rulers' borders weren't theirs. The rulers' world was not the same as the world of the common people.

Other cultural regions had more relevance for Johannes Hooss, and they influenced his life from the time he was very small. I have assembled some of them in figure 7 (p. 45). Seen in their entirety, these maps should emphasize to us what little basis of comparison there was between even the smallest areas because every one was entirely different from the others in some way. Given this background information, the inevitable question about how representative any village, borough, hamlet, or farm was becomes an irrelevant one. Every tiny region was unique, and the lives of the individuals in it were not interchangeable with the others. There was a multitude of little worlds, and none of them could claim to be representative.

The center of the world in the first small map is Leimbach, and with it the Vältes Farm on which Johannes Hooss was born, lived his whole life, and eventually died. In this case the word *world* simply means a rectangular section of a topographical map. The map stretches a good thirty kilometers from east to west and twenty-five kilometers from north to south. The lowlands of the Schwalm region stand out clearly, lying virtually level at an elevation of 200 to 250 meters and being protected all around and favored by a good climate. One is almost tempted to say that it lies like a child cradled in its mother's lap. The lowlands are ringed all around by higher elevations, ridges, and hills: the Keller Forest, the Keller Forest Foothills, the Upper Hessian Hills, the Arnshain Heights, the Schwalm Ridge, the Ottrauer Mountains, the southern and northern Knüll Foothills, and, finally, behind them all, the Hochknüll. What are pretentiously called the "mountainous areas" and the "Hochknüll" never reach more than 700 meters in elevation: the Knüll itself was 634 meters, and the highest point, the Keller Forest, was a mere 675 meters. All of the other heights were even more modest in elevation.

About forty kilometers south of this lowland area on the northern edge of the Vogel Mountains are the headwaters of the Schwalm. The river flows from south to north and still gives its name to the region today. The main highway follows the river's course to Alsfeld and then goes on to the fortress of Ziegenhain and the territorial capital of Kassel. Roads were seldom used exclusively for peaceful purposes in the past. They served not only as trade routes, as highways for travel and news, but they repeatedly became the strategic line of march for soldiers as well. They were also the arteries that spread human and animal diseases and the communication lines that carried terrifying rumors. Extreme remoteness or certain topographical conditions could effectively isolate a region, and this could either work to the advantage or disadvantage of its villages, hamlets, farms, fields, and inhabitants. The isolation was an advantage insofar as it kept the region out of the way of military maneuvers and horrible plagues. But at the same time the remoteness was a disadvantage since the residents were out of the mainstream of economic development, market ties, innovations, the development of novel curiosities, and the spread of news.

The idea that a landscape influences a people, physically as well as psychologically, has long been acknowledged. Narrow and cramped mountainous areas affect people differently from wide-open river landscapes and stretches of coastal area. These days we can no longer see the effects on people in the past of another part of the landscape, namely, the forests, or we at least have to make an effort to comprehend it. I have therefore drawn on figure 7b the divisions in the Schwalm between open areas and forests as we know them for the seventeenth and eighteenth centuries. Forest boundaries are generally ancient boundaries; they are "structures of long duration." The cry "Protect our forests!" is hardly a discovery of our age, even though it has been made at different times for different reasons. Even for the period after the Thirty Years' War, no essential reforestation of the landscape took place despite the losses in population, the abandoned farms, and the overgrown fields. The edge of the forest advanced here and there and clearings were closed in again with woods, but nowhere did a fundamental redivision between open land and forest take place between 1650 and 1750.

Combining the forest and topographical maps enables us to see that the entire lowlands of the Schwalm in the past was situated in an area completely free of forests and formed into a single wide and unobstructed hollow. In this open lowland area surrounded by forests, everyone knew each other. They knew how many horses one had and who owned only cows or goats

7.   Schwalm region in the seventeenth and eighteenth centuries. *A,* surface area map; *B,* distribution of open land and forest; *C,* towns, villages, and hamlets; *D,* land use: pastures and arable; *E,* property holding: common lands, inherited land, cleared land, rented lands, and usable lands from noble properties; *F,* farm size. *Source:* Martin Born, *Wandlung und Beharrung ländlicher Siedlung und bäuerlicher Wirtschaft: Untersuchungen zur frühneuzeitlichen Kulturlandschaftsgenese im Schwalmgebiet,* Marburger Geographische Schriften, vol. 14 (Marburg: Selbstverlag des Geographischen Instituts der Universität, 1961), 9, 11, 94, 101, 119, 133, and maps 1, 2, 7, 8, 11, and 16.

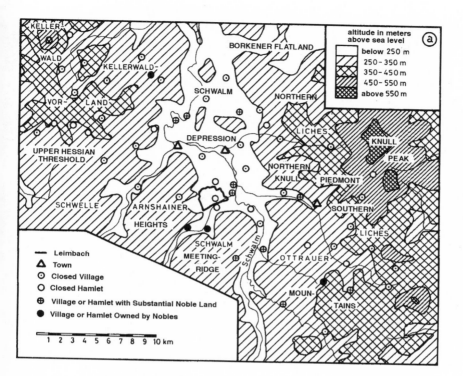

KELLER
WALD
KELLERWALD-
VOR-
LAND
UPPER HESSIAN
THRESHOLD
SCHWELLE
ARNSHAINER
HEIGHTS
SCHWALM
MEETING-
RIDGE
BORKENER FLATLAND
SCHWALM
DEPRESSION
NORTHERN
LICHES
NORTHERN
KNULL
PIEDMONT
KNULL
PEAK
SOUTHERN
LICHES
OTTRAUER
MOUN-
TAINS

altitude in meters
above sea level
below 250 m
250 - 350 m
350 - 450 m
450 - 550 m
above 550 m

ⓐ

— Leimbach
△ Town
⊙ Closed Village
○ Closed Hamlet
⊕ Village or Hamlet with Substantial Noble Land
● Village or Hamlet Owned by Nobles

Schwalm

1 2 3 4 5 6 7 8 9 10 km

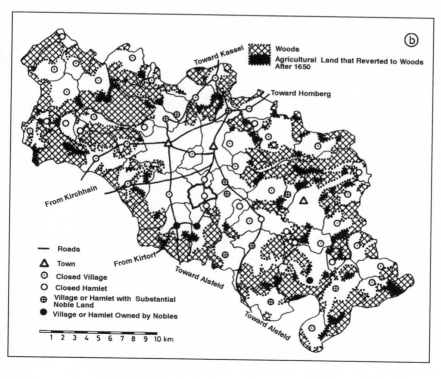

Toward Kassel
Toward Homberg
From Kirchhain
From Kirtorf
Toward Alsfeld
Toward Alsfeld

Woods
Agricultural Land that Reverted to Woods
After 1650

ⓑ

— Roads
△ Town
⊙ Closed Village
○ Closed Hamlet
⊕ Village or Hamlet with Substantial Noble Land
● Village or Hamlet Owned by Nobles

1 2 3 4 5 6 7 8 9 10 km

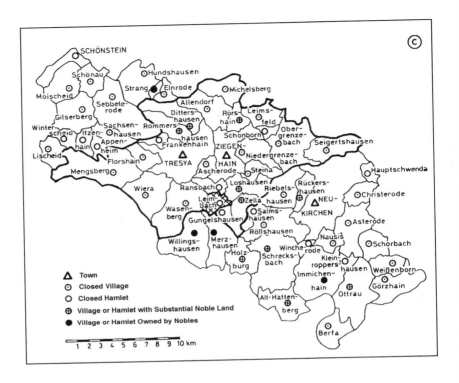

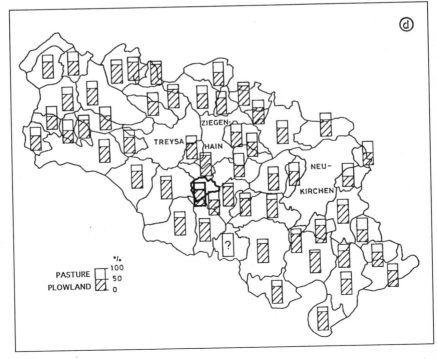

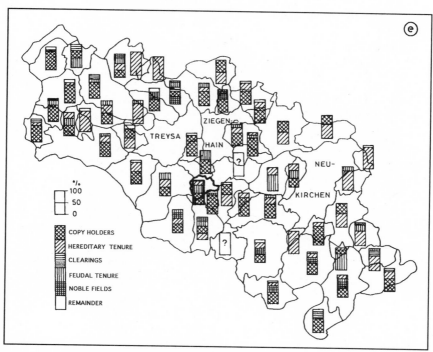

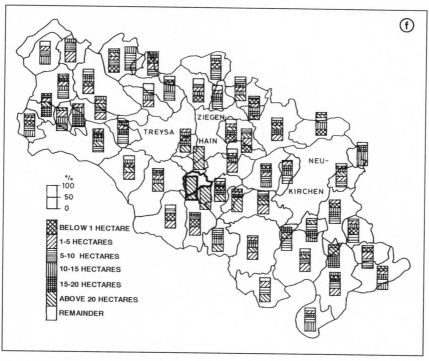

that had to be pastured on the side of the paths. By the same token, they also knew when someone introduced something new—perhaps when potatoes were first planted or lucerne cultivated—and what kind of success or failure he had with it. Everyone talked about it and maybe someone tried it out in the following year.

The more people were separated from the world on the other side of the forests, the more foreign everyone living on the other side became to the residents of the Schwalm. Sprawling and shady forests are mostly recreational areas for us today. We go for walks or have picnics in them and walk around in them without fear. Our ancestors, however, experienced them very differently. In their time the woods aroused fear in people, this despite the greater economic role that the woods played as a supplier of firewood and building materials and, to the poor, as a source of food for goats and pigs who foraged in the underbrush. This was not simply because of the threat posed by wild animals that are now extinct, like wolves, rapacious boars, and wild pigs. Like these animals, highwaymen preferred not to operate along open stretches of roadway that were easily scanned. Instead they waited in ambush under the light cover of the forests. It was easy to suddenly attack a herd of livestock and quickly drive the animals out of sight right and left into the underbrush. Where could they drive them to in an open field? Where could they possibly hide them?

Anyone who takes the reading of fairy tales, myths, and legends seriously will remember that the woods were not simply full of the evil deeds of people and wild animals. At one time trees and bushes too were animate, and one never knew whether they were well disposed or not. Today we concede that plants are alive when we say that this tree is living, that one dead, and a third one awakens to new life in the spring. But for us they no longer have a soul. We claim that only humans have souls. Our environment is poorer because of it since trees, bushes, animals, and plants naturally no longer talk to us. And they too no longer understand us as they once understood Francis of Assisi. When he preached the birds listened religiously.

Anyone who wants to put himself back into this lost world, a world that abounded in life everywhere at the time, turns to the Grimm's children and household fairy tales for examples. They originally appeared in two volumes between 1812 and 1815. It is fortunate for us that Wilhelm (1786–1859) and Jacob Grimm (1785–1863) collected the largest part of these fairy tales in Hesse, especially in and around Kassel.[1] We need not worry about the fact that some of the stories were not Hessian, or even German for that matter, that they had essentially old French and Swiss origins. New research by German literature and folklore specialists has shown that the circle of the most important of Grimm's informants centered on two families in Kassel and a tailor woman from the nearby village of Niederzwehren. All of them had more or less direct roots in French- and Swiss-speaking areas, whether it was through parents or spouses. The Wild family, for example, had close ties to family members in Bern and Basel, the Hassenpflug family to Huguenot relatives in the Dauphiné. Frau Dorothea Viehmann of Niederzwehren, on the other hand, whose maiden name was Pierson, even grew up speaking French as her native tongue.

It is small wonder then that a collection of the fairy tales known to us as Grimm's is to be found in an older French collection from a hundred years before: Charles Perrault's (1626–1703) *Stories* of 1697.[2] One finds "Sleeping Beauty" there as "La Belle au bois dormant," "Little Red Riding Hood" as "Le Petit Chaperon rouge," "Puss 'n' Boots" as "Le Maître Chat ou le Chat botté," "Cinderella" as "Cendrillon ou la petite pantoufle de verre," and "Thumbellina" as "Le Petit Poucet." The Hassenpflugs and Piersons had known this collection of fairy tales since they were children. In their new home they passed them on, not only to their own children but to anyone who would listen. Radio and television did not compete for public attention at the time, and there were no inexpensive comics and picture books yet.

Despite the French origins of the tales, I believe we can still use the content of Grimm's fairy tales for our purposes. Here I want to quote a specialist on the tales, the folklorist Ingeborg Weber-Kellermann of Marburg (Hesse): "After their introduction the tales became partially domesticated in Hesse. They were repeatedly told and adapted by authors who felt at home in Hesse. And so the great woods in which Hansel and Gretel got lost and in which Little Red Riding Hood met the wolf were undeniably thought of as Hessian woods. The hollow tree where Little Brother and Sister Unterschlupf are found, the grass that Little Sister needs for her deer: all of this smacks of the Hessian landscape [from her introduction in the first volume, p. 15]." Reading further in the introduction of the Weber-Kellermann edition, we find an additional illustration. It contains a number of drawings made for Grimm's collection of fairy tales toward the end of the nineteenth century by the Marburg painter Otto Ubbelohde (1867–1922). Weber-Kellermann notes:

With his ink drawings Ubbelohde built up a Hessian landscape. In the fairytale of the Bee Queen one recognizes the inner courtyard of the palace of the landgrave at Marburg. Sleeping Beauty slept for a hundred years in the castle at Weilburg. The peasant folk in the Golden Goose come from the Schwalm region, since clever Gretel was wearing the broad costume of the Schwalm girls and the mother, while mourning at the grave of the willful child, wore the common evening bonnet and the oval-shaped mourning shoebuckles on her shoes. Snow White and Rose Red appear as peasant girls from the Schwalm and ride around on their bears with open cape strings. Clever Hans wears an otter pelt cap worn by the boys of the Schwalm, and Hansel and Gretel meet in the forest in a Hessian elders' house. (15–17)

It is one thing to cite Grimm's fairy tales and the Ubbelohde drawings in order to illustrate the great psychological importance of the woods, as, for example, the "deep dark woods" in the "Frog King." It is quite a different matter to interpret the substance of the fairy tales for the purposes of social history, agrarian history, or even psychohistory, that is, to use them as sources. Despite all of the caution needed here, one cannot escape the fact that these fairy tales frequently mentioned things well known to the professional social historian. The parents of "Mary Child" were so poor that, perhaps during one of the frequent crop failures of that time, they "no longer had their daily bread." On the other hand, when the characters ate lavishly or to excess they did not feast on roasted and smoked meats, but instead, as in those meat-poor times, they ate butterbread and cakes as in "The Three Little Men in the Forest."

Above all we are repeatedly witnesses to the classic conflict between stepparents and stepchildren and between stepbrothers and stepsisters. This was not at all unlike frequent disputes occasioned by the very high mortality rates and the remarriage of the surviving partner that followed the death of a spouse. People at the time could relate plenty of examples from their own experience to the following story: "The brother took his little sister by the hand and said: 'Since our mother died we don't get any relief. Every day stepmother beats us, and when we go to her she kicks us away. We eat only the leftover hard crusts of bread. May God keep our mother from knowing about this! Come on, let's run away from home' ("Little Brother and Little Sister").

I am reminded here of little Johannes Hooss, who lost his mother when he was seven. Shortly after that, Elisabeth Stumpf, a stranger from another village, became his stepmother. On top of that, he soon had five stepbrothers and -sisters. All of them, supported by their mother, could lay claim to the Vältes Farm. To be sure, Johannes did not run away from home as in the fairy tales. But his brother, Hans Class, disappeared after he was confirmed and never came back, and this might have been related to his uncertain prospects for the future.

If you look at it from a certain point of view, things also happen all of the time to us in the same way that they do in a fairy tale. If only we were to observe things around us carefully enough, the fairy tales suddenly come to life. They start to speak to us and explain things. But let's not digress too much from our six maps, even though I have provided them for the purpose of stimulating just such ideas.

Figures 7c through 7e illustrate one more time the theme of how many little worlds existed in the past. Figure 7c shows how the region, that is, the land known as the Schwalm, was divided into its smallest political and administrative units, that is, towns, villages, and hamlets. The borders of the Schwalm region essentially coincide with those of the old county of Ziegenhain, a county that, for its own part, encompassed the three districts of Neukirchen, Schönstein, and Ziegenhain. With the exception of the towns of Ziegenhain and Treysa and the Huguenot colony of Frankenhain, founded in 1699–1701 and located near Treysa, the following places belonged to the latter district: Leimbach, Gungelshausen, Zella, Loshausen, Ransbach, Ascherode, Steina, Niedergrenzebach, Obergrenzebach, Seigertshausen, Schönborn, Rörshain, Leimsfeld, Michelsberg, Allendorf, Dittershausen, Rommershausen, Florshain, Mengsberg, Wiera, and Wasenberg.

The district of Neukirchen that bordered it on the south included, in addition to the town of Neukirchen, the communities of Riebelsdorf, Rüchershausen, Salmshausen, Röllshausen, Asterode, Schrecksbach, Wincherode, Nausis, Kleinropperhausen, Görzhain, Ottrau, Alt-Hattendorf, and Berfa. To the north the adjoining district of Schönstein encompassed, in addition to the town of Schönstein, Lischeid, Winterscheid, Appenhain, Itzenhain, Sachsenhausen, Gilserberg, Sebbeterode, Schönau, and Moiseid. In addition, I have included four villages still in noble hands, namely, Strang, Willingshausen, Merzhausen, and Immichenhain. To round things off I have finally added in a few communes under the jurisdiction of the old courts of

Jesberg and Oberaula that belonged to the Landgraviate of Hesse-Darmstadt. They were Einrode, Hundshausen, Weissborn, Schorbach, Christerode, Hauptschwenda, and Holzburg.

This assortment of different towns, villages, and hamlets, whether belonging to districts in the Landgraviate of Hesse-Kassel, noble enclaves, Hesse-Darmstadt, or the areas hedged in by Jesberg and Oberaula, reveals the richly colored tapestry of worlds made up of the tiniest administrative units. It clearly shows that also with regard to politics and administration we are dealing with a diversity of cultural areas. The subjects of the Landgraviate of Hesse-Kassel were not the same as those from the neighboring village of Merzhausen that was dominated by the nobility, let alone the same as those in nearby Holzburg under Hesse-Darmstadt. There was a multiplicity of types of villagers in the Schwalm region.

The differentiation did not stop here. The region that was popularly identified as the Schwalm region was not at all the same thing as the region known as the traditional Schwalm in folklore. This was a smaller area and essentially encompassed only the communities of the Ziegenhain and Neukirchen Districts. Finally, the area that has achieved a certain notoriety among anthropologists and geneticists as "the Schwalm isolate" is smaller yet and defined by their extensive research as an area of close intermarriage and the inbreeding that has resulted from it. This includes only the villages of Wasenberg, Ransbach, Loshausen, Zella, Leimbach, Gungelshausen, Merzhausen, and Willingshausen.

For figures 7d through 7f I have used the layout of the communes from 7c as a model and in each case highlighted a specific feature that directly contributed to economic differences from place to place. In figure 7d there is land use, in 7e the distribution of land, and in 7f average farm size. All of the maps refer to the period around 1750, the first time statistics appeared everywhere in sufficient detail. They depict the layout of the region toward the end of Johannes Hooss's life (d. 1755).

The fact that the last three maps reveal a number of connections between topography (7a), the distribution of open land and forest (7b), and communal jurisdictions (7c) is self-explanatory. In the first chapter we noted how the largest property-holding peasants, each with a sizable portion of cultivable land in the Landgraviate, owed carting and carrying services to the lord's estate in Ziegenhain, and that they met these obligations with horses. It is no surprise that the three villages with the largest farms (Leimbach, Gungelshausen, and Ransbach) owned at the same time the largest stables of horses.

In these villages the average size of the farms was fifty acres (7f), and they encompassed at least half of all of the cultivated land (7e). When a peasant was free from carting and carrying services, he did not work the horses in the meadows or put them out to pasture. They were used to plow the fields. Arable land comprised 252 out of 383 acres (66% of the land) in Gungels-hausen, 450 out of 583 acres (77%) in Leimbach, and even more in Rans-bach, 667 out of 761 acres (88%) (7d).

Looking at these maps, one is also not surprised to discover that the rural world around the three prosperous villages, that is, Merzhausen, Will-ingshausen, and Loshausen, was completely different and comparatively poor. The starkest contrasts appear on the map that depicts farm size (7f). Instead of the black columns that represent large properties, the villages show a predominance of cross-hatched and striped columns signifying small, even minute farms of less than seven and a half acres. The explanation is to be found once again in maps 7c and 7e. Merzhausen and Willingshausen were in the possession of the nobility, and Loshausen was among the villages with the second-largest concentration of noble properties. Subtracting the consid-erable areas that the nobles worked directly from the total arable in these communities meant that relatively little land was left over for the other farms.

Given this background, it starts to become clear why the sons and daugh-ters of Leimbach's large peasants did not look for marriage partners in Merzhausen, Willingshausen, or Loshausen, even though they were from neighboring communities. They were more interested in young men and women from Gungelshausen, Ransbach, Wasenberg, and Ascherode, or even Steina, Niedergrenzebach, and Obergrenzebach. These communities, especially the latter ones, may have been located much farther away, but the map of farm sizes shows that large farms predominated in these villages, and these peasants, for their own part, were less interested in marriage ties with small peasants within their own community than in alliances with peasants with large holdings elsewhere. Such marriages united partners who came from the same social and economic worlds and not neighbors who had land and pastures next to each other (compare this with fig. 23, p. 120, "Marriage network of the Vältes farmers, 1600–1800").

The landscape of the Schwalm—the lowland itself and the heights and forests that surrounded it—therefore shaped the social horizons of Leim-bachers just as it did the other inhabitants of these low-lying lands. Within this cultural world defined by the landscape, life was hardly the same every-where. There were large peasants with large farms, small peasants, and even peasants with smaller lands yet. Some worked with horses, others ploughed their fields with oxen, and there were still others who had nothing at all to plough with. The lands they worked, whether their own or those of others who hired them, were burdened with a variety of obligations. In addition, some lived in villages, some lived in towns, while some were subject to entirely different political authorities. The majority of them were Calvinists from the Landgraviate of Hesse-Kassel. Next to them lived Lutherans in Holzburg, belonging to the rival house, the Landgraviate of Hesse-Darmstadt. Over and beyond that and living in Frankenhain were Huguenots who had emigrated as religious refugees from the Dauphiné and Languedoc after the revocation of the Edict of Nantes in 1685.

It was among these communities, woven together like a colorful tapestry, that a person made his or her way through life. The distinctive features of life that are reflected in the maps—and these represent only a sample of them—formed the framework for every individual as networks of personal ties were made, improved, expanded, reconsidered, and broken up over the course of a lifetime. The way so many boundaries and cultural areas within the Schwalm lowlands crisscrossed each other, each of them extending out different distances and exercising a different influence, contributed to the fact that no one boundary line, not even those that extended out beyond the lowlands, was a hard and fast one. No matter where the boundaries were laid down, the other side always exercised a certain power of attraction. Marriages could therefore be contracted on occasion with villagers from Arnshain or Mönch-Leusel, on the other side of the mountains. In 1775 Johann Jost of the Hooss clan even married his second wife, Maria Catharina Michel, from the Lutheran village of Holzburg! Even the smallest worlds were not hermetically sealed off from the outside world.

I would like to introduce another subject using another map and with it bring into the discussion a few more fundamental questions. This was not a map that was drawn physically but one that existed in the spirit. I have not depicted it because such a map might pretend to a degree of certainty that is misleading. In terms of subject matter this is a map of the religious confessions. When a confessionally mixed marriage was made with the villager from Holzburg, I was puzzled since it ran counter to the cultural boundaries. Did it involve what we would call religious toleration? Should we interpret it as the beginning of a process of "de-confessionalization" or even "de-Christianization"?

To be sure, historians have turned in recent years to the delicate subject of the history of religious mentalities and its related source problems. They have done so with understandable hesitation and a great deal of caution. What did religion really mean to the Leimbachers and the Holzburgers, both before and after the Reformation? What did they believe, and what relevance did their religious ideas have to the life they had to lead in the village? Generally speaking, we know only what the official teaching about this or that subject was. Young clergymen had to learn this body of doctrine from the confessionally oriented universities, but it was another matter what they actually preached in their sermons and passed on in their lessons to their "believers." And what the Leimbachers or Holzburgers eventually made out of it was something else again.

In this context one thinks about the ambiguousness of the position of people like Johannes Hooss's uncle. This man, whose name was also Johannes Hooss, was born on the Vältes Farm in 1631 and was steeped in its worldview for twenty years while he was growing up. In 1651 he enrolled in the Royal Collegium Adelphico-Mauritianum in Kassel, founded in 1618, in order to study theology. After finishing his studies in 1658 he assumed responsibility for his first parish in Oberbiel, near Wetzlar. For seven years he had been indoctrinated at a strict orthodox Calvinist university, living in what was to him an alien world. One wonders whether, when he took up his duties in the parish, he actually denounced and banned everything he saw there as the superstitious beliefs of ignorant peasants or as immoral behavior that ought to be punished, just as it had been drilled into him in Kassel. He saw the villagers of Oberbiel every day and probably knew, if he were a good pastor and really cared for their souls, much more about their needs and worries than the urban professors of theology did. The worlds of Oberbiel and the Vältes Farm were, after all, more his worlds than the world of the intellectuals at Kassel in the Collegium Mauritianum.

What could these intellectuals and their secular colleagues possibly understand about peasant life? Let's take one concrete example, sexuality, to illustrate the problem. What did they know about what it was like to stay unmarried for ten or twenty years, and sometimes for an entire lifetime, as so many peasant boys and girls, servants, maids, old uncles, aunts, young widowers and widows did, and to suppress their sexuality as the church and state wanted them to? Unlike townspeople, rural youths, single men, and widowers lived in constant contact with animals, whether they were living with them under the same roof or in the next stall or whether it was out in the green meadows or in the thickets of the woods. Bestiality, that is, sexual relations between humans and animals, was punished by urban officials and their subordinates in the countryside much more severely than was extra-marital sexual intercourse. Well into the modern period men paid for this crime with their lives. The animals were burned. Yet it was reported so infrequently that one can confidently assume that not all of the crimes were reported. In the eyes of those who had to report it, namely, peasants themselves and pastors who had grown up in the countryside, the crime obviously did not deserve capital punishment. Besides, no one was burdened with any undesirable social consequences such as illegitimate children and the difficulty of finding a home for them.

From 1749 on one can easily and systematically survey all of the legal accusations, convictions, and punishments involving one of the most thoroughly peasant societies anywhere in Europe at the time (Sweden) and, in this way, investigate the circumstances involving such cases. After the first statistical office in the world opened that year in Stockholm, every Swedish pastor was required not only to report regularly every death in the parish but to fill out printed forms providing details concerning the causes of death. Looking through the mass of forms that were filled out, one finds hardly any cases of bestiality, at least according to the pastors who filled out the reports. In this case the pastors' world coincided with that of the peasants, their sons, daughters, servants, and serving girls, even when they often flew into a fit about the peasants' cursing and drinking and interpreted some epidemic as the righteous punishment of God.

In those cases in which the solidarity of the community broke down, when the network of the parish split apart and a case of bestiality was publicly reported to the authorities, it appears to me to have been frequently accompanied by a settling of old scores between families, groups, and individuals who were hostile to each other. Moral outrage over violating the norm hardly seemed to be the issue. Moreover, a report and the intervention of the authorities in the affairs of the community that followed it was a double-edged sword. Anyone who filed a report was eventually delivered into the hands of the authorities along with everyone else in the village, since the authorities claimed responsibility for even the most intimate affairs involving their subjects and eagerly used the occasion of any report to exercise a thorough and harsh social discipline on the population. (Anyone who objects that I should substitute "complicity" for "solidarity" should consider whether by doing so one hastily and uncritically assumes the perspective of the authorities and shows the same lack of understanding that they did.)

There is still little enough known about such "history from the bottom up," even if much more of it has been written in recent years. A historian in need of assistance should therefore turn to colleagues in folklore studies who have worked longer with such sources, even if they do so with entirely different purposes in mind. I would like to cite one of them who has examined the history of religious mentalities: Pieter J. Meertens of Amsterdam, who represents a nation that has been Calvinist Reformed as it is commonly defined since the end of the sixteenth century. Concerning the "survival of pre-Reformation religious practices in the Netherlands during the Reformation," Meertens wrote in 1972:

> It is at first sight a curious phenomenon that in a land that felt the call of Protestantism since the time of the Reformation so many remnants of the pre-Reformation past remained. What at first seems strange to us becomes understandable when one considers that the Reformation was less firmly established than the Protestant-minded historical writings of the nineteenth century thought and maintained. By the end of the sixteenth century and shortly thereafter, a large portion of the Dutch people were a long way from renouncing Catholic beliefs and accepting the teachings of Calvin. Especially the flat countryside remained Catholic for a long time. The North and South Dutch Synods of 1635 declared that decrees and ordinances amounted to nothing because no one obeyed them.[3]

After Meertens describes in detail a large number of these remnants in the form of feast days of the saints such as Martin, Nikolaus, and the Three Kings and other customs celebrated during the year such as Carnival, May Day, Easter, and Pentecost, he concludes briefly and succinctly: "It is wrong to characterize the Netherlands as a Calvinist nation as it is commonly done" (409).

A historian, especially one of collective mentalities, would certainly see things differently and formulate these views differently from the way a folklorist would. He would perhaps avoid generalizations like this: "The great mass of the people cultivated, and still cultivate, until recently a conservative attitude especially with regard to religion" (396). A historian would be more inclined to look into the origins and significance of the so-called "conservative" attitudes, how long they persisted, and how they were repressed, denounced, and broke apart. One would be more inclined to see in them a way of dealing with everyday life in a particular region at a particular time.

I do not at all mean to suggest that I could explain this any better. Quite the contrary! If I can do so then it is because the folklorists with their usually ahistorical way of seeing things—and who holds that against them?—have stimulated me to think about such issues much as they did above with regard to cultural regions. It is worthwhile for us social historians to listen to the folklorists. They have a number of stimulating ideas, and discussions with them are often fruitful.

It was no accident that a Dutch folklorist was speaking in this case, and that his subject was the superficial establishment of official Calvinism in the sixteenth and seventeenth centuries and even in our own time. At least in the eyes of the authorities, the Landgraviate of Hesse-Kassel, including the Schwalm region, was also Calvinist Reformed ever since Landgrave Moritz issued the so-called "Improvement Points" decree in 1605 and introduced the creed and catechism (1607) and the consistory ordinance (1610). Moreover, an official delegation from Hesse-Kassel took part in the Synod of Dordrecht in 1618–19, joining the European community of Reformed churches and publicly making the break with Lutheranism.

Landgrave Moritz and his theologians certainly did all of this. But what about the Leimbachers and the people from the Vältes Farm? Were they "Calvinists" too? Were they Calvinist more than in the sense that it now appeared on their baptismal certificates or that they celebrated a new form of the Eucharist, receiving not hosts but the bread mentioned in the words of the institution by the evangelists? How many of us are really what appears on our baptismal certificates, if we even have one? What did the Leimbachers take away from sermons in which the nature of Christ was no longer discussed in great detail but was supposed to be illustrated with the plain words of the Bible? What did they believe in their everyday lives and not simply on Sunday in the short time of the church service? Couldn't we substitute the people of the Schwalm for those from the Netherlands? Weren't the people of the Schwalm just as "conservative," "especially in matters of religion," as they were? To borrow Meertens's words, could we claim that the majority of the population of the Schwalm at the beginning of the seventeenth century and later had not completely renounced the old beliefs and adopted the teachings of Calvin?

I don't know and I don't pretend to have the answer. In the end the historian can't good-naturedly slap our ancestors on the back and ask them about their religious beliefs or their doubts, especially not when they preferred to remain silent about them. And they often remained silent. What I aim to do here is to stimulate readers to think on their own about things that have hardly been explored yet, much as reading Meertens's study did for me. Let me quote the Dutch folklorist once again:

> As Christianity advanced into the Germanic world, it adapted itself to the dominant customs and habits of the people so long as they did not openly contradict the new teaching. The Reformation, by contrast, intentionally avoided this adaptation. Reformers had no understanding of the meaning of popular festivals in which the members of the community, especially the younger ones, could satisfy their needs for joyful celebrations. Calvinism failed to understand that one could not eliminate certain values in traditional popular life without substituting new ones in their place. Because this chance was missed, it had to fight an unnecessary and hopeless battle in which it triumphed only partially. (409–10)

What interests me is not popular festivals or communal celebrations but everyday life. I would like to take one key concept from Meertens: adaptation. We can assume that the Leimbachers and other inhabitants of the Schwalm then and now took as much from official Calvinist teaching as they needed for everyday life and that for their own benefit they incorporated this into their own everyday worldview. If the Reformation refused to accomodate the people's dominant habits and customs, then the reverse was the case: the people adapted the Reformation to their own habits, customs, and everyday needs.

I would like to illustrate this point once again with the example of Johannes Hooss's world. As was often the case, he left behind no direct sources, so we have to proceed indirectly. I invite the reader to look at three pictures with me. The originals all hang in the London National Gallery, only a few galleries apart from each other, so that on a single morning or afternoon one can walk comfortably from one to the other and compare them in all their glory and think about them.

The three paintings (figs. 8, 9, 10, pp. 62–64) are from the Netherlands in the middle of the seventeenth century, that is, the period following the upheavals of the Reformation era. Two of them were painted in the northern part of the country, which had become Calvinist. The third, on the other hand, was painted in the southern part of the country, which had remained Catholic, that is, modern-day Belgium. Each of them depicts a family grouping. The question that occurs to us while looking at them is a simple one: Does one find depicted here differences in family size due to differences in religion?

Let me interject here that recent historical research has uncovered a great deal of conclusive evidence showing that family planning and birth control started much earlier among Calvinist populations than among Catholic ones. In staunchly Calvinist Geneva, for example, it was already practiced in the seventeenth century and in every social class. Historians ascribe this to the fact that Calvinism made parents responsible, to a certain extent, for the number of children they had and for their futures. Fewer children meant generally better-fed, more carefully reared and educated children, ones endowed with more property and married more advantageously. In parish registers of Geneva one can easily follow how the birth intervals at the time compared with those from an earlier period, how they doubled and then tripled in length. Long before the fertile part of their lives came to an end, women stopped giving birth. Soon families of two or three children were no longer a rarity. Before the Reformation families had had six or eight children like everywhere else, as was still the case in Catholic Europe well into the eighteenth and nineteenth centuries. In these areas the number of children was largely left to Providence. Catholic parents also felt responsible for their children, but this was expressed by baptizing them quickly so that through baptism a newborn child might enter the Christian community and therefore, should it die young, might have a reasonable chance at eternal bliss.[4]

Little is known about the painters of the three paintings. One therefore cannot assume that they have portrayed families that were actually alive at the time. Artists have always taken the liberty to paint in accordance with their own imaginations, and this makes the content of these paintings even more interesting for our purposes. They might have involved real families, a mother and father with their children, a portrait done on commission comparable to our modern family pictures for a photo album. But this was not necessarily the case. They might have involved imagined realities. Then we would be dealing with family groupings stemming ideally from the imagination or the convictions of the artist, perhaps in accordance with family norms conditioned by religion. In Dutch painting at the time we know that many paintings ostensibly dealing with themes from everyday life and painted for average people from this milieu contained an easily discernible moral message. One such message might have been, "Have only a few children and take good care of them!"

The first painting lends itself to this kind of interpretation (fig. 8). It comes from the hand of Jan Steen (1625/26–1679). Steen was not only one of the most prominent representatives of Dutch genre painting at its peak but also one who almost always used a moralizing tone in his works. Born in Leiden, Steen spent his entire life there or in the immediate area, in Utrecht, Haarlem, Den Haag, and Warmond. Even if the work's title, *Blessing at Table,* was not his own, the religious significance of the painting comes through unmistakably in the little girl folding her hands and the boy holding his hat before him. This family with only two children certainly did not belong to the upper classes. The girl may have been four, the boy eleven years old. The interval between their births would therefore have been seven years, and the woman does not appear to be pregnant again. The interval until the birth of the next child, should it come, would therefore have been at least five years.

This was not at all "natural." The interval between births at that time averaged, in the absence of family planning, between two and two and a half years. One might possibly object that one or two of the family's children may have already died in infancy. This was possible but still unlikely in this case. Even though the meal is not a lavish one, neither malnutrition nor famine is evident here. On the contrary, all of the members of the family look well nourished. It *was* easier to feed and care for two children than for six or eight of them, just as it was easier to provide clothing, education, and individual religious instruction. Each child could have his or her own toys, suggested here by the boot on the floor with the pull string that had just fallen from the little girl's hand. It is tempting to speak in this case about a fully developed "intimate family" in the middle of the seventeenth century, with marriage partners of the same age and loving devotion to child-rearing: a small family in the modern style, planned, affectionate, and intentionally created.

The upper-class family that the Flemish portrait and narrative artist Gonzales Coques (1614/18–1684) painted at the same time looked entirely different (fig. 9). Coques was associated throughout his life with the Catholic city of Antwerp and enjoyed a good reputation there as a portrait artist preferred by the well-to-do middle class. In this painting the subjects are not even looking at each other, let alone displaying loving attention. There is no

8. Jan Steen (1625/26–1679), *Blessing at Table*, 40.6 × 35 cm on wood. Reproduced by courtesy of the Trustees, The National Gallery, London. Family with two children painted in Calvinist Holland after 1660.

trace of warm feelings or tender affections, not even in the younger sisters who are being pushed forward in a stroller. Someone must have stifled it. Six chidden are depicted. All of the five younger ones seem to have been born in quick "natural" birth intervals. The oldest daughter is picking roses, perhaps as a sign of her imminent marriage and departure from the family, that is, the beginning of its eventual end. She no longer stands in the half

9. Gonzales Coques (1614/18–1684), *Family Group in the Open Air*. Oil on canvas, 64.2 × 85.5 cm. Reproduced by courtesy of the Trustees, The National Gallery, London. Family with six children painted around 1664 in the Catholic city of Antwerp.

circle of the family but is standing in the background separate from them. This is not a portrait of an intimate small family like Steen's but rather one of the divinely and state-supported institution of marriage and the family. Children were born into it as God willed, and this was pleasing to the state since it was believed at the time that its most precious treasure was a large population.

More crowded yet is the last painting, of a father, mother, and eight children (fig. 10). It was the work of Frans Hals (1581/85–1666), recognized as one of the great Dutch painters. Even today we like to visit the museum dedicated to him in Haarlem, a house where he worked in his own time. You might be surprised to know that he was Dutch and lived in the northern part of the Calvinist Netherlands, in Haarlem. The painting of the largest family with the largest number of children comes from this part of the Neth–

10. Frans Hals (1581/85–1666). *Family Group and Landscape*. Canvas, 148.5 × 251 cm. Reproduced by courtesy of the Trustees, The National Gallery, London. Family with eight children painted in Calvinist Holland around 1650. Frans Hals was born in Catholic Antwerp and remained Catholic his entire life.

erlands? All of the children must have followed each other in short "natural" birth intervals, and this has clearly left its mark on the appearance of the mother. Her face and body seem much older than her husband's.

It is true that during his lifetime Frans Hals painted in Haarlem, and yet he was born, like Coques, in Catholic Antwerp. At a young age he then settled in Holland with his parents. He also remained loyal throughout his life to the Catholic faith that he had inherited. He did not have to explain this to everyone all of the time, but it can be unmistakably found on occasion in his work as part of a fundamental attitude, which sometimes had to be expressed.

Keeping this in mind, let's return to Johannes Hooss. The fact that he doubtlessly lived from cradle to grave in the bosom of the Calvinist church of Hesse-Kassel can be demonstrated using the baptismal and death registers from the main parish of Zella. Changing this statement a bit, would it perhaps be more accurate to say that he was in the bosom of the church only four times: first in the cradle, a second time on his death bed, and two other times at the altar when he got married, first in 1689 and again in 1700? We indeed know more about Hooss: that he served the church as an elder much as he served the secular authorities as a court assessor. The fact that he held these offices says nothing about his religiosity or his political loyalty, however, only that he was not liable for military service in either case. Obviously personal esteem, prestige, and power accrued to him within the context of his little world as a result, and this may have been more important to him than the offices themselves.

Given all of this, it puzzles me that Hooss had sixteen children, four from his first marriage and twelve from his second, as was mentioned in the first chapter. Even if you look closely at the birth intervals, you could hardly conclude that there was an effort to limit the number of children in his case. The interval between the births rarely exceeded an average of two to two and a half years. Indeed they were repeatedly below the average. Should we conclude from this that Johannes Hooss, like Frans Hals, may have lived in a Calvinist land but that he stayed Catholic in his heart or that he shared in centuries-old Catholic attitudes? Have we stumbled in both cases across the survival of "pre-Reformation practices" of the kind that Meertens discussed in his work?

Perhaps our question, on the other hand, does not really get to the heart of the issue. From the "Catholic" family portrait by Frans Hals one can see that having many children cannot in any way be equated with indifference toward children, even if there were a lot of them, as was the case with Coques. The married couple painted by Hals may have had four times as many children as the small and intimate family portrayed by Jan Steen. Yet doesn't his portrait overflow with warmth, devotion, mutual sympathy, and a sense of belonging to an affectionate family group? No one stands apart, withdrawn, posing grudgingly against his or her will, simply playing a family role dictated by the church or state. All of the brothers and sisters, the mother, and the father are open to each other and do not stand around lonely and lost.

It could have been the same thing with sixteen children, or it might have been. For of the sixteen children of Johannes Hooss, only nine survived the early years of infancy. Other children died when they were two, six, and seven. He was left with six daughters: Anna Catharina (1696–1724) from his first marriage; and Gela (1701–60), Catharina (1703–42), Anna Gela (1709–84), Elisabeth (1720–42), and Martha Elisabeth (1723–94) from his second. Not one of them went away empty-handed during their lives. In 1716 the oldest one married Andreas Riebeling of Zella, an heir to a farm and later the *Grebe,* that is, village headman. In 1721 the second married Johannes Hahn, the son of a peasant from Gungelshausen. The third married wealthy Johannes Hooss, also from Gungelshausen, who by means of this marriage and his purchase of the farm became Hooss's successor on the Vältes Farm in Leimbach. The fourth daughter married the heir to a farm in Zella, Johannes Knauff, in 1730, and the fifth married Johann Jost Fenner, a peasant boy from the Grebe Farm in Niedergrenzebach, in 1741. The sixth daughter, finally, married another Johannes Hooss, now a widower but still the proprietor of the Vältes Farm, in October 1743. His first wife, Catharina, had died in May 1742.

Family planning does not always unconditionally mean simply restricting the number of births. Only in modern times when practically all of those who are born survive and have predictable life courses ahead of them have the two terms become synonymous. In a time in which families averaged six or eight children, sixteen was just as "unnatural" as only two or three at the other extreme. To achieve either result parents had to struggle "more than the average." This same sense of responsibility for the family could lead either way: to having many children or to having only a few. Only in the cases where the family had little or nothing to pass on to the children was the "Calvinist" statement above—"fewer children are better provided for, better cared for"—really true.

A sense of responsibility to nurture a network of strong social ties could also lead to family planning with above-average numbers of children. For centuries the Leimbachers, for example, strictly maintained the impartibility of the farm. The good placement of a number of children on the Vältes Farm therefore depended upon the family's and the farm's standing. In no way did this create problems. In none of the cases did it lead to a social decline for the children. On the contrary, by following a systematic and well-thought-out marriage strategy that was oriented around social prestige, the family only consolidated and expanded the social network that was bound to it.

It was therefore not at all a question of whether to have a small "Calvinist" family with few children or a large "Catholic" family with large numbers of them. It was not even a question of whether Johannes Hooss followed basic Catholic principles in his heart. If providing for and taking better care of children were virtues for responsible parents that were primarily Calvinist, then Johannes Hooss behaved in a thoroughly "Calvinist" way. Yet the principles had to meet his needs and not the other way around. He took as much from the official teaching of the church as he needed to master *his* everyday life. He adopted those parts of it that were useful *to him*. These were the things he integrated into his world.

CHAPTER 3

Dangers

I N CHAPTERS 1 AND 2 we reconstructed, step by step, the little world of Johannes Hooss as well as a whole series of other little worlds. Despite the existence of the protective hills and the ring of protective forests surrounding the Schwalm lowlands, these worlds were hardly safe and secure places. In this chapter I will discuss the massive threats from the outside that these little worlds faced back then. They were primarily of three types. For centuries our ancestors prayed and begged that they would not be devastated by them: "Protect us, oh Lord, against plague, famine, and war!"

These three scourges of humankind were held in check in the Schwalm region about as well as anyplace during the period of the seventeenth and eighteenth centuries that concerns us. When they struck they ravaged entire stretches of the countryside, sweeping across entire territories and continents. This had happened repeatedly in the centuries before Johannes Hooss lived and continues to happen today, even though the scourges look different. In this chapter we must therefore survey broader expanses of time and space than we have up to now. This doesn't mean that we will examine in detail all of the plague epidemics and military campaigns. Nor will we examine exactly who suffered from famine or where and when it happened. Plague, famine, and war ravaged the population at various times and places and invariably singled out some people more than others. If we went into the details we would quickly lose sight of the important connections.

In this chapter I am interested in showing that our forebears had more reason to ask for God's mercy from these three scourges in the seventeenth and eighteenth centuries than for long periods before or since. Simultaneous outbreaks of plague, famine, and war reached a peak during this time. It is often tempting to call this period a watershed, even though some areas were more seriously affected than others. To this idea let me add two more thoughts that will then be more fully developed in chapter 4. If I am correct in assuming that human beings by their nature have never given in to outward dangers without a struggle, then our ancestors must have shown unusual courage in dealing with the dramatically more uncertain times of the seventeenth and eighteenth centuries and created, in spite of it all, a measure of stability for their insecure lives. And in regions more seriously afflicted than others, they must have managed with even greater tenacity. At the very least they must have behaved differently. Let us then briefly look at the histories of the three scourges.

"Oh Lord, protect us from the plague!" Figure 11 is based on the authoritative two-volume work on the history of this disease published by the French physician and historian Jean-Noël Biraben in 1975–76. In his appendix is a summary that is useful for our purposes. Using all of the sources and the literature available to him at the time, it lists year by year all of the places known to have been visited by the plague. If to us it seems like a virtually endless list, to our forebears it was one that brought anxiety, fear, and terror.

In order to make this unending list of plagues more meaningful and easier to grasp, I have arranged the information in a graph, beginning, on the left, with the great wave of plague that swept over Europe and Asia between 1346 and 1350 and then following the outbreaks that occurred over the next five hundred years. For the time between 1350 and 1850 I have arranged the recorded outbreaks of plague into twenty-five-year periods. Europe and all of the adjacent regions visited by plague have also been divided into a series of three zones. Behind this idea is the assumption that our forebears were concerned wherever the plague may have broken out. If we imagine a circle drawn around Central Europe with our ancestors living at its center, then (according to Biraben) they lived in the area most directly and seriously affected by plague whenever it broke out in Germany, Switzerland, Austria, and Bohemia. The frequency of the outbreak of plague in this zone appears in the upper part of figure 11. Once the plague broke out here, any measures to contain it were already too late. One could, of course, pray and beg for mercy, make a pilgrimage, and perhaps appeal to St. Roche to intercede on one's behalf with the Almighty. Otherwise fear seized the people, the fear that one's fate was sealed as soon as the black boils appeared that put an end to one's earthly existence. The sand had run out of the hourglass.

Around this core area came a circle of lands that acted repeatedly as com-

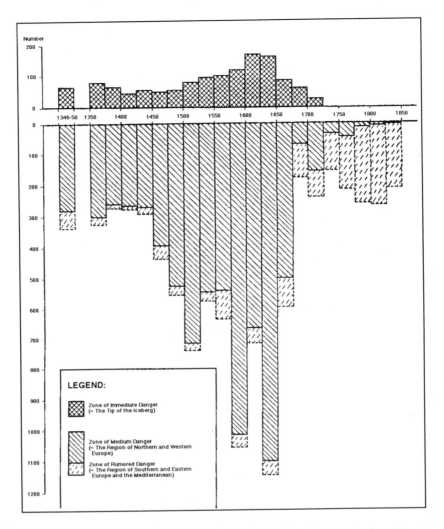

11. Plague in Central Europe: actual fear and general anxiety, 1346–1850. The places ravaged by the plague at the time of the Black Death (1346–50) and in subsequent periods have been grouped in three zones: (1) Zone of imminent danger, with a real and manifest fear of the plague: Germany, Switzerland, Austria, and Bohemia (upper half of the graph). (2) Zone of intermediate danger, with outbreaks of the disease in a ring of bordering regions, mainly in the north, west, and south: Poland, the Baltic States, Finland, Sweden, Norway, Denmark, Iceland, England, Scotland, Iceland, the Netherlands, Belgium, Luxembourg, France, Spain, Portugal, and Italy. These regions fostered a constant and general worry about the specter of plague (cross-hatched areas in the lower half of the graph). (3) Zone of distant danger, primarily in southeast Europe and the broader Mediterranean region: the Balkans, Turkey, Syria, and the area from Lebanon to Morocco (dotted lines in the lower half of the graph). *Source:* analysis of appendix 3 of Jean-Noël Biraben, *Les hommes et la peste en France et dans les pays européens et méditerranéens,* vol. 1 (Paris: Mouton, 1975), 363–74, and notes to pp. 118–29. My "zone of immediate danger" corresponds to the lands in Biraben's Group VI, the "zone of intermediate danger" to Groups I–X (including VI), and the "zone of distant danger" to Groups XI–XV.

munication zones of the disease, transmitting it primarily by sea and water routes. I would describe this area as one of indirect or intermediate danger. It stretched from Poland across the Baltic and the northern European lands of Finland, Sweden, Norway, Denmark, and Iceland around to England, Scotland, and Ireland, then down to the Netherlands, Belgium, Luxembourg, and France, and finally to Spain, Portugal, and Italy. If the plague flared up anywhere in these regions, the danger arose that sooner or later it would spread back to Central Europe. This didn't always happen, but it wasn't an impossibility either. The epidemics of plague in this circle of lands (up to eleven hundred of them in the twenty-five-year periods depicted in the graph) kept the underlying fear of plague alive in Central Europe.

Beyond this circle lay another ring of yet more distant lands where new waves of plague frequently originated or lands that suffered first when a new wave of plague swept out of Asia. Included among these lands were the regions of southeastern Europe and the larger Mediterranean basin: the Balkans, Turkey, Syria, and the coastal region from Lebanon to Morocco. Central Europe was not directly threatened by outbreaks of plague in these regions. The epidemic would possibly weaken before it ever reached the area of indirect danger. But our ancestors still were not always spared from outbreaks that originated even in these distant areas. True, nothing definite was known about them. But rumors about them spread through merchants, peddlers, travelers, beggars, soldiers, and artisans who traveled about, and in the news that spread this way the number of victims and the places visited by the plague tended to grow rather than to diminish. Those who had news to tell wanted to impress other people with the novelty of their stories, and stunned or horrified listeners were hardly inclined to check them out. Rarely did more informed people deny the rumors. The specter of plague stayed alive this way and was constantly renewed. It didn't arouse so much a concrete fear as a vague, underlying anxiety. Accordingly I have called this outer ring the area of rumored or distant danger.

One can distinguish between an immediate fear and a latent and vague kind of anxiety that resulted from the plague. The first occurred when plague flared up in the core region, the second when it came to the area of intermediate danger or to the periphery of the region. By "fear" I mean real and concrete fears, such as the feeling of panic when the plague broke out in one's own village, house, or family; the dread of famine that came when the crops failed and the sparse grain was already starting to disappear at the beginning of the winter; the terror spread by soldiers who were plundering, burning, and murdering, who had already completed their vile work in the next community and who were now on the march toward one's own; and the fear of robbers rumored to be in the forest that one had to pass by in order to bring cattle to the market. By "anxiety," on the other hand, I mean to signify worries that were aroused by vaguely perceived and lurking dangers, such as the anxiousness about the recurrence of plague on the other side of the territory's border or its rumored recurrence among the pagans; the worry about the Turks who might yet overrun Europe after one of their countless attempts to do so, bringing war and gruesome carnage as they rolled over it; and the apprehensiveness about the grain not ripening during the summer after days of continuous rain and cool weather, leaving hardly anything for humans or animals to eat at harvest time.

The more one thinks about it, the more one realizes that a fundamental transformation has taken place since our ancestors' time. In their age real fears about daily life burdened their thoughts more than did the vague worries about distant events. Our environment and everyday life, by contrast, have become safer, more secure. We no longer fear that we might suddenly die from the plague either today or tomorrow. We no longer suffer from famine because of the abundance of food in our supermarkets and the constant agricultural surpluses of the European Community. Moreover, hordes of soldiers do not stand at our doorsteps. And yet the more the fears of once real dangers subside, the more they seem to be replaced by steadily growing but vague anxieties about less immediate but more dangerous threats to our lives. It is much more difficult for us to deal with this kind of anxiety than it was for our forebears to handle fear in their own time. We will return to this change in the last chapter.

If we look at figure 11 and the half a millennium between 1350 and 1850, it is strikingly evident that the largest number of plague outbreaks occurred between 1575 and 1650. This was true for the core zone in Central Europe as well as for the adjacent circle of lands where the danger was indirect. If we look simultaneously at the upper and lower segments of the graph, the whole appears like an iceberg with a small, visible part above and a much larger, invisible threat below.

We began this chapter trying to find out not only the times when the plague broke out most frequently, but also which parts of our core region were more seriously afflicted than others. To find the answer I have depicted all of the occurrences of plague mentioned for Central Europe between 1575 and 1650 on the maps in figure 12. The specific details involving the differences from place to place are easy to discern, but they are not what really concerns me here. Transportation hubs, busy ports and trading centers like Bremen, Danzig, Dresden, Leipzig, Nuremberg, Basel, Frankfurt am Main, and Cologne were naturally more threatened by disease than remote and isolated places. As a result they turn up more frequently as areas visited by plague. Aside from this obvious point, I call the reader's attention to the maps in order to introduce a specific concept: the traumatization of a local population.

Let us assume that the plague ravaged the population of one community repeatedly over the years. Each outbreak of plague took the lives of a number of children and young and middle-aged people, ripping apart marriages, leaving behind dozens of widows and widowers, extinguishing entire families, erasing whole neighborhoods, disrupting community life, and even threatening the survival of the population. The inhabitants of another place experienced only smaller outbreaks of plague between much longer intervals of time and never lost more than a few inhabitants during any given epidemic. When compared to the significantly higher mortality rates elsewhere, they would hardly be worth mentioning. Fear of the plague not only must have been much greater in the first place than in the second, the two populations must also have associated very different types of dangers and threats to their lives with the same expression "plague." Gradually the differences would have been expressed in behavior and attitudes about everyday life, especially in aspects having to do with the fragility of life, the length of marriage, the survival of the family, planning for the future, and death. It might be an exaggeration to say that a certain indifference about these matters may have taken hold in the first community. In the second community, however, where repeated visitations of plague did not have the same numbing effects, it would have been more worthwhile to invest in all aspects of life, both emotionally and materially. The plague did not always threaten human existence in the same way.

Plague epidemics displayed two characteristics that traumatized a local population: first, they threatened the very existence of the whole community; second, they often repeated themselves over relatively short intervals. Only in this way could the plague leave a deep and enduring impression on the collective memory of a community. Over time this led to fundamental differences in collective attitudes and behavior, marking an adaptation to the

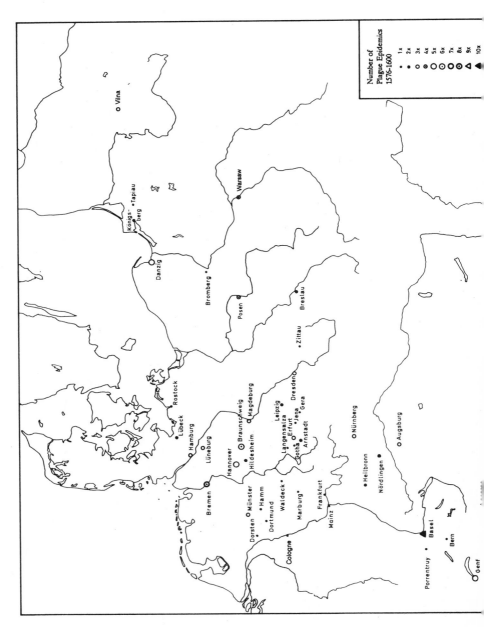

○ Vilna

• Warsaw

Königs- • Tapiau
berg

Danzig

Bromberg •

Posen ○

Breslau

• Zittau

Rostock

Dresden

Lübeck

Magdeburg

Hamburg ○

Leipzig

Braunschweig ⊙ Langensalza

Lüneburg

Nürnberg ○

Hannover ○ Hildesheim ○ Gotha • Jena • Gera
Erfurt • Arnstadt

Augsburg ○

Bremen ○

Münster ○ • Hamm

Waldeck •

Heilbronn •

Dorsten •

Dortmund

Marburg •

Nördlingen •

Frankfurt ○

Mainz ○

Cologne ○

Basel ▪

Bern •

Porrentruy •

○ Genf

12. Places in Central Europe ravaged by the plague during three twenty-five-year periods, 1576–1600, 1601–25, and 1625–50. *Source:* analysis of appendix 4 of Jean-Noël Biraben, *Les hommes et la peste en France et dans les pays européens et méditerranéens,* vol. 1 (Paris: Mouton, 1975), 412–15 (the lands in Group F: "Germany—Central Europe"), 424–26 (Group H: "Poland—East Prussia—Lithuania—Latvia—Estonia").

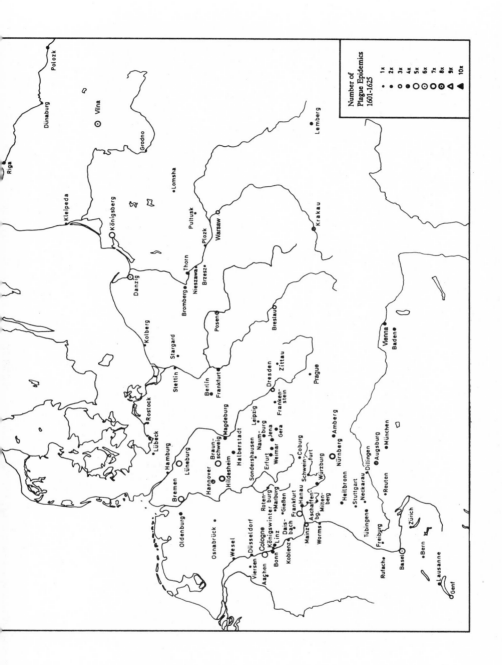

Number of
Plague Epidemics
1601-1625

- 1x
- 2x
- 3x
- 4x
- 5x
- 6x
- 7x
- 8x
- 9x
- 10x

Polozk
Vilna
Dünaburg
Grodno
Riga
Kleipeda
Königsberg
Lomsha
Lemberg
Pultusk
Thorn
Warsaw
Plozk
Niesszawa
Brzesz
Danzig
Bromberg
Krakau
Kolberg
Posen
Stargard
Stettin
Breslau
Berlin
Frankfurt
Vienna
Baden
Rostock
Dresden
Zittau
Frankenstein
Prague
Lübeck
Magdeburg
Leipzig
Hamburg
Braunschweig
Naumburg
Jena
Amberg
Lüneburg
Halberstadt
Erfurt
Weimar
Gera
Nürnberg
München
Hanover
Hildesheim
Sondershausen
Coburg
Bremen
Marburg
Schweinfurt
Augsburg
Oldenburg
Rotenburg
Gießen
Hanau
Würzburg
Reuten
Osnabrück
Königswinter
Frankfurt
Aschaffenbg.
Heilbronn
Dillingen
Wesel
Düsseldorf
Dais-bach
Mainz
Miltenberg
Stuttgart
Neckarau
Viersen
Cologne
Bonn
Linz
Koblenz
Worms
Tübingen
Zürich
Aachen
Freiburg
Bern
Rufach
Basel
Lausanne
Genf

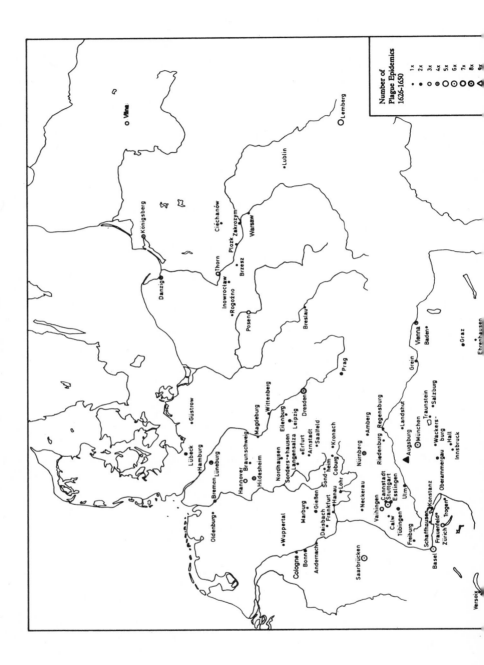

Number of
Plague Epidemics
1626-1650

- 1x
- 2x
- 3x
- 4x
- 5x
- 6x
- 7x
- 8x
- 9x

Vilna

Königsberg

Danzig

Ciechanów

Płozk Zakrozym

Thorn

Warsaw

Inowrocław

Rogoźno

Brzesz

Posen

Lublin

Lemberg

Breslau

Güstrow

Lübeck

Hamburg

Bremen

Lüneburg

Oldenburg

Hannover

Braunschweig

Hildesheim

Magdeburg

Wittenberg

Eilenburg

Leipzig

Dresden

Nordhausen

Sonders-hausen

Langensalza

Erfurt

Arnstadt

Saalfeld

Kronach

Prag

Wuppertal

Marburg

Gießen

Sond-heim

Coburg

Nürnberg

Amberg

Riedenburg

Regensburg

Cologne

Bonn

Andernach

Daisbach

Frankfurt

Hanau

Lohr

Neckerau

Vaihingen

Cannstadt

Stuttgart

Esslingen

Landshut

München

Traunstein

Salzburg

Augsburg

Wackers-burg

Hall

Innsbruck

Saarbrücken

Calw

Tübingen

Ulm

Freiburg

Schaffhausen

Konstanz

Oberammergau

Basel

Frauenfeld

Zürich

Trogen

Grein

Vienna

Baden

Graz

Ehrenhausen

Versoix

special disease environment and the advent of attitudes and behavior that were no longer always spontaneous but which were passed down from one generation to the next. Our French historian colleagues have recently worked intensively on collective mentalities, and they speak here about a *non-conscient collectif*, a "collective unconscious."

One does not have to imagine two such villages visited by the plague in such different ways, since a number of them actually existed. I have selected two contrasting examples from my own research: Gabelbach in South German Swabia, and Hesel in North German East Frisia. They were introduced briefly in the first chapter in order to point out the stark contrasts in living conditions between the rich Gabelbach peasant boy, Matthäus Burkhart, and the wretchedly poor day laborer from Hesel, Gerdt Peter. These two places figure more prominently in the discussion that follows. They are not only better known to me than other communities from my years of work on them, but they turn out to have had village populations that differed sharply from each other in behavior and attitudes. It is only natural to inquire about the sources of such differences.

One would search in vain for Gabelbach and Hesel on one of the three maps concerning the plague. As tiny settlements they were too insignificant for anyone to note their everyday history. Because it was equally unlikely that anyone would have documented the possible outbreaks of plague in them, I have looked in both cases at the next largest town in the area, assuming that an occurrence of plague would not have been restricted to that city's population but would have spread out into the countryside surrounding it. Gabelbach lies about twenty-five kilometers west of Augsburg, Hesel about forty kilometers northwest of Oldenburg. These two cities do appear on our maps, but in very different ways. The plague visited Augsburg three times between 1575 and 1600 (1585, 1592, 1593), four times between 1601 and 1625 (1607, 1608, 1624, 1625), and ten times between 1626 and 1650 (1626, 1627, 1628, 1632, 1633, 1634, 1635, 1646, 1647, 1648). In the first period Oldenburg was spared completely from any outbreaks of plague. The town suffered two outbreaks in the second period (1611 and 1623) and only one (1637) in the third.

Located at a crossroads and sought out from every direction, Augsburg suffered the ravages of the plague seventeen times over a seventy-five-year period, that is, once every four to five years on average. If our assumptions are correct, then the same would have been true for Gabelbach. The residents of the more remote town of Oldenburg, and probably also those from the still more isolated village of Hesel, experienced the plague only three times over this same time span, an average of only once every twenty-five years.

Gabelbach and Hesel differed from each other not only in the frequency with which plague swept through their populations, but also in the way that war affected them. Because of its recurrence and violence, war had the same traumatizing effect on the population as the plague. Turning now to the subject of war, another member of our trinity of scourges, we will study it with maps in the same way.

"Protect us from war, oh Lord!" Figure 13 (p. 79) is made up of four map sections that depict Bavaria as a war zone between 1546 and 1813. The first map depicts the Schmalkaldic War (1546–47). At the time, Emperor Charles V was opposed by the Schmalkaldic League, made up of an alliance of Protestant imperial estates, among them the imperial city of Augsburg in Swabia. The three other maps all depict wars on a broader, European-wide scale: the Thirty Years' War (1618–48), the War of the Spanish Succession (1701–14), and the wars of the Napoleonic era (1796–1813).

One need not be a military strategist to be able to pick out on a map of Europe and Germany the areas that were particularly vulnerable in time of war. Over the centuries these were always the routes for troop maneuvers, the natural river crossings, and the avenues of attack into other regions, and they stand out much more than places that were in the shadows of war, like East Frisia. The names of these latter places are not found in the annals of war. One does not have to know a great deal about history to know that Bavaria, hemmed in by the two great powers of the day, Habsburg Austria and France, would suffer during every European war. Bavaria's strategic and political location excluded the possibility of neutrality from the start, making it virtually inevitable that Bavaria would serve repeatedly as a theater of war, whether as an ally of the emperor during the Thirty Years' War or as a confederate of France, as in the War of the Spanish Succession and the Napoleonic Wars.

Eastern Swabia, that is, the region from Rain am Lech to Augsburg and south to Füssen, was among the regions threatened by war most of all. Every enemy army had to force the crossings of the Danube and Lech Rivers that lay in this area in order to push into the heart of Bavaria. In every war the highways here became military roads, the towns embattled fortresses, the open landscape battlefields and foraging areas for friend and foe alike—so long, that is, as there was something to take. One need not dwell on the

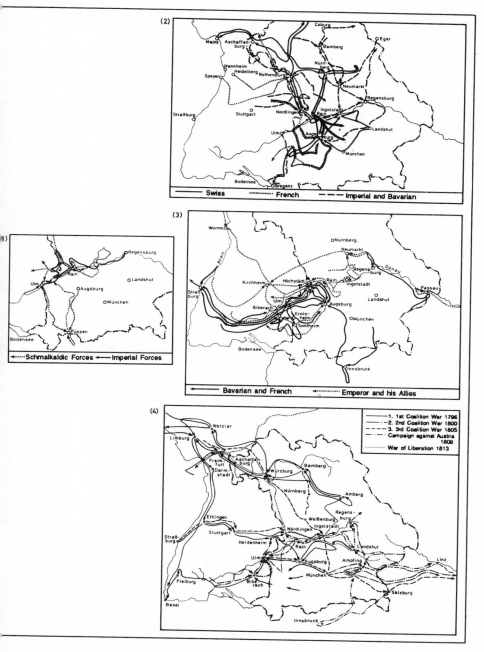

13. Bavaria as a war zone, 1546–1813. (1) Schmalkaldic War, 1546–47. (2) Thirty
Years' War, 1618–48. (3) War of the Spanish Succession, 1701–14. (4) The campaigns
of 1796–1813 during the Wars of the First and Third Coalition against Napoleon and
the Wars of Liberation, 1796, 1800, 1805, 1809, and 1813. *Source:* Max Spindler, ed.,
Bayerischer Geschichtsatlas (Munich: Bayerischer Schulbuchverlag, 1969), 29, and the
commentary by Th. Straub, 95–97.

details. One needs only to find the area around Rain am Lech and Augsburg on each map. Their experiences testify eloquently to the political and strategic threat to the region. The military movements themselves also don't interest us so much as does the traumatization of the population as the region was drawn repeatedly into the events of war, this in contrast to other regions that lived in peace for generations at this same time.

If we apply the criteria we developed earlier to this case, then these military events represented a second shock to the population of the Augsburg region and Gabelbach. Recent research on population losses during the Thirty Years' War makes it clear in this context that the village lay precisely in the zone that suffered such steep losses that the very survival of the community was threatened. In many places the losses were between 30 and 50 percent, usually higher than lower.[1] The Imperial-Bavarian Army even suffered its last defeat of the war at Zusmarshausen, a village only a few kilometers northeast of Gabelbach in the direction of Augsburg. Hesel, these same studies make clear, belonged to one of those rare parts of Germany that suffered no population losses during the Thirty Years' War.

The second aspect of war that traumatized the community was the way it became a recurrent threat to the existence of the community. This Gabelbach doubtlessly experienced. Of course there were times of peace, whether for shorter or longer periods of time, but they were never long enough to allow the terrible events of the last war to be forgotten before a new war began. Besides this, Gabelbach peasants lived with the awareness that they lived on the most exposed forward front in case of war. When the clouds of war gathered, they knew they would be among those to suffer first; thus they lived in permanent fear for their lives.

We turn now to the question we asked concerning the outbreak of plague: What effect did the constant threat of war have on a population? Gabelbach was exposed at the same time to two dangers—plague and war—and continuously suffered from them over the centuries. Hesel suffered from neither of these scourges, however. In the first village not only was one's own life constantly at risk, but those of others as well: spouses, parents, children, dependents, relatives, friends, servants, and serving girls. All of one's property was also at risk: household goods, farmhouse, barns, arable fields, crops, stores in the cellar and the barn, pigs, horses, cattle, sheep, chickens, and geese. When troops approached, one never knew what would be left standing the next morning or the day after that. In the second village death certainly took its toll, and frequently, too, given the conditions of the time, but it was not as arbitrary and brutal. When one built a house or even just a wooden hut in the village, it would still be standing after a generation if it had not collapsed or burned to the ground.

If it was true that the trauma inflicted on this village population resulted in behavior and attitudes toward daily life fundamentally different from a population spared such trauma, then the modern historian should be able to find these differences long after the fact. Even though our ancestors never wrote about these changes, even if they did not constantly reflect about them since they had long since passed into a collective unconscious and become a self-evident part of everyday behavior and conduct, still such attitudes, behavior, and ways of acting always left behind their traces, effects, and consequences. With patience and good luck we can eventually come across them lingering even into our own times.

Among the obvious differences between the two village populations, I first want to discuss those that were particularly revealing about earlier attitudes toward life and survival. Perhaps the most astonishing discovery I made was that newborn infants apparently had a much greater chance of survival in Hesel over time than was the case in Gabelbach. This certainly could not have stemmed from the fact that the peasants in the first village enjoyed better general economic conditions than those in the second. On the contrary, agricultural conditions on the less fertile and sandy soil were notoriously difficult in the region known as the East Frisian Geest. The villagers from Hesel were commonly known in the area as poor people. The conditions were equally poor in Gabelbach, where peasants lived mainly from growing grain. Available land was in short supply, and the upper limits of additional land clearing had long since been reached.

The infant mortality rate in Hesel amounted to only 13 percent, that is, half the rate historical demographers generally assume as the average for this time. Infant mortality in Gabelbach, however, averaged 34 percent, almost three times the rate in Hesel, and far above the norm. One has to rely upon numbers for the period between 1780 and 1899 because calculations going further back than this cannot be reliably carried out due to the lack of older birth and death registers. Since experience informs us that we are dealing here with "patterns of long duration," one can assume that both the absolute numbers and the relationship between them were probably valid for much earlier periods as well. One of our arguments is that the most far-reaching traumatization took place primarily in the seventeenth century and that the patterns that originated through plague and war continued to have effects until the end of the nineteenth century and even on into the first half of the twentieth century. At the beginning of this century parents in Gabelbach still buried one in every three newborn children, who lived only a few days, weeks, or, at the most, months. More likely than not, some families had more relatives in the cemetery than in their homes. In this same period only one in every eight infants died in Hesel.

That is not all that is surprising. Looking more closely at the sizes of the families in the two villages, we notice that they were about the same in both cases. To be more precise, families from both villages had about the same number of children who survived to their first birthday. An average of 4.5 infants survived their first year of life in Gabelbach, 4.6 in Hesel. Mothers in Gabelbach, however, had to bear on average 6.8 children in order to reach this number, since their children suffered significantly higher infant mortality rates. By contrast, all it took was 5.3 births in Hesel. Nothing less than a different attitude toward life and survival among mothers and their husbands lay behind these statistics. In one village it took expression as greater reverence for life, in the other as less regard for it. Naturally the conditions that accompanied birth in Hesel were no better than in Gabelbach. Studies show that almost the same number of mothers died in childbirth in both villages between 1780 and 1899; when expressed in modern terms, 152 mothers died per 10,000 births in Hesel, and 158 per 10,000 in Gabelbach.

If one wanted to safeguard the lives of pregnant women in the past, regardless of whether the initiative came from mothers or from husbands concerned about the welfare of their wives, this could only come about through fewer pregnancies so that women confronted the dangers associated with childbirth less often. This is exactly what happened in Hesel, as a historian can demonstrate today. The mothers from this village gave birth to one or two fewer children over their lifetimes than did the mothers from Gabelbach. There were accordingly fewer chances for death during childbirth. If we compare the maternal death rates between the two villages again, this time calculating the number of deaths per 10,000 mothers and not, as above, per 10,000 births, a considerable difference emerges. In Hesel 794 mothers (per 10,000) died in childbirth or, as the saying went at the time, "within the seven weeks," that is, up to forty-one days after the last birth. In Gabelbach, in contrast, 1,068 died, fully one-third more.

Naturally one will inquire into the techniques responsible for the superior performance of the Hesel villagers, or, to ask a more basic question, What was the deeper reason for their fewer pregnancies and births? What was the source of their "deeper reverence for life"? Simply to refer to the fact that the Heselers were Lutherans, not Catholics, that they no longer left everything to divine providence, including the number of children born to a marriage, is no longer satisfying after questioning in the last chapter our forebears' adherence to official confessions of faith. Besides, from the vantage point of the parents of Hesel, this was not a matter of having fewer children. The unfavorable economic conditions might suggest this view, but, despite the differences in numbers of births, both villages still had the same number of living descendants.

The other probable cause for this difference therefore becomes more credible. The villagers from Hesel developed a greater respect for the lives of wives and mothers, or, seen from the point of view of mothers, a greater fear of death from childbirth. Substantial support for this thesis comes from the major work of Johann Peter Süßmilch (1707–67), Royal Prussian Consistorial Councilor and founder of the modern science of demography in Germany. In his own time he noticed differences in the nursing customs among German mothers, especially the practice in the countryside around Berlin of nursing children for an extensive period of time. This practice was actually one of the most frequently employed methods known to women for delaying a subsequent pregnancy. In his main work, bearing the awkward eighteenth-century title *Divine Order as Seen in the Changes of the Human Race, Demonstrated from Births, Deaths, and Propagation of the Same* (1761), Süßmilch wrote, unabashedly:

> Proof of the fear of the dangers of childbirth among rustic people is the long period in which it is customary to nurse children. I believe that it is very good for the strength of the body in fact when children can enjoy the very best nourishment possible, mother's milk, not simply for one year but for a time beyond that. But one should observe moderation here, and I think it's enough when children have come far enough along that they can eat stronger and more solid foods without danger to their health. What does one do with mother's milk when the children can already enjoy other foods? Many in the countryside persist in nursing for two or three more years. Rural preachers assure me that it has to do with the recurrent fear of having many children. Since experience teaches that women rarely become pregnant while nursing, it is easy to understand why long nursing periods are the cause by which marital fertility is declining. (Cited according to the second, revised edition, Berlin, 1761, p. 194)

The fear of the hazards associated with childbirth and the renewed danger of having many children led these *mothers* to practice birth control. They were clearly concerned for their own lives first; only after that did they think of having fewer children for reasons of family planning. The fact that extending the nursing time kept more newborns alive because they received "the best nourishment," that is, mother's milk, was actually only a side effect of behavior aimed primarily at reducing the death rates among mothers.

It should also not be overlooked that the longer periods of nursing brought about closer mother-child relationships and higher rates of survival for children in these regions. This, in turn, may have gradually led to a different relationship to children compared to regions in which nursing ended sooner and the survival rates of newborns were significantly lower. In these areas parent-child relationships did not become as close or they did not develop in this direction from the same early age on.

The postponement of conception through nursing was clearly a form of birth control employed by women and mothers. The other method frequently employed at the time, coitus interruptus, the man's withdrawal of his penis before ejaculation, presupposed the initiative of men or of women who urged their men to practice it. There are signs, moreover, that where women and mothers cared more for their own lives, nursing longer periods of time in order to have fewer children, not only did men approve of this behavior, but it seems to have led to more mutual respect between married couples. In Hesel widows and widowers therefore waited significantly longer periods of time to replace a partner who had passed away than in Gabelbach. Widowers waited in Hesel on average twenty-eight months, widows thirty-six, to remarry between 1780 and 1899. In Gabelbach widowers waited only seven months, widows nine, before remarrying. Greater affection for someone in this life carried over into his or her being memorialized longer after death. Did such different mourning behavior represent an expression of fundamentally different kinds of relationships between married couples in the two villages?

One can assume that the knowledge Süßmilch ascribed to women in Brandenburg, and apparently also known to peasant women in East Frisia, was widespread and had been known just as long in South Germany. Why women from Gabelbach remained ignorant of these birth control practices stems from age-old patterns of behavior, predating any observations by physicians, and passed down from generation to generation, from grandmothers and mothers to their daughters and granddaughters. The difference lay in the simple fact that this knowledge was used in one village but not in the other.

Looking at the reports of South German physicians from this same time dispels any doubts. Doctors were generally not only keen observers, they also knew what they were talking about. They knew their patients' lives intimately. One sample report comes from 1822 from the region around Sigmaringen in Württemberg, where the infant mortality rate at the time had reached a horrendous 50 percent and exceeded even that of Gabelbach's:

> Pregnant women perform heavy labor until the last minute before giving birth, and then they return to it almost immediately afterward. Sexual intercourse takes place up until the end of pregnancy and then starts again immediately after it. Mothers show great indifference for the feeding of their children, especially with regard to nursing. They sell the very best cow's milk while they and their children eat wretched watered-down soup. The neglect of newborn children is such that it would offend any compassionate observer. Already a few days after the birth, mothers let their children lie around the house and scream while they spend most of the day working in the fields. The resistance of the people to health measures is great, above all against smallpox vaccination. A doctor will hardly ever be called to tend a sick child.[2]

Here we clearly confront for the first time that basic attitude of indifference toward life that we expect as a consequence of the traumatization brought about by frequent epidemics of plague and the repeated devastations of war. These complaints run like a common thread through dozens of reports by doctors from this time: "Pregnant women are not protected. They work hard until shortly before giving birth and then return to their work shortly after it. Nursing is neglected. Children eat from dirty plates. Cleanliness is lacking. Small children grow up in filthy living quarters. Parents do not care how many children they have."[3]

The contrast with the attitudes and conduct of the villagers from Hesel could hardly have been starker. In these villages one finds neither evidence of safeguards for the lives of women and mothers, nor evidence of mutual regard between married couples, nor intimate mother-child relationships, nor any evidence at all of the use of deliberate strategies of survival through long periods of nursing. The demographic consequences of such insensitivity have already been noted in Gabelbach: three times higher infant mortality than in Hesel, a significantly larger number of mothers dying in childbirth, and shorter periods of mourning for widows and widowers.

But this is only one side of the coin. One cannot easily skip over comments like this one: "The population stiffly resisted medical measures, especially against smallpox immunization." This behavior is really puzzling, since it is one thing to be indifferent toward one's physical health but something entirely different to resist health measures that save lives. Smallpox vaccination, the first really effective safeguard against one of the most deadly of all killers of infants and small children, was available everywhere on the European continent since the beginning of the nineteenth century. Parents could hardly have been unaware of the fact that vaccinated children were in fact protected from the disease and outlived other children. And they resisted this measure? That many of them did so is amply demonstrated through other sources.

One might explain this behavior in any number of ways. Vaccination involved drastic intervention by the state, one could argue, and was accompanied by massive state propaganda, creating a degree of distrust among many people. Some villagers may also not have wanted their children to be treated and vaccinated, one after the other, by some educated stranger, and this without the children even being sick. For villagers it may have sufficed up to that time to be treated by a neighbor or someone else in the village knowledgeable about healing, but then again perhaps not.

All of this points toward a much deeper conflict, however, nothing less than the clash of two worldviews. Villagers did not simply let children "die," and the people in the Bavarian countryside didn't either, if we mean here by "dying" the modern sense of the word as the final extinguishing of a life. We would describe this state of affairs as showing indifference toward life, but this is an attitude that comes only with hindsight. For our ancestors, who were part of an entirely different world and worldview, this behavior had a fundamentally different meaning. For them "dying" represented only a passage, a transition from the worldly to the otherworldly life, and the otherworldly life was naturally much more important. The younger a child died in a state of innocence, the more certain one could be of its entrance into eternal salvation. Why begrudge children this blessing and keep them alive by unnatural means? Was this not trying to play God by intervening in his plans? Gabelbach was totally Catholic according to the baptismal register. Among other reasons so many children were born here was the prohibition

by the Catholic Church of any form of birth control as illegitimate intervention in divine providence and counter to nature. One heard no protests from
the church, however, when many children died shortly after their birth or
baptism, joining the heavenly hosts as little angels. This was a kind of godly
family planning after the fact.

With this religious context in mind, what we call indifference toward life,
at least the less important, worldly part of life, appears in a different light.
For a complete understanding of this now largely archaic worldview, a
broader analysis will be necessary. This will be undertaken in a larger setting
in the next chapter, so the reader should be patient. Let us close this chapter
by turning to the middle part of the plague-famine-war trinity.

"Protect us from famine, oh Lord!" Figure 14 depicts another long-term
trend much like figure 11, which dealt with outbreaks of plague. The graph
spans the five hundred years between 1450 and 1950. I am again interested
in showing that our ancestors had more reason to beg for their daily bread
between 1550 and 1700 than had generations either before the middle of the
sixteenth century or after the end of the seventeenth century.

The graphs cannot directly depict the occurrence of famine. They depict,
however, the most important conditions that affected the harvest, that is, the
weather and climate. Figure 14 has three parts. The top graph charts the
weather conditions affecting the ripening of grain, the most important food
source of the time. What is considered is the rainfall during July and August,
the two months of the summer when the grain ripens and is harvested. If
sources noted heavy and especially long-lasting periods of rainfall, I listed
the month as "rainy" and gave it one point. Those months that were not
mentioned in the sources receive a half a point, and sunny and dry ones
receive no points. The entire five hundred years is summed up in fifty ten-
year periods. A completely rainy decade would receive a maximum of
twenty points, ten for July and ten for August. When the rainy and sunny
months balance each other out the total would come to ten points. I have
used this average of ten points in the top graph as a baseline and graphed the
results as deviations from it. The columns above the line point to decades
with largely wet summer months. Columns below the line point, however,
to sunny and dry periods.

A close inspection of the graph makes evident that the second half of the
sixteenth century and the majority of decades in the seventeenth century
had summers wetter than average. The decades between 1560 and 1590, the
1600s, 1620s, 1660s, and the 1690s must have been particularly catastrophic

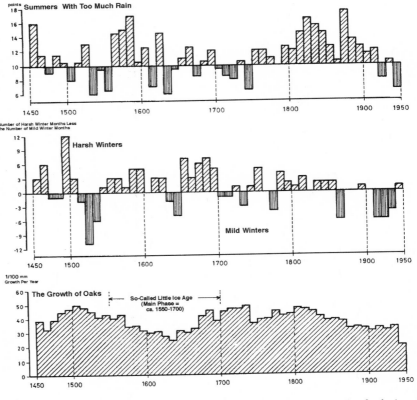

14. Rainy summers, severe winters, and differences in tree ring growth of oaks in Germany over the last five hundred years (1450–1950). *Top:* rainy summers. The months of July and August were the subjects of the study. Rainy months received one point, those that were not particularly noteworthy a half a point, and dry summers zero points. The total number of points per decade has been recorded (with a maximum of twenty possible points). Region: 50° N latitude, approximately 12° E longitude; the Fichtelgebirge, northeast of Bayreuth. *Middle:* severe winters. The months of December, January, and February were the subjects of the study. The number of months of severe winter weather minus the months of mild weather per decade have been recorded (with a maximum of thirty possible points). Region: same as above. *Bottom:* growth of oak trees. The growth rings of long-living oak trees in the Spessart region were examined (ca. 50° N latitude, 9.5° E longitude). The study is based on 10 to 150 cross sections of oak trees, depending on the period. The average growth in hundreds of millimeters per year has been recorded for each decade from 1450–59 to 1940–49. *Source:* H. H. Lamb, *Climate: Present, Past, and Future,* vol. 2: *Climatic History and the Future* (London, 1977), 562–65, 599–602. One should also note the large historical climate study by the Swiss historian Christian Pfister at the University of Bern. See his "Die Fluktuationen der Weinmosterträge im schweizerischen Weinland vom 16. bis ins frühe 19. Jahrhundert: Klimatische Ursachen und sozioökonomische Bedeutung," *Schweizerische Zeitschrift für Geschichte* 31 (1981): 445–91.

for agriculture. Flooded fields, stalks and heads of grain that were crushed to the ground and rotten, meager and unripe harvests, and grain of hardly any value must have been common in these periods. "Protect men and animals from famine, oh Lord!"

Hard winters, as represented in the middle graph, did not damage the winter wheat that was sown in the fall so long as a thick layer of snow didn't cover the ground. They would hardly have affected the summer grain crops, sown in the spring. But hard winters tended to be long, and this accordingly shortened the growing and ripening seasons. Several more cloudy days and a few more days of rain in summer were often enough to keep the grain from ripening. If the winter then came early the meager crops had to be harvested wet, often from under a blanket of snow.

The middle graph is a study of the months of December, January, and February. When the sources point to a lot of snow and low temperatures for a given month it receives a point. If neither is mentioned then it receives a minus point. The maximum number of points per decade would be plus or minus thirty points. None of these extreme cases occurred in any of the fifty decades. Still, the graph clearly points to the period from the middle of the sixteenth century to the end of the seventeenth century as a time with a heavy predominance of hard winter months. The two decades of the 1630s and 1640s were exceptions; they were the only ones with more mild winters than severe ones.

The coincidence of hard winters and rainy summers resulted in a long series of years with extremely unfavorable growing conditions and very poor prospects for the harvests. A long and sunny summer might have been able to compensate for an extremely long and cold winter. The devastating consequences, however, are clearly summed up in the bottom part of the figure. This graph charts the growth rings of ancient oak trees. The harder and longer the winter and the shorter, the wetter, and the cooler the growing season, the smaller the growth rings for that year. It is hardly surprising that the whole period from 1550 to 1700 comes off as having exceptionally bad growing seasons. The graph reveals a clear trough with small and extremely small rates of growth. Studies in climate history mention a "little ice age" in this context, the main part of which occurred in this century and a half.

I would like to stress once again that this evidence doesn't give an accurate picture of famine over time. It only highlights the prospects for the crops, whether favorable or unfavorable. One should also not overlook the fact that the graphs only reflect conditions in the regions in which the studies were undertaken: the Franconian Fichtelgebirge northeast of Bayreuth; and a stand of oaks in the Spessart between Aschaffenburg and Würzburg, its tree rings revealing rainy summers and hard winters. As anyone knows, and as weather forecasts confirm every day, rainfall and temperatures can vary greatly from place to place. Winter also does not begin at the same time in all of Germany and Central Europe. In the Upper Rhine Valley—that is, in the warmest part of Germany—apple trees normally start to bloom between April 10 and 20, but on the Baltic Sea between May 15 and 20, and in the higher elevations of the Mittelgebirge, later yet.

Were one to consider all of the differences in weather and climate and draw up dozens of illustrations and maps, one would still not have a true picture of famine in the past. In every period crop failures affected different groups of people in varying ways, even within the same village. Day laborers suffered differently from peasants with storehouses still full from last year's harvest. Old and frail people were not affected in the same way as youths at the peak of their strength who may have had to work three or four times as long to earn their bread but who still were physically able to care for themselves. Even taking into account all of the differences between social classes, villages, and regions, I believe that the trends suggested by the figures are accurate. For most of Central Europe's population, the years between 1550 and 1700 were not easy ones, let alone years of plenty, even with regard to daily sustenance. Even when everything went as well as in the fairy tales, this only provided for butterbread and cakes, as in the Grimm's fairy tale about the "Three Little Men in the Woods."

The discussion in this chapter has centered on plague, famine, and war as the three most dangerous threats to human existence and how all of them reached a peak at the same time between 1550 and 1700. Careful consideration of figures 11–14, their interconnections, and the historical background should give us a somewhat more realistic picture of people's fear and anxiety in an age cursed by the three scourges. But if these illustrations fail to do so then perhaps our imagination needs to be inspired by evidence from other sources. All of the suffering, the threats to daily existence, the destruction of property and goods, the killing, and catastrophes of every description hardly left contemporaries feeling indifferent about life. Instead they were moved, touched to the core, and angered by it all, and so were those who came after them.

It is therefore not surprising that poets and artists repeatedly drew upon these tragic experiences, giving them artistic shape through their creative power. One might gaze today at Arnold Böcklin's terrifying painting *The Plague,* at the Basel Museum of Art (fig. 15), with its picture of the Black Death as a blind skeleton, riding through the air on a fire-breathing and hissing monster, its poisonous and rasping breath withering every human life it touched. Böcklin (1827–1901) painted this picture in 1898, more than a century and a half after the last European occurrence of the plague in Marseilles. The disease that spread fear and anxiety may have died out in the 1720s, but the traumatic collective memory of this deadly scourge apparently lived on. Even today, 250 years after its disappearance, figures of speech survive, and are rooted in our collective memory, that everyone understands without the slightest explanation. Who hasn't called out at least once after smelling a terrible, penetrating odor, "That stinks like the plague!" In the past decomposing bodies may have polluted the air of homes and streets in entire communities for days or weeks, since the survivors often couldn't bury the dead fast enough. And this stench of death was an awful smell, unlike any other, even for country people who were generally less fussy about odors.

For a literary description of these tragedies one might turn to the introduction of Grimmelshausen's *Simplicius Simplicissimus.* Written about the Thirty Years' War (1618–48), which took place in the middle of our period and became the longest war in German history, the work describes how marauding troops could brutally treat peasant families:

A number of soldiers began to slaughter, to boil and roast things, while others, on the other hand, stormed through the house from top to bottom. Others still made a large pack out of linens, clothes, and all kinds of household goods. Everything they didn't want to take with them they destroyed. A number of them stuck their bayonets into the straw and hay, as if they didn't already have enough sheep and pigs to stick. Many of them shook out the feathers from the bedcovers and filled them with ham. Others threw meat and other utensils into it. Some knocked in the oven and the windows, smashing copper utensils and dishes. Bedsteads, tables, stools, and benches were burned. Pots and cutting boards were all broken. Our servant girl was so badly handled in the barn that she couldn't move any longer. Our servant they tied up and laid on the ground and rammed a funnel in his mouth and then poured a ghastly brew full of piss down his throat. Then they started to torture the peasants as if they wanted to burn a bunch of witches. (book 1, chapter 4)[4]

While such graphic descriptions, striking paintings, and abstract figures and graphs make it relatively easy for us to understand these calamities, the next step is a bit harder to take. I want to pick up the history of "religious mentalities" that was introduced in the last chapter. Up to this point we have listened to the plea of our ancestors—"Protect us, oh Lord, from plague, famine, and war!"—and acted as if these three scourges were the only things that threatened their world. By comparison the cry "Oh Lord!" seems to point to something fixed and unmoving in the midst of so many awful turns of fate, a secure place of refuge, a rock against which the waves of the storm crashed. What if that wasn't the case for some of them, or perhaps for many of them? What if even this bastion in their lives wavered? What if the calm certainty that radiated out from such faith began to disappear?

Certain statements are difficult to make about religious beliefs in the past. One may assume, however, that for the majority of our forebears in the sixteenth and seventeenth centuries life involved not simply one physical existence but an earthly life, more or less short and threatened, and a much more important and longer, even eternal, afterlife. In theory every believer who was baptized and a part of the Christian community had a hope of resurrection after death and an eternal life in the countenance of God. That was in theory. But just as there were bodily dangers on earth like plague,

15. Arnold Böcklin (1827–1901), *The Plague.* 149.5 × 104.5 cm on wood, 1898. Öffentliche Kunstsammlung Basel, Kunstmuseum, Loan of the Swiss Gottfried Keller Foundation 1902, photo by Martin Bühler). In this vision of terror Böcklin took up a theme at the end of his life that was constantly close to him and which touched his life in different ways. In 1855 he and his wife became sick from cholera in Rome. Later typhus almost took his life. Four of his children did not survive similar epidemics. In 1873 another cholera epidemic broke out in Munich from which Böcklin sought refuge in Florence in 1874. Two years later he made his first sketch, called *Cholera* (today in the Hessisches Landesmuseum in Darmstadt). As with the plague, cholera involved an infectious disease that made few distinctions regarding age, sex, or social status of the individual but instead struck equally every man, woman, and child on the street. Even the image of the Mother of God in the small niche in the wall appears powerless before the power of this fate. Today we no longer die publicly in the streets or from infectious diseases that kill swiftly regardless of age. Instead, most of us die in places screened off or hidden from view, largely at an old age of seventy, eighty, or more years and after long, painful, and chronic suffering. Death and dying have changed in fundamental ways. We no longer die from the Black Death but from the White Death.

hunger, and war that threatened human existence, so there were spiritual dangers and threats to the hope of salvation in the eternal life.

Extremist representatives of the history of religious mentalities may argue that a thorough Christianization of broad parts of the population never took place in the West. One cannot, as a result, talk about the beginning of the eighteenth century as the start of de-Christianization or even, returning to Meertens's study of pre-Reformation remnants, as the rigidification of Christianity at some earlier stage of development. To sum up the argument, it is said that in the period that interests us our forebears were not so completely different from us today in matters of belief or even unbelief. I am not so sure of this, or at least I look at it differently given how strongly they embraced notions about the other world and how closely they related the microcosm to the macrocosm, their little worlds to the entire universe, as we can see everywhere. The next chapter and the concluding one will give us an opportunity to return to this theme.

Naturally we are not talking here about official religion, dogmatic theology, confessional hairsplitting concerning the matters of faith, and elite souls on the way to perfection. What interests us instead are the religious needs of everyday people who, living in a rural world in which up to 80 or 90 percent of the people were peasants, made up the majority of our forebears. Our task is to try to imagine what "Christianization" offered them in life. The centuries-old institutional church, first of all, accompanied every person, generation after generation, through the most important moments in life, from baptism and first communion to confirmation, marriage (and re-marriage if necessary), and, finally, to death and burial. In this way it progressively integrated a person into the church and society, offering a number of opportunities for distinction in the eyes of the community: an honorary church office; a seat of particular distinction in the church near the high altar or across from the pulpit; and a grave in a choice location in the cemetery, perhaps even up front in the church itself, thus guaranteeing, by virtue of one's closeness to the saints, that one would be among the first of those resurrected on Judgment Day to enter heaven. Or the church could simply emphasize a man's role as head of the family and household by his leading the obligatory walk from the farm to the church on Sundays.

There was, on the other hand, the church as a secular authority with its power to command and forbid, its power to tax through the tithe and exercise juridical powers of punishment and reprimand. Not least was the church's ability to make life better or worse, or even unbearable, by means of bestowing blessings and honors through its official representatives.

The church also controlled the liturgical year with its many days of worship and feasting. Some were serious, others celebratory or dramatic, giving flight to the heart and soul or soothing them through services of thanksgiving, commemoration, and expiation. By "opening up" certain times of the year and "closing off" others, the church not only allowed weddings at one time and prohibited them at others, as during Advent, it also impressed its own rhythm on the course of the year, transforming the natural work year of the peasant into a unified agro-liturgical year. That it came to conflicts here and there is easily understandable, as it did, for example, after a long rainy period in the summer if the pastor wanted his flock's unconditional attendance in church for a certain service, but they preferred instead to harvest the hay or grain on the first sunny days, ignoring the fact that it was Sunday or a feast day. There were, moreover, other opportunities according to one's religious confession: processions, confraternities, quiet personal prayer, open congregational prayer, and singing, the latter often satisfying more social than religious needs.

The material side of the church, finally, left its mark as well: a parish church, modest as always, with a cemetery and charnel house, and various other Christian signs on the pathways, houses, barns, stalls, and fields. For a long time there were many more of them: monasteries, abandoned monasteries, religious orders, and proscribed religious orders. There were no longer simply Christians, Jews, and pagans, but, after the division of Christendom, a number of religious confessions. They sometimes warred with each other and sometimes were tolerant. Among them one could find internal missionary efforts, growing pressure on believers in a particular church as it became intolerant and forcibly imposed its confessional view up to the point of religious war.

The question that interests me is this: How did the church and its representatives, coercive and obtrusive on as many levels and in as many ways as they were, shape the everyday lives of our ancestors? What kind of a spiritual climate resulted from all this? The people that I mean are again those 80 or 90 percent of the population who lived on the land. Complete literacy was unknown to them, so "Christianization" took place for them through what they saw and heard. Above all they listened to sermons, and one of the most pressing research tasks is to look at the collections of sermons of rural pastors from this period. In this regard French scholars speak unhesitatingly about the traumatizing of the faithful in the seventeenth and eighteenth centuries through increasingly fantastic descriptions of hell and the punishments that awaited them there, and the progressive demonization of a purgatory once considered to be relatively harmless. Prescriptions to perform twenty years of penance there, even for the most harmless trespass, were no longer unusual.

They could also look at what the simple parish church offered them as they passed the graves in the cemetery and entered the front door. First came the baptismal font with several symbolic carvings of baptized souls being saved from eternal darkness and damnation, graphically portrayed as monsters and fabulous elongated creatures grabbing at them (fig. 16). Farther toward the front of the church came perhaps paintings depicting the two high points of the church year, Christmas and Easter, a statue of the Virgin with Child, and a cross with the Savior, who was either martyred or triumphant. If the church offered more than this they were equally simple and contained lessons as easily understood as those in a picture book: a scene from the Scriptures that illustrated the morning sermon; a statue of a saint and his or her legend; and on an altar maybe a creature from hell in the

16.   Demonic and monstrous images in the churches of the Christian West. Our forebears understood demonic and monstrous sculptures and pictures as embodiments of the powers of darkness and evil who had come into the world through the Fall and who threatened and endangered their salvation, even though they were visible symbolically in their churches. The baptismal font made of fir (top), dating from around 1200, was originally in the village church of Alnö near the small town of Sundsvall in northeastern Sweden on the Gulf of Bothnia. Along with two dozen other pieces, it is part of one of the finest collections of this type in Statens Historiska Museer in Stockholm. The altar table, *The Damned Will Be Driven into Hell* (bottom), an illustration of the revelations to St. Birgitta, can be seen at the same place. Originally it was located in the village church of Tönevalle in Östergötland in southeastern Sweden. It was probably made at the end of the fifteenth century in Lübeck.

Even though these two illustrations come from parts of northern Europe, this does not mean that plastic representations in sculpture or painting were limited to these areas. They are found throughout Western Christendom. An impressive example from Central Europe, for example, is the *Last Judgment* over the main portal of the cathedral in Bern (created 1490–1500) and the monumental fresco on the same theme on the northern wall of the nave of the village church of Raron in Wallis (1512–15). The large collection of reproductions (sculptures and wall paintings) in the Musée National des Monuments Français in the Palais de Chaillot in Paris is impressive and, at the same time, instructive.

shape of a dragon into which the eternally damned, heavily chained, are tumbling or are being dragged (see figure 16).

Were our rustic forebears to visit a town on a market day they would find that the pictures in the numerous churches were, in our eyes, generally more refined, artistically more challenging and multifaceted. The message, however, was still the same: the coming of the Savior to save the world, his death on the cross, and his Resurrection and triumph over death and darkness. The dangers to one's soul were everywhere portrayed with extreme realism in the form of wild animals and demons who signified the loss of paradise and the coming of evil into the world through the fall of man.

Naturally the normal churchgoer at that time had no access to the art treasures, the fine paintings and choice woodcarvings hidden away and difficult to find and look at. They would have been located, for example, at the far front of the church, closed off from view behind screens in the chancel or sacristy. Today we can let them amaze us close-up in air-conditioned museums, letting them work on us as delightful and refreshing images from times long since past.

But what I am referring to are the contemporary works of art located in the most visible places. A favorite example to be found in a number of variations in the nearest cathedral would be the struggle between St. George and the dragon. It is located on the main facade of the cathedral in Basel and is impossible to overlook. Elsewhere in the same church one can see a dragon with a raging red head in the floor of the nave, and symbols of animals, clearly drawn and easily visible, on the outside walkway around the choir. For peasants who looked up at them these symbols affirmed the omnipresent relationships between humans and the natural world, the web of reciprocal influences between everyday life, the little world or microcosm, and the larger world or macrocosm of the universe. For the peasant at the time this wasn't a necessary reminder but an affirmation of what was self-evident.

Please do not respond to my point with superficial arguments from the history of art and architecture, playing down these pictures because of their origins in a world of pictures and myths from the High Middle Ages and claiming that this world had long since disappeared by the period 1550–1700. Such an argument would further claim that these images had lost their meaning, mystery, and mythical power centuries before at the hands of the Gothic style, a trend that would lead eventually to the modern world with its lack of imagination. By that time the demonic and the monstrous had been distinctly banned to the lower zones, to pedestals, gargoyles, and stone supports. However true this objection might be, the monsters, fabulous creatures, these pictures of the animal world and the heavens, were still in place as late as the period 1550–1700, and they have remained there. We can still be charmed today by the puritanical and iconoclastic views of Bernard of Clairvaux (1090–1153), the eloquent founder and abbot of the Cistercian order, later canonized and elevated to the status of teacher of the church, who stormed against the symbolic world of the Middle Ages in 1125:

What are these laughable monstrosities, these unbelievably deformed beauties and ugly oddities doing in the cloisters among monks who can read? What are foul apes doing there? Wild lions? Monstrous centaurs? Half-humans? Tigers? Battling warriors? Horn-blowing hunters? Beneath a head you find a number of bodies, and on top of a body a lot of heads. On a mammal you see the tail of a snake, on a fish the head of a mammal. Over there is a beast with a horse's front and a goat's behind; or an animal with horns in the front and a horse's behind. In a word, you find such a wonderful diversity of creations everywhere that you would rather look at these chiseled pieces of stone than at written works. You prefer to concern yourself with these all day long, by God, to muse about them than to think about God's Law! As if the foolishness of it all is not already embarrassing, why not at least repent the costs?[5]

How could our ancestors relate to this position, or even share it, when they did not even have the alternative of reading the "written works"? Closely related to this was the fact they weren't supposed to reflect on the articles of faith. At that time belief meant, above all, practice. This statement speaks much more to those of us who "muse about them" today than it could have to our ancestors with their entirely different way of seeing things.

It is one thing to devote ourselves to works of art from the Middle Ages and the early modern period that have been taken completely out of their context and placed in art museums or to enjoy the sheer pleasure of looking at them in magnificently reproduced picture books. We gaze at a sculpture of St. Roche, St. Florian, or Mary with Jesus, and right next door stands a pharmacy stocked with wonder drugs, a fire station with efficient fire-fighting equipment, and a modern children's clinic. It meant something entirely different to our ancestors to seek out the statues of the saints and the Virgin in the parish church as an epidemic of plague raged, fire threatened, or after the death of their only child, appealing to them in their need and uncertainty as powerful intermediaries with the Lord and waiting for help. Haven't we degraded churches and cathedrals into museums and objects of mere artistic interest, even if their paintings and statues are still standing in their original locations? How can these works have the least bit of power anymore for mere art lovers, and how could they still provoke associations connected to the history of religious mentalities? We can no longer perceive their meaning, since our beliefs have totally changed.

These short discussions should remind us that our forebears' spiritual world, and not just their external world, was threatened. We need to focus our attention not only on the timing of local outbreaks of plague, famine, and war but also not lose sight of this inner world at the same time. For the threats to their physical environment that multiplied between 1550 and 1700 coincided precisely with an equally troubling time in the history of religious mentality. Even doubting how deeply Christianized the peoples of Europe were, a simple glance at a confessional map of Germany for any year between 1550 and 1700 reveals why. Looking at the crazy quilt of splintered territories, a hodgepodge of Catholic, Calvinist, and Lutheran lands, raises the question of how the confusion of religious confessions affected our forebears. It was no longer enough just to believe what they were told by generations of ecclesiastics, even if they were so inclined. For these officials were no longer united among themselves about what was true and false in matters of belief. One time they believed this, another time that. Here the truth was one thing, over there something else, and in a third place something entirely different. One can justifiably conclude that the confusion led to new converts, the spiritually reborn finding a new certitude about salvation, while others became deeply insecure in matters of faith. Still others may have turned even further from official religion between 1550 and 1700.

In closing this chapter and leading over into the next one, I ask the reader to look at another painting (fig. 17). In the previous chapters we have been discussing the everyday lives of our present ancestors between 1550 and 1700. While I have tried to describe their fears and troubles and bring the unusual fragility of their existence closer to home for the reader, these peasants may still seem bloodless, abstract, and remote.

I would be among the first to want to know much more about the reality of everyday life for our ancestors. What did they physically look like? How did they dress? Since we are today better nourished from the moment of conception on than they were, it would be interesting to know how much smaller they were than we. How did they sit at table? What did they eat and

17.   Joint composition of the three brothers Antoine, Louis, and Mathieu Le Nain (ca. 1588–1648, ca. 1593–1648, 1607–77), *Peasant Family* (also known as *Pleasant Mealtime, Family Mealtime, Family Union, The Young Flageolet Player,* and *Peasant Family at Home*). Oil on canvas; 111.3 × 159.5 cm; 1640s; Musée du Louvre, Paris. See the description of the painting and commentary in the exhibition catalogue *Les Freres Le Nain, Grand Palais Paris, October 3, 1978–January 8, 1979* (Paris: Editions de la Réunion des Musées Nationaux, 1978), 13, 185–89. The Le Nain brothers' pictures are eye-catching favorites on the dust jackets of books about peasants by French historians. See, for example, *Paysans devant leur maison* on the cover of Jacques Dupâquier, *La population rurale du bassin parisien à l'époque de Louis XIV* (Paris: Ecoles des Hautes Etudes en Sciences Sociales, 1979), or *La charrette ou le retour de la fenaison* on the cover of Pierre Goubert, *La vie quotidienne des paysans français au XVIIe siècle* (Paris: Hachette, 1982).

drink, and how? Did women, children, servants, and serving girls receive the same portions as the head of the family? What were the consequences of poor dental hygiene, the loss of teeth, and painful toothaches? What marks were left by illnesses that were not treated, poorly healed wounds, broken bones, and war wounds? How much more quickly did women age than men due to bearing on average six to eight children? How did those with poor eyesight make do without glasses? With what sensitivity did they react to the smells of sweaty and unwashed bodies? How did they dress in summer and winter? Did they wear the same clothes all the time, or did they change into others? Was it common to wear shoes, or did they mostly go around indoors and outdoors without shoes, their feet itching from all the scratches?

How did their houses look? Were they gray upon gray, brown upon brown, or did they have a sense for color? If they did, did they have the same meaning as the liturgical colors—violet, purple, green, and black—during the church year? Were their rooms heated? Which ones? Did one room always serve as the living room, day and night? Which rooms were lit, and what with? What role did the senses—seeing, tasting, smelling, feeling, and hearing—have in a world where immediate sense experiences counted for more than mental reflection? What noises were heard during the day? What noises at night? What role did elders play as role models in an age without year-round schooling? What role did bodily gestures and rites play? Rituals and ceremonies? What were their symbols? Honors? On what did they bestow prestige, value, and attention? What offended them? And what elicited revenge? What constituted fun, joy, festiveness, and playfulness among young and old? What was their sexuality like? What constituted force and brutal violence? What was considered gluttonous and drinking too much? What were their curses? To sum it up, I want to know about everything that was spontaneous and unfettered.[6]

One question after another comes to mind. If we are to know what necessities of life and simple pleasures people enjoyed, which groups of people had them or only a part of them, where these conditions were threatened and destroyed, and how long they lasted before they were replaced, each question would actually have to be answered on a regional basis for every period in history.

In looking at a painting this time, I have a different goal in mind. I do not want it to yield a mass of new information or even describe one particular case in detail. The goal instead is to arrive at a general statement about everyday life in the past. I have chosen a French painting from the 1640s, *Peasant Family,* or *Peasant Mealtime,* by the three French brothers Antoine (ca. 1588–1648), Louis (ca. 1593–1648), and Mathieu Le Nain (1607–77). Because of its prominent location in Paris in the Louvre and its reproduction on hundreds and thousands of postcards, collections of artworks, history books, and schoolbooks, the painting has achieved a degree of familiarity in France comparable to some of the most often reproduced and displayed "peasant pictures" in Germany, such as Albrecht Dürer's copperplate engraving *Peasant Men and Women at the Market* (1519). Yet it may take an outsider, someone not familiar with the picture, to see it with new eyes. Doing this is much more difficult with a painting from one's own country.

The Le Nain brothers often worked together on the same painting and depicted a number of aspects of peasant life. Since their works largely date from the first half of the seventeenth century, they suit our purposes perfectly. Still, one must look at the painting carefully and critically so as not to judge it hastily as a simple mirror of contemporary realities. After a quick observation of the work, it is obvious to the eye of a social historian that a few things are out of place and some are missing. The upper-class lapdog painted at the bottom left, for example, certainly has no business in a peasant room at that time. This may have been a gesture toward the patron, who, one assumes, came from a well-situated and financially better off social class. The white tablecloth also belongs in this picture about as much as the romantic shepherd's flute music the youth is playing and the thin, finely made wineglass in the hand of the older woman.

What does the title, *Peasant Mealtime,* signify here anyway? I see no evidence of a meal except the bread, wine, and salt, that is, unless one wants to interpret them in this way symbolically. There is a more basic question yet. How does one know with certainty that the title refers to a real peasant family? One looks in vain for typical peasant tools, instruments, or utensils in the picture. Are we simply projecting onto this painting our preconceived notion of peasant life at that time, letting it become a "peasant family" or a "peasant meal"? After we have fabricated the source ourselves in this way, we then cite it as an authentic portrayal of "peasant" life from the first half of the seventeenth century. That's making a fool of yourself!

Reflections like these inevitably lead to doubts. The social historian then gladly turns to the advice and knowledge of a colleague in art history. By keeping one's purpose in mind and asking carefully worded questions, one can learn more than by consulting commentaries that might be knowledgeable but which dwell on painting technique and color. As a specialist he or she can place this one painting within the context of the complete works of the Le Nain brothers and, by doing so, point out, for example, that lapdogs and peasant children playing music frequently appeared in their paintings. Their value should not therefore be exaggerated. To mention only a few points, the specialist can draw on a rich general knowledge and, with a knowledge of the theories about art current back then, can consider the themes that were preferred at the time. The specialist, moreover, is familiar with the secular and spiritual patrons who often influenced the content of paintings. Assuming mutual open-mindedness and understanding, a patient questioning, answering, and listening on both sides can gradually lead away from the narrow confines of one's discipline toward a common basis for interpreting a work.

Such a discussion, jointly carried out at an interdisciplinary level, might illustrate how to determine the appropriateness of the title, *Peasant Mealtime*. One shouldn't initially leap to a judgment about its appropriateness but instead discuss cautiously how peasant conditions at that time were written down and communicated. What resulted from one such discussion was the theme of the succession of the ages and the generations. Therefore the painting doesn't revolve around the peasant family itself so much as it does around people generally at a time in which a sudden outbreak of plague, famine, and war was always possible. Now the picture begins to speak to us. It appears as if this family has just narrowly escaped such an experience. They have something to eat, drink, and clothe themselves with, perhaps not lavishly and with much variety, but they have it all the same. The fire in the background also gives off heat so that those going barefoot don't have to freeze. The hearth provides not only warmth and light, and a place to cook meals, but also reminds us of the constant danger of devastating fires, even in times of peace.

One face after another in the painting also tells us, in the most expressive terms, about a whole range of potential human experience. Moving from one to the next, one can hold imaginary conversations with them. There is the uncomplaining boy on the floor, his legs sprawled out, looking unaffected by it all. Then comes the girl, seated and with a somewhat open blouse, who shows all of the modest life and role expectations of a young peasant woman. There are finally the bitter faces of the husband at the end of his years, broken by his providing the daily bread for the family, and, at the left, his wife, the mother of the children, looking resigned and detached after all of the toil, joy, and suffering she has endured in her full life. It is as if we were back in Leimbach with Johannes Hooss and Elisabeth Riebeling, with their worries about life and survival in the little worlds of that time, concerned about the next generation and the one after that, the strategies for marriage, and passing on the farm as they grew weak.

This interpretation perhaps restricts the meaning of the picture and might disappoint the expectations of some readers. The limitations, however, are inherent in the painting itself. What is left, it seems to me, is a great deal considering the tediousness and difficulty of reconstructing, one small piece after another, the mosaic of the worlds of our ancestors.

CHAPTER 4

The Search for
Stability

OME BECAME HARDENED under these circumstances, of course, and tried to defy the hard blows dealt out by fate, much as the father does in the Le Nain brothers' picture. That might have helped in the short term and could be interpreted as a sign of an unbroken will to survive. In difficult times, however, stability could never be achieved in this way. If someone wanted to survive in his little world and not be ruined, not be overwhelmed by the dangers of the larger world, even more had to be done. Long-term plans were needed. The persistent pursuit of strategies of survival became an absolute necessity.

Let me first illustrate this search for stability within the context of the little world of Johannes Hooss. For this purpose I have drawn up four figures (fig. 18, 20, 21, and 23), all of which follow the same scheme. A broad half circle, representing a continuously turning wheel of time, sweeps around a circle at the center of the graph. Figure 18 depicts the 100 years between 1670 and 1770, figures 20 and 21 the 450 years between 1520 and 1970, and figure 23 the 200 years between 1600 and 1800.

At the center of figure 18 is Johannes Hooss as ego. The time starts with

18. Johannes Hooss (1670–1755) (ego) at the center of a constantly changing social network. Its beginnings, expansion, peak, and contraction over the course of his life are easily visible. A total of thirty-six people were involved (see their names and dates in the lower part of the figure). *Sources:* Gottfried Ruetz, comp., *Hessisches Geschlechterbuch,* vols. 18, 19, 20, Schwalm vols, 1, 2, and 3, Deutsches Geschlechterbuch, vols. 157, 159, and 176 (Limburg an der Lahn: C. A. Starke, 1971, 1972, and 1977). Additional genealogical material and databank at the Friedrich-Meinecke-Institute at the Free University Berlin.

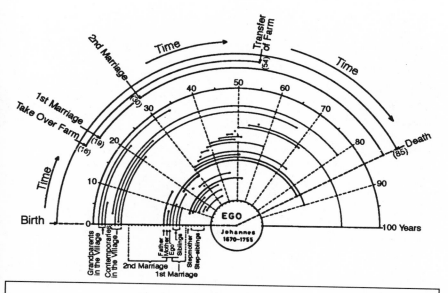

	Dates of Birth and Death	Presence at Vältes Farmstead During the Lifetime of EGO	
EGO: Johannes	1670-1755	(1670-1755)	Owner of the Farmstead 1686-1724
			First marriage 1689-1699
			Second marriage 1700-1755
Father	1626-1686	1670-1686	Owner of the Farmstead to 1686
Mother	1636-1677	1670-1677	
Siblings			
Anna Catharina	1661-1747	1670-1681	Married out to Ransbach in 1681
Anna	1665-1726	1670-1688	Married out to Ascherode in 1688
Hans Class	1677-?	1670-1680	Confirmed 1680--Death date unknown
Stepmother	1650-1723	1678-1723	Married in from Wasenberg in 1678
Stepsiblings			
Johann Valentin	1679-1761	1679-1707	Married out to Obergrenzebach in 1707
Hans Henrich	1680-?	1680-1694	Confirmed 1694--Death date unknown
Johannes	1681-1743	1681-1708	Married out to Obergrenzebach in 1707
Johann Adam	1683-1688	1683-1688	Died in childhood
Catharina	1685-1760	1685-1706	Married out to Wasenberg in 1706
First Marriage			
Wife--Catharina	1672-1699	1689-1699	Married in from Rausbach in 1689. Died in childbed 1699
Children			
Anna Catharina	1691-1692	1691-1692	Died as infant
Anna	1693-1693	1693-1693	Died as infant
Anna Catharina	1696-1724	1696-1716	Married out to Zella in 1716
stillbirth	1699-1699	1699-1699	Female stillborn--caused death of mother
Second Marriage			
Wife--Elisabeth	1681-1760	1700-1755	Daughter from Leimbach--Farmstead 2
Children			
Gela	1701-1760	1701-1721	Married out to Gungelshausen in 1721
Catharina	1703-1742	1703-1742	Inherited the Farmstead; Married 1724 at the Farmstead
Anna	1705-1705	1705-1705	Died as infant
Elisabeth	1706-1709	1706-1709	Died in childhood
Anna Gela	1709-1784	1709-1730	Married out to Zella in 1730
Johannes	1711-1719	1711-1719	Died of dysentery in childhood in 1719
Johann Valentin	1714-1721	1714-1721	Died in childhood
Johann Henrich	1717-1718	1717-1718	Died as infant
Johannes	1719-1719	1719-1719	Died as infant
Elisabeth	1720-1742	1720-1741	Married out to Niedergrenzebach in 1741
Martha Elisabeth	1723-1794	1723-1755	Married in 1743 to the widower of her sister Catharina at the Farmstead
Johannes	1726-1726	1726-1726	Died as infant
Men of Same Age as EGO in the Village			
Hans Henrich (Farmstead 5)	1666-1746	(1670-1692)	Married out Wasenberg in 1692
Johannes (Farmstead 5)	1671-1737	(1670-1737)	Married in 1700 to the inheritor of Farmstead 3 in Leimbach
Johannes (Farmstead 6)	1670-1698	(1670-1696)	Married out to Wasenberg in 1696
Helwig (Farmstead 6)	1673-1750	(1673-1750)	Married in 1697--Owner of his farmstead 1697-1745
Grandparents in the Village			
Hans (Farmstead 2)	1607-1676	(1670-1676)	Owner of Farmstead 2, 1626-1676
Elisabeth (Farmstead 2)	1614-1692	(1670-1692)	Married in from Gungelshausen in 1634
Catharina (Farmstead 1)	1611-1704	(1670-1704)	Married in from Mönch-Leusel in 1636

his birth in 1670 and ends with his death in 1755. Other important events in his life are noted at the outer edge of the half circle: his inheritance of the farm at 16, marriage at 19, becoming a widower at 29, his second marriage at 30, retirement at 54, and, finally, his death at age 85. Altogether his life was a long one, one that was rich and full of changes. The inner half circle depicts his network of personal relationships over a number of years as it developed, expanded, matured, and then contracted. Someone who lived as long as Hooss easily outlived not only his closest childhood friends, but also his spouse and the majority of his children. His social network was most extensive during his adult years, the circle of people closest to him increasing when he was between thirty and fifty. After that, however, it rapidly declined. At the end of his life old Johannes died virtually alone.

I need not describe the complex structure of this figure in detail. In the bottom half of the figure one can find a list of thirty-six individuals who were a part of his life, along with their names, dates, the time they spent on the Vältes Farm during Hooss's life, and other details about their lives. One of the most important conclusions to be drawn from the figure is that Hooss's social network encompassed six different groups. The first group included his father and mother and, leaving aside the siblings who died very young, two sisters and a brother. The second group involved his stepmother, four stepbrothers, and a stepsister. In the third were his first wife and his four children by her. The fourth group was made up of his second wife and the twelve children from this marriage. The fifth included his four friends of roughly the same age. Finally, the sixth group comprised members of his grandparents' generation in Leimbach, who were experienced in the ways of the world and who passed on their wisdom by storytelling.

These six groups differed in size and lasted different lengths of time. Some of them overlapped with other groups, while others succeeded one another. Only a few accompanied Hooss for a long time during his life: two friends from his youth, Johannes from the George-Hinrichs Farm and Helwig from the Konrads Farm; later, his second wife, Elisabeth; and the next-to-last child from his marriage with her, Martha Elisabeth. Only two out of the thirty-six outlived him: his wife, who lived five more years until 1760; and his daughter, who died in 1794.

Since no one could count on the survival of close friends and relatives in this age, even in times of peace, strategies for stability had to revolve around more than a specific individual. It was no different when considering oneself.

It made no sense to make yourself the center of the world, to have everything revolve around yourself, to cling to worldly possessions regardless of the costs. The more I look at landscape paintings in the age of Johannes Hooss, the more it seems no accident that they often depicted people crossing bridges without railings, bridges that had collapsed or which were rickety at best. Today we would either make a long detour around them or, if we used them, we wouldn't lean on the railings for support (see fig. 19). Like these bridges, life in the past had no firm handholds. Life might end abruptly at any moment. This understanding of the outward circumstances of life apparently corresponded so closely with the inward realities that no one seemed bothered by the fact that there was nothing to hold on to. Otherwise someone would have repaired all the dilapidated railings and equipped the bridge with solid planks. But this was not done, even though people repeatedly fell off and drowned on account of them. Over and over again in the burial registers one reads, "Fell into the water during the night, lost his way in his sleep and was found half dead—died a half hour later without saying a word."[1]

This accident didn't happen just anywhere, and the deceased wasn't just anyone. He was a close relative of Johannes Hooss: Johannes Hooss of Ascherode, the Leimbach peasant who bought the Baste Farm in 1675. He died on January 21, 1699, when he was only fifty-one years old. This wasn't the only entry like it at the time. It was yet another manifestation of what earlier seemed, at least to us, people's indifference toward worldly affairs and especially toward the earthly part of life.

Still, people created some stability in the little worlds of that age, and did so in ways that seem almost incredible to us today. The most important starting point was a lesson drawn from everything we have discussed up to now: Don't make your own fragile self the center of affairs in a world full of uncertainty. Instead, look at yourself as temporarily filling a role, and serve this role for whatever part of life you need to. At the center of the next three time wheels I have therefore placed not an individual but an idea, a task, a role. For our purposes the Vältes Farm in Leimbach assumes this central position. Everything revolves around the farm, not any of the individuals who temporarily possessed it; the different people related to each other circle around it like dancers spinning around in a round dance. Figure 20 (p. 111) makes this point clearly by setting in the middle of the circle a house inscription often found on older peasant farms from the Schwalm region. It contains the key idea behind the thought and behavior of the house and farm:

19. Meindert Hobbema (1638–1709), *Village Road under the Trees.* Canvas, 97 ×
128.5 cm; 1667/1670; cat. no. 1984, Staatliche Museen zu Berlin Preußischer Kulturbesitz, Gemäldegalerie, Berlin (West). Bridges in Hobbema's time often had unsafe
railings. In this way they resembled the lives of the people who crossed them. As an
example of a bridge without any railings at all see Jacob von Ruisdael (1628/29–
1682), *Landscape with Footbridge* (The Frick Collection, New York); and of a bridge
with collapsed railings, Jan Brueghel the Younger (1601–78), *Cour de ferme* (Musée
du Louvre, Paris). In the same museum see also François Boucher (1703–70), *Le
moulin,* in which a man is leaning backward against the railing of a bridge that is so
rickety that one wonders how he has not yet fallen over. This was also a traditional
theme with a number of variations by the well-known seventeenth-century landscape painter Claude Gellée (1600–82) (often called Claude Lorrain, after his home
in Lorraine), since the main subject of his paintings was the depiction of landscapes
and architecture in association with water. The retrospective to commemorate the
three hundredth anniversary of his death, in 1982 in the National Gallery in Washington and February–May 1983 in the Grand Palais in Paris, enabled me to devote
myself to this little-noticed aspect of his work with all the freshness of a new discovery. I am not convinced by the view of art historians, expressed through interdisciplinary discussions, that bridges without railings were more attractive themes than
those with intact railings. Certainly I would not want to argue that we are dealing
here with natural depictions of conditions at the time. In general it seems to me that
we have before us an artistically created mirror of an inward and outward reality.
Moreover, there were almost certainly scenes of bridges with intact railings from this
age that would have been just as pleasing.

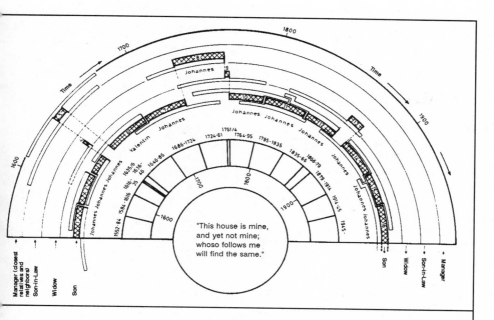

Period	Name	Dates of Birth and Death		Age at Succession/Transfer/Death			Relationship
1. 1552-1584	Johannes Hooss	ca. 1520	ca.1584	ca. 32	64	64	Son of Johannes Hooss
2. 1584-1616	Johannes Hooss	ca.1560	-15.07.1616	ca. 24	56	56	Son of Johannes (1.)
3. 1616-1635	Johannes Hooss	ca. 1585	-25.12.1635	31	50	50	Son of Hohannes (2.)
4. 1635/1636	Margarethe Hooss	?	-30.05.1636	?	?	?	Wife of Johannes (3.)
5. 1636-1646	Georg Hooss and	1589	-02.05.1673	47	57	84	Brother of Johannes (3.): Farmsteader in Asherode
	Johannes Riebling (joint administration)	05.03.1607-23.08.1676		29	39	69	Neighboring Farmsteader in Leimlich
6. 1646-1686	Valentin Hooss	22.06.1626-13.06.1686		20	60	60	Son of Johannes (3.)
7. 1686-1724	Johannes Hooss	17.08.1670-30.12.1755		16	54	85	Son of Valentin (6.)
8. 1724-1761	Johannes Hooss	02.01.1704-29.12.1761		20	57	57	Son-in-law of Johannes (7.)
9. 1761-1764	Martha Elisabeth Hooss	25.7.1723-07.03.1794		38	41	71	Wife of Johannes (8.)
10. 1764-1795	Johannes Hooss	02.02.1734-25.07.1817		30	61	83	Son of Johannes (8.)
11. 1795-1835	Johannes Hooss	14.07.1773-19.06.1838		22	62	65	Son of Johannes (10.)
12. 1835-1866	Johannes Hooss	14.01.1812-24.08.1866		23	54	54	Son of Johannes (11.)
13. 1866-1879	Anna Katharine Hooss	30.11.1814-10.07.1883		52	65	69	Wife of Johannes (12.)
14. 1879-1914	Johannes Hooss	08.02.1854-17.04.1920		25	60	66	Son of Johannes (12.)
15. 1914-1945	Johannes Hooss	13.07.1880-05.08.1970		34	65	90	Son of Johannes (14.)
16. 1945-	Johannes Hooss	31.05.1915-		30			Son of Johannes (15.)

Source: Deutsches Geschlechterbuch, Bd. 159, 1972, S. 8, 11; Bd. 176, 1977, S. 12, 13, 14, 15, 66, 118, 119, 131, 132, 133.

20. Sixteen tenants of the Vältes Farm in Leimbach, 1552–1977. *Sources:* same as in figure 18. The household inscriptions in the middle of the circle comes from a house in the Schwalm community of Wasenberg. See *Schwälmer Jahrbuch* 1976, p. 85. On this subject see also Robert Tuor, *Berner Hausinschriften,* Berner Heimatbücher, vol. 127 (Bern: Paul Haupt, 1981); and on the subject of the thinking that transcended the individual and centered on the farm from the side of folklore studies see Dietmar Sauermann, "Hofidee und bäuerliche Famlienverträge in Westfalen," *Rheinisch-Westfälische Zeitschrift für Volkskunde* 17 (1970): 58–78.

This house is mine,
and yet not mine,
whoso follows me
will find it the same.

Looking ahead at the outcome of this master plan for stability, in this case carried out to its logical conclusion, the results are astonishing: the house endured more than four hundred years without a single break! Figure 20 depicts the ownership of the Vältes Farm and its sixteen owners between 1552 and 1977 as spokes of a wheel, each of which corresponds to the length of time the owner held it. At the bottom is a list of the owners' names, their dates, the ages at which they succeeded to the farm and passed it on, their ages when they died, and their relationship to their predecessor. As far back as this farm's history can be traced, it was never divided up among the heirs, as has already been mentioned. From the middle of the sixteenth century onward it was always passed on as a unit to one person from the next generation. For the good of the farm, the claims of all of the other children were subordinated to this strict principle.

In the majority of cases, that is, eleven out of sixteen times, a son inherited from his father, just as one would expect. These cases are drawn in as an inner ring of Vältes Farm peasants turning around the center. On three occasions a son was not yet old enough to take over the farm when his father died. In these cases the mother, a widow, held it for a few years. These widows assume a place in the next ring. On one occasion no male heir was available and the farm passed at that time through the female line to a son-in-law. His place is depicted in the third ring. Finally, on one other occasion, the widow possessing the farm died only a few months after her husband died, and therefore a long time would pass before a son reached the age of inheritance. In this case, the deceased man's brother, a peasant and farm-holder in Ascherode, and a neighbor from Leimbach—someone with knowledge of the village—stepped in as joint administrators of the farm until the heir reached the age of majority. They have been given a place in the outermost ring.

A close look at the graph and the table reveals two patterns, both of which are closely related to the search for stability. They seem important enough to me to merit a separate study with their own illustrations (see figs. 21, p. 114, and 22, p. 117). First, one notices that the farmholder's life span did not correspond with the time he held the farm. The cross-hatched blocks in figure 20 indicating possession of the farm naturally follow each other without a gap. The life spans of the individual farmholders, however, often overlapped with the time they possessed the farm by only a few years or decades. Only when a farmer died young did the age of death correspond with his retirement from the farm. A few Vältes Farm peasants became old, some even very old, reaching eighty-three, eighty-four, eighty-five, and even ninety years of age. Yet none of them managed the farm beyond his sixty-fifth year. Instead they managed the farm during their best years, a term good both for them and for the well-being of the farm.

This pattern predates the introduction of uniform pension and retirement ages by the state and conformed with a conception of the stages of life dating far back in time. If one believes the following proverb, this popular conception of life is still common in many places today. As one would expect, it can be easily documented with illustrations from different sources:

> Ten years a child,
> Twenty years young and wild,
> Thirty years his manhood won,
> Forty years is very well done,
> Fifty years he's standing still,
> Sixty years he's over the hill,
> Seventy years his old age shows,
> Eighty years the memory goes,
> Ninety years children poke fun,
> Hundred years by God's grace is done.[2]

Figure 21 takes into account these traditional stages of life and clearly shows that a Vältes Farm peasant would never have considered retaining control over the farm once he was "over the hill" and "showing old age," that is, once he was between sixty and seventy years old. How was a seventy- or eighty-year-old man or one with failing memory supposed to manage a large farmstead with the necessary strength to guide it through dangerous and difficult times and not come to harm? Were he to reach the age of ninety he would become the butt not only of children's jokes but of jokes from the entire village as well.

Once again we confront behavior that is difficult for inveterate individualists like us to comprehend: gradually letting go, giving up the main role and turning it over to someone else, retreating into the background once one's

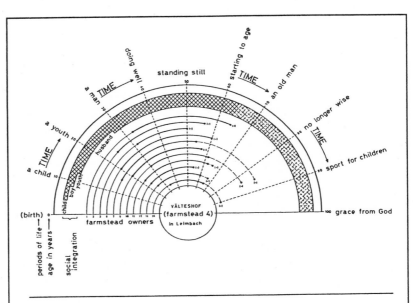

The diagram labels (reading around the arc):

a child · a youth · a man · doing well · standing still · starting to age · an old man · no longer wise · sport for children · grace from God

TIME (repeated around arc)

child · boy · youth · husband

VÄLTESHOF (farmstead 4) in Leimbach

(birth) — periods of life — age in years — social integration

farmstead owners

Years of life of the farmstead owner			Farmstead owner from ... up until ... year of life				Death of farmstead owner at the age of	
1. Johannes Hooss	1520 – 1584		from 32.	to 64.	(+)		64	years
2. Johannes Hooss	1560 – 1616		from 24.	to 56.	(+)		56	years
3. Johannes Hooss	1585 – 1635		from 31.	to 50.	(+)		50	years
6. Valentin Hooss	1626 – 1686		from 20.	to 60.	(+)		60	years
7. Johannes Hooss	1670 – 1755		from 16.	to 54.			85	years
8. Johannes Hooss	1704 – 1761		from 20.	to 57.	(+)		57	years
10. Johannes Hooss	1734 – 1817		from 30.	to 61.			83	years
11. Johannes Hooss	1773 – 1838		from 22.	to 62.			65	years
12. Johannes Hooss	1812 – 1866		from 23.	to 54.	(+)		54	years
14. Johannes Hooss	1854 – 1920		from 25.	to 60.			66	years
15. Johannes Hooss	1880 – 1970		from 34.	to 65.			90	years

Die Stuffenjahre des Menschen.

Fünf Jahr ein Kind.
Zehn Jahr ein Knab.
Zwanzig Jahr ein Jüngling.
Dreißig Jahr ein Mann.
Vierzig Jahr wohlgethan.

Frühling Sommer.
Herbst   Winter.

Fünfzig Jahr Stillstand.

Sechzig Jahr gehts Alter an,
Siebenzig Jahr ein Greiß.
Achtzig Jahr Schneeweiß.
Neunzig Jahr der Kinderspott.
Hundert Jahr Gnade bei Gott.

physical strength begins to fade. How easy or difficult it was for someone to do this in that age I cannot say. What is evident to me, however, is that several peasants gave up the farm at a time in their lives that was prescribed neither by nature nor by the proverb, that is, around age sixty, and in the case of Johannes Hooss, at fifty-four. At that time three decades of "retirement" lay before him.

I have drawn in one more development in the individual life cycle in figure 21: the farmholder's integration into his society from his early stages in life up to the time of his greatest vigor and on to his decline and fading away. This draws our attention to another connection between the time one was a property holder and that phase of life in which the broadest social integration takes place. In the graph this is the outermost band with cross-hatching. At the beginning it is narrow, then gradually it becomes broader, and then, as age progresses, it thins out. A newborn infant was slowly incorporated into the Christian community through baptism, naming, first communion, confirmation, and marriage. He slowly was accepted among people like himself through these rituals until, finally, a number of the residents of the village bore him off to his grave. The process was the same for a boy, an adolescent, or a young man growing up in the world of the family, the neighborhood, the village, and the society beyond the village. He sought out contacts with the outside world and developed an ever growing social network, just as he was drawn increasingly into the different networks of

21.   Property holding and the stages of life. The peasants on the Vältes Farm managed this large property only during their best years, when they were the best connected socially. The division of life by decades has a long tradition behind it. It can easily be documented in funeral sermons and single-leaf broadsides for the entire period this study encompasses. Each depicts a couple climbing up the steps to their fiftieth year and then descending toward the grave. Two easily accessible works on exhibit from places far apart from each other and from different time periods: *The Antiquity of Human Life,* woodcut, Schleswig, eighteenth century (after a model from the seventeenth century), in the Landesmuseum Schleswig, Schloß Gottorf; and, reproduced here in the lower half of the figure, *Man's Staircase of Years,* hand-colored print from Switzerland (Basel?), ca. 1830, Schweizerisches Museum für Volkskunde, Basel. I am grateful to Dr. Paul Zubek of the Schleswig-Holsteinisches Landesmuseum, and Dr. Christine Burckhardt-Seebass and Dr. Theo Gantner of the Schweizerisches Volkskundemuseum Basel for permission for new photographic reproductions. *Sources:* for the upper part of the figure, as for figure 18; for the lower part of the picture, the Schweizerisches Museum für Volkskunde, Basel.

other people. Marriage and inheritance of the farm anchored him in the most solid way possible in the society. It was then that he developed the widest circle of relationships and experienced the broadest social integration in his life: family contacts with new relatives, economic ties with buyers of his products, and legal agreements with the holders of neighboring farms. Depending upon his knowledge of people, his patience, toughness, and tact, he accumulated a fund of esteem and prestige at this time, whether large or small, that could be used for the benefit of the farm.

As he grew old this mosaic of social relationships came apart piece by piece. Within the network, older and younger people left the stage, leaving behind them gaps that were increasingly difficult to fill because of the growing age differences with those who came along behind them. A once broadly integrated network contracted. A person growing old might keep his esteem and prestige for a while, but the gap between him and the young grew. Much in the same way that he had been integrated into society a step at a time at the beginning of his life, now at the end of life he saw himself increasingly excluded, pushed aside, marginalized, perhaps only sought out by curious youngsters with questions about the past. Wasn't it time to make room for the next generation?

The second part in the master plan for creating stability over the centuries is already evident in figure 20. It involved names, or, to put it briefly, it involved *the* name. Setting aside the three widows and the two administrators of the farms, for more than four hundred years all of the Vältes Farm peasants, with only one exception, carried the name of Johannes Hooss. The exception was Vält, the father of our Johannes, and that was so only because his older brother—also called Johannes!—died at age twelve. Considering the enormous infant and childhood mortality rates of the time, it struck me at first as very odd that a Johannes always survived and came of age to take over the farm. A study of the first names given to the Hooss children quickly solved the puzzle, however. The amazing results are summed up in figure 22. The Hooss family usually had not one but several sons with the name Johannes at the same time. No fewer than twenty-nine of the thirty-nine male children were baptized Johannes, some simply as Johannes, Johann, or Hans, others as Johannes coupled with another name, like Nicolaus, Clas, Jacob, Jost, Henrich, Valentin, Adam, or Georg. If we look at their dates, it is obvious that an older Johannes didn't first have to die before a younger brother could be baptized with the same name. By naming two, three, four, and, in extreme cases, nine boys Johannes the family guaranteed that despite

Farmstead Owner	Period	Sons (Heir is underlined)	
Johannes Hooss	ca. 1562-1584	1. Curt	1562-?
		2. Georg	1560-1612
		3. Johannes	1560-1616
Johannes Hooss	1584-1616	1. Johannes, Sr.	1585-1635
		2. Georg	1589-1673
		3. Jost	1595-1629
		4. Johannes, Jr.	1598-1670
Johannes Hooss	1616-1635	1. Johannes	1624-1636
		2. Valentinus	1626-1686
		3. Johannes	1629-1631
		4. Johannes	1631-1669
		5. Clas	1632-1677
Valentin Hooss	1646-1686	1. Hans Clas	1677-?
		2. Johannes	1670-1755
		3. Johann Jacoo	1673-1673
		4. Johann Jost	1674-1674
		5. Johann Henrich	1675-1675
		6. Johann Valentin	1679-1761
		7. Johann Henrich	1680-1694
		8. Johannes	1681-1743
		9. Johann Adam	1683-1688
Johannes Hooss	1686-1724	1. Johannes	1711-1719
		2. Johann Valentin	1714-1721
		3. Johann Henrich	1717-1718
		4. Johannes	1719-1719
		5. Johannes	1726-1726
Johannes Hooss (Son-in-law from Gungelshausen)	1724-1761	1. Johannes	1728-1728
		2. Johannes	1734-1817
		3. Johann Jost	1744-1792
		4. Conrad	1747-1750
Johannes Hooss	1764-1795	1. Johannes	1773-1838
Johannes Hooss	1795-1835	1. Sebastian	1801-1858
		2. Johann George	1803-1805
		3. Johannes	1812-1866
Johannes Hooss	1835-1866	1. Sebastian	1801-1843
		2. Johannes	1854-1920
Johannes Hooss	1879-1914	1. Johannes	1880-1970
		2. Sebastian	1885-1966
Johannes Hooss	1914-1945	1. Johannes	1915-
Johannes Hooss	1945-		

22. First names given to male descendants on the Vältes Farm in Leimbach, 1550–1950. *Source:* as for figure 18.

high infant and child mortality rates someone named Johannes always survived in the end, making it possible for the farm to be managed by someone bearing the same personal and family names. Even on the one occasion that a son-in-law succeeded to the farm, his name was Johannes Hooss, in this case a man from a close branch of this large family in Gungelshausen.

Parents' belief today that every child must have his or her own personal name stems from our idea of individualism. Each of us would probably have wanted to keep our parents from giving our names to a brother or sister, since it would have threatened our sense of individuality. But our forebears not only had no restrictions against such a practice, they repeatedly baptized their children with the same names from generation to generation. What was important was not the individual, who lived only a certain length of time, but the name that the individual carried. One might just as well change the house inscription in the Schwalm to read, "This name is mine, and yet not mine, and whoso follows me, will find it the same." Just as one person followed another, fleetingly playing the role of the Vältes Farm holder, one male descendant after another slipped into the name of Johannes and played the part of Johannes the farmholder. In this way the Vältes Farm remained in the possession of Johannes Hooss not simply for ten, twenty, or even thirty years, but continuously from 1552 to the present day. What endured was the name. The person who carried the name simply changed as someone slowly grew old or died before his time.

Did this role-playing also meet the needs of each individual Johannes? Did it help him to come to terms with his own life? Everyone is alone today and performs a life's work that lasts only for the time of one's own life. Consequently it is done hurriedly, hastily. In our age every single death is a tragic event that terminates someone's life work. This was not the case with the "collective" Johannes Hooss, who was composed of a number of men following each other in succession from 1552 down to the present day. It was also certainly not the case with each individual who bore the name of Johannes Hooss at any single moment in time. Just as Johannes Hooss carried the same name as his precursors, so he lived on in the lives of his successors. It was not a question of doing "his" own life's work so much as one of good stewardship and the development of "their" common life work. Wasn't it easier, then, given this fact, to pass on the farm to the next Johannes at age fifty-four, to leave center stage and move into the elders' house? Wasn't death then faced more calmly, regardless of when it came, whether in the fullness of life, tomorrow or the day after tomorrow, whether at age seventy, eighty, or ninety?

"More easily" and "more calmly": the contrasts with our own day are striking since we have such a difficult time coming to terms with death. Even in that age I would not say that death was met "easily" or "calmly." There have always been only a few people who faced death easily or calmly even in an age in which death was a daily occurrence, a frequent visitor in every household. The awareness of death was kept alive in the recommendations for a good death that were more widespread and more commonly followed when the belief in an afterlife was more vital, and when the individual was viewed only fleetingly as the center of the world. Still, all of these conditions appear to me to have been better suited than modern conditions in helping people manage their everyday lives, and this includes the final departure from life's stage.

The last of the four time wheel graphs illustrates one additional and long-lasting strategy on the part of the holders of the Vältes Farm. It contributed significantly to the stability of their world. In figure 23 I have identified the home villages of all of the marriage partners of the Vältes Farm peasants and the communities that the noninheriting children married into between 1600 and 1800. If you study the places and names in detail, it is evident that no one ever married someone from just any village at any particular moment. There was always a specific and carefully balanced marriage strategy at work in the interests of the Vältes Farm.

Leaving aside the six farms from Leimbach itself, the area involved in this marriage market included the villages of Ransbach, Loshausen, Zella, Gungelshausen, Merzhausen, Wasenberg, Ascherode, Steina, Niedergrenzebach, and Obergrenzebach, and the town of Treysa. All of them were located within a radius of about ten kilometers from Leimbach and were therefore reached in a one- to two-hour walk in case one should need something quickly or want to get extra family advice. On only one occasion was this network in the Schwalm region broken. As we know, the younger brother of Vält Hooss, Johannes (1631–69), left the farm to study theology in Kassel and became a pastor in Oberbiel near Wetzlar. He also married there. Otherwise the plan involved without exception the reciprocal placement of family members on large and prestigious peasant farms. This was even true in the case of the neighboring village of Merzhausen, a village that was otherwise avoided, as figure 7f, depicting farm size, suggests. A nephew

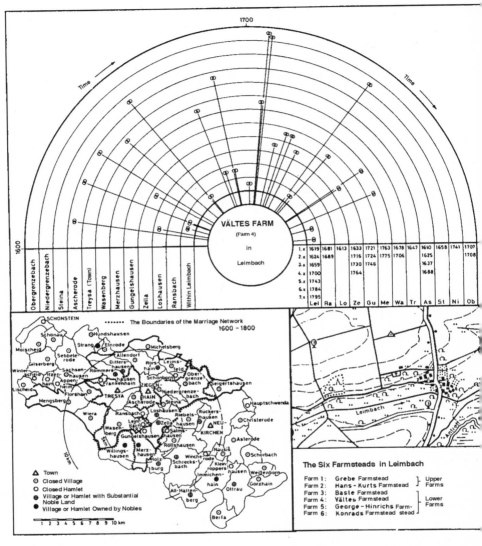

23. Marriage network of the Vältes farmers, 1600–1800. The figure includes the places of origin for all of the Vältes Farm peasants' marriage partners and the places to which noninheriting children moved when they married. Only one marriage took place in this entire period outside this area, that is, in Oberbiel near Wetzlar, where one of the Hoosses had become a minister in 1658. *Sources:* as for figure 18, and, in addition, Martin Born, *Wandlung und Beharrung ländlicher Siedlung und bäuerlicher Wirschaft: Untersuchungen zur frühneuzeitlichen Kulturlandschaftsgenese im Schwalmgebiet,* Marburger Geographische Schriften, vol. 14 (Marburg: Selbstverlag des Geographischen Instituts der Universität, 1961), map 1, p. 9.

of our Johannes, Johann Jost (1744–92), married into that village and settled there in 1763 on one of its few sizable properties, that of his bride, Anna Catherina Geissel. The farm was soon named the "Hooss Farm" after him. When his wife died young in 1774, Johann Jost no longer considered moving away, and in the following year he married once again in Merzhausen. As a result of his doing so, this village appears in our network a second time in 1775.

Just how single-mindedly the Vältes farmers pursued a *peasant* marriage strategy focused on rural property in their marriage ties is revealed in the fact that they didn't consider town girls and women for marriage. This was true despite—or even because of—the fact that the peasants must have known townswomen from their visits to the market or from the time in the Thirty Years' War when they sought refuge behind the town walls. Only once during these two centuries, in 1647, did a marriage take place between a son of the Vältes Farm, Johannes Hooss the Younger (1598–1670), and the daughter of a townsman from Treysa, Eulalia Giebelshausen (1596–1668). (He by the way never left Leimbach but became the holder of the Konrads Farm next door.) This was not a normal marriage, however. For the aging Johannes it was already his third. In 1635 his first wife, who came from the "more proper" village of Zella, died from the plague, and his second wife, Catherina Spor, from the equally "proper" village of Ascherode, had died in childbirth in 1643. Male heirs were readily available from the first two marriages, while in the case of his third marriage it must have seemed unlikely from the start that additional children would be born. Eulalia was fifty-one, after all! Perhaps for this reason the forty-nine-year-old Johannes, now twice widowed, could afford the luxury of marriage with a townswoman that would clearly remain childless.

Towns in general seem to have acted as boundaries for rural marriage markets. In the south the boundary of the marriage network for the peasants of the Vältes Farm largely coincided with the boundary of Ziegenhain District. To the north, however, a large gap stretched between the farm and the district boundary (see the bottom left of fig. 23, the political and administrative fig. 7c, and the commentary with it). One simply did not marry anyone beyond the towns of Treysa and Ziegenhain, just as one didn't marry people from the surrounding area living on the other side of the forest. There were certainly farms that were large enough on the other side of Treysa and Ziegenhain, in Schönborn and Leimsfeld, for example, or, farther to the west, in Wiera and Mengsberg (see fig. 7f on farm sizes once again).

Once more we can see that the Vältes Farm was the center of a little world. This time it was not simply restricted to Leimbach but included a dozen other places. If one looks over figure 23 and thinks about it, one can hardly argue that the noninheriting children left empty-handed. True, they couldn't stay on their parents' farm and acquire it, but all of them were still placed in accordance with their social status. The enduring and undiminished prestige of the Vältes Farm therefore worked to their advantage as well. For this reason it is unlikely that they questioned the strict impartibility of land. Instead they voluntarily submitted themselves to this venerable custom and supported it over the centuries. By the same token, those on the Vältes Farm could count on the lasting goodwill of family members who already had moved away, and, when they needed it, their help in a crisis.

The departure of children from the farm without harming anyone's interests and the continual exchange of young people between specific farms within a firmly circumscribed and easily managed marriage market created one more stable and centuries-long link of support across the generations. None of these places was so far away that the difficult task of managing the property couldn't be taken over, at least temporarily, should the holder of the Vältes Farm suddenly die and leave only minors behind. Georg Hooss of Ascherode did this when his brother died in 1635, and his widow followed him the next year, leaving the farm suddenly with only orphaned minors. The social network was kept intact. Stability was assured. The railings of the bridge didn't collapse.

Leaving behind the little world of Johannes Hooss and looking elsewhere for similar methods of assuring stability over the generations, I turn for help to a simple but powerful example, one that only at first glance seems far removed: the preference for weddings on certain days of the week. In this case there were no carefully planned strategies involved like the ones at work in such a sophisticated way among the Vältes farmers. Instead it involved one of those countless little things from the depths of the collective unconscious that are no longer thought about, something that made everyday life easy in an inconspicuous way but which also provided a framework for and sustained everyday life.

Since most peasants in those days married after the harvest was brought in, any day of the week late in the year could have been chosen to hold weddings. All of the farm work at that time of the season—threshing, carting manure out to the fields, preparing the fields for the winter sowing, carrying out repairs on the farm—could have been interrupted or postponed for a day or two. In principle this was also true for the other months of the year, when weddings took place less frequently. A study of contemporary practices clearly reveals, however, that wedding days were rarely chosen randomly. Naturally people rarely held weddings on Sundays, since churchgoers would have been lured away to these more festive celebrations. But in areas that tended not to hold weddings on Sundays, not all of them preferred holding them at the same time, whether on Saturdays or Mondays or any other day of the week. Instead people in one area preferred to marry on Mondays, in others they did so on Tuesdays or Saturdays, and at still another place people held their weddings on Sundays. But whenever it was, whether on Monday, Saturday, or Sunday, it stayed that way for centuries.

Let us take once again as our examples Gabelbach in Swabia and Hesel in East Frisia, two peasant communities located far apart. For both villages I have analyzed the weekdays on which all weddings were held between 1680 and 1899. The results appear in figure 24 (p. 124). The top part of the graph represents Gabelbach, the bottom Hesel. Both parts are organized in the same way, once again using a time wheel. Each half wheel has been divided into five periods of time. The seven circular bands represent the days of the week. The cross-hatched areas indicate the percentage of marriages that took place on the different days of the week during each period. Beneath every half circle in the figure there is also a small table listing the total number of marriages.

At first glance the two parts of the graph look very much alike. Each of the outer bands contains the largest cross-hatched areas, indicating that the largest number of weddings took place on these days of the week. But a closer look reveals fundamental differences between the two. In the upper graph the days of the week are read from the outside band in, from Monday to Sunday. In the lower graph, however, they are read in the opposite direction, that is, from the inside out, from Sunday to Monday. According to the graph, for over two hundred years one generation after another of Gabelbachers tended to marry on Mondays. In Hesel, by contrast, people married just as often on Sundays, Saturdays, and, if need be, Fridays. Weddings took place on other days of the week, but the numbers were not of much consequence in either village.

Why was this? "Because that's the way it's done!" This explanation does not strike us as an enlightening one today, but for dozens of couples from these two communities between 1680 and 1899 it was a good enough reason to hold their weddings on these days. It is relatively easy to understand, of

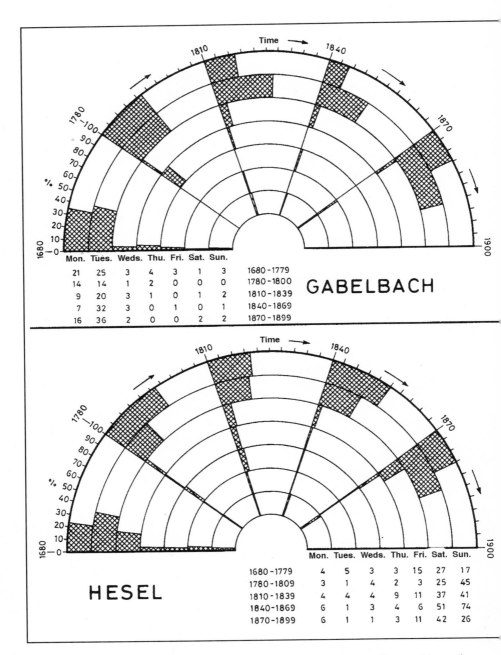

	Mon.	Tues.	Weds.	Thu.	Fri.	Sat.	Sun.	
	21	25	3	4	3	1	3	1680-1779
	14	14	1	2	0	0	0	1780-1800
	9	20	3	1	0	1	2	1810-1839
	7	32	3	0	1	0	1	1840-1869
	16	36	2	0	0	2	2	1870-1899

GABELBACH

HESEL

	Mon.	Tues.	Weds.	Thu.	Fri.	Sat.	Sun.
1680-1779	4	5	3	3	15	27	17
1780-1809	3	1	4	2	3	25	45
1810-1839	4	4	4	9	11	37	41
1840-1869	6	1	3	4	6	51	74
1870-1899	6	1	1	3	11	42	26

24. Sources of stability in the everyday lives of our ancestors as illustrated by wedding day preferences. Frequency distribution of marriages (first marriages and remarriages) on weekdays in Swabian Gabelbach in Bavaria (top) and Hesel in East Frisia (bottom), 1680–1899. *Source:* Databank at the Friedrich-Meinecke-Institut of the Free University Berlin, based on the genealogical books for Gabelbach, compiled by Franz Hauf (Frankfurt am Main, 1975), and Hesel, compiled by Ludwig Janssen and Hans Rudolf Manger (Aurich, 1974).

course, that in Catholic Gabelbach one did not marry on Fridays, since Fridays carried the burden of being meatless fast days, or on Sundays, since the priest had other duties to perform. This obstacle was less important in Lutheran Hesel, or it didn't matter at all. Why did the villagers from Gabelbach and Hesel not marry on Wednesdays or Thursdays? Since as peasants working conditions didn't restrict their choice of weekdays, why did the people from Hesel not celebrate weddings on Mondays or Tuesdays?

Naturally I am once again not the first person to note these curious differences, even though they impressed me as enduring preferences for holding weddings on certain days of the week. This practice caught the eye of folklorists long ago, and they documented these conditions earlier in their studies. Folklore atlases of Germany, Austria, and Switzerland show large regions with clear tendencies for weddings to take place on certain days of the week. In South Germany, Austria, and Catholic Switzerland people tended to marry on Mondays and Tuesdays; in North Germany, however, they preferred Fridays.

One explanation folklorists have advanced for this pattern has to do with church regulations, the rules and proscriptions of the different religious confessions already mentioned. What is also often evident, however, is that scholars' explanations seem to be influenced by their times. Depending upon whether the studies appeared during the last century or at certain times in this century, a Germanic view has sometimes been offered. According to this view, Tuesdays (or *Ziischdig*) and Fridays were preferred as days honoring the Germanic gods Ziu and Frija. At other times, interpretations stressing relationships with classical antiquity have been put forward: Fridays in honor of the Greco-Roman goddess Aphrodite (Venus) as "governess" of this particular day of the week. Finally, especially today, one looks to deeply rooted popular superstitions about certain weekdays bringing good or bad luck, blessings or misfortune, as responsible for the practices.[3]

Our ancestors would have listened with amusement, if not with surprise and contempt, to all of these academic theories. They would have challenged from the very start the scornful condescension with which we discuss the fossil-like mentality of peasant society. Granted, they couldn't choose to hold a wedding on just any day of the week for a long time. They conformed instead with what was self-evident and had been done for a long time. Moreover, they did so voluntarily, as is proven by the number of those who didn't conform. But our forebears didn't create unnecessary problems for themselves by repeatedly asking about the reasons for choosing a certain day of the week, demanding an explanation for it as curious know-it-alls do today. It was simply one custom among many that created stability and endured for generations, thus making it easy for our ancestors to shape and manage their everyday lives. The preferences for holding weddings on certain days persisted for such a long time that they survived of their own accord. As times changed and Saturday became increasingly a rest day from work, for example, this day became suitable for weddings. Wedding days also endured when marriage license bureaus opened only on the morning or afternoon of certain days of the week, thereby making these times appropriate for weddings as well.

Up to this point, the examples in this chapter have dealt essentially with outward forms of stability and continuity: repetitive behavior, rhythms of time, the social networks created by marriage alliances, and traditions. In an age when the individual's life was insecure, they provided support during the transition from one generation to the next by passing on the same first name for centuries, holding weddings on the same day of the week, and supporting collective role-playing that corresponded with the stages of life.

If the need for stability was as pronounced as this among our ancestors with regard to the external world, then it would hardly have been less so when it involved things related to the inner life. In the following example I want to approach this delicate issue by looking at an everyday reality that most of our ancestors had to deal with in some way right up to the beginning of the present century: the shockingly high rates of infant mortality. Taking into account the variations from place to place and region to region over time and between classes, roughly one-fourth of all newborns lived no longer than a year.

The question is a simple one: How did mothers and fathers deal with this appalling fact? Please do not say that our grandparents and great-grandparents looked on the large number of infant deaths with indifference, that the children who died were easily replaced with new ones, or that we were the ones who discovered maternal and paternal love and that it was not a part of their reality. Even when one cites the tens of thousands of known cases of death because of wet-nursing as "evidence" of alleged indifference and the absence of love on the part of parents, this argument strikes me as extremely shortsighted. Particularly in France, but also in other European countries well into the nineteenth century, infants were put out to wet nurses shortly after their birth, and, since death was almost certain because of the lack of proper care, the children usually never returned to their parents. This argument follows too much our modern way of looking at things. If we look more carefully at actual conditions, things quickly look different. At the very least, it keeps us from asking the wrong question at the outset.

One example illustrates what I mean. In 1513 the first son of Jean de Gennes in Brittany was born. He came into the world on February 28 between six and seven o'clock in the morning. At around eleven o'clock that morning he was baptized and given the name Jean, and, without being brought home, was immediately turned over to a wet nurse by his father. He died in her care. On August 1, 1518, another son followed. This one received the name of Sebastian, and he soon died on August 2 in the care of his substitute mother. The same pattern repeated itself with three more children. With the wet nurse not one of them survived the second day after baptism.[4]

Like other parents at that time, Jean de Gennes and his wife naturally understood that children put out to a wet nurse would probably not return. This was an ancient experience, one repeated hundreds of thousands of times. It would be premature to conclude from this, however, that these parents had not yet "discovered" their children. Even though they did not pay attention to the child's physical existence as we do today, they certainly had already "discovered" that their children possessed a soul. Birth, *baptism,* sending the child out to a wet nurse, and then very probably a swift death: this was the sequence of events, and for them the only proper sequence of events. Parents felt responsible for the baptism of their children, not for their physical existence. The beginning and the end of this existence was determined by God. Baptism opened the gates of heaven for the little ones. Without it the deceased would never see divine glory, and the parents would be to blame for it.

Since infant mortality rates were so high at this time, it was not unusual for the proper sequence of events to break down during or shortly after a child's birth; that is, the child died before he or she could be baptized. For their children's sake, as well as for their own relief and peace of mind, the parents in these cases did everything possible to reverse the events and do what was right. What could they do?

Let me elaborate a point here that has come up before and which this example illustrates: how certain parts of the church's teaching were picked up and then altered to fit our ancestors' worldview so that they could master *their own* problems in everyday life. In this case it involves, first and foremost, the church teaching that baptism was required for the admittance of a new-

Anno io 80 an Creis mitwoch als dem 14 may ist mir Martin Wierer von
naath Ehrwirdin Catharina Wiererin gebor ne obr wednern am fonna Sochter aut die
[illegible cursive text]

25.   Children's life signs on a votive tablet from the parish church of Abfaltersbach
near Sillian in eastern Tyrol, 1680. A stillborn child is brought back to life so that it
could be baptized and then buried in the consecrated ground of the cemetery. *Sources:*
the votive tablet is located today in the Museum der Stadt Lienz in Schloß Bruck,
eastern Tyrol. I am thankful to the director of the museum, Dr. Lois Ebner, for
permission to make a new photographic reproduction in the summer of 1982.

  According to the inscription, Martin and Catharina Wierer's stillborn little boy lies
on the altar before a picture of the Annunciation of the Virgin. After the beseeching
pleas of the kneeling men and women, he briefly comes back to life. The little body
gave two "signs," a reddening of the cheeks and the appearance of beads of perspira-
tion. While alive the little boy could be baptized by the midwife, and then after his
immediate death he could then be buried in the consecrated ground of the cemetery.
The inscription reads: "Anno 1680 on Cross Wednesday the 14th of May, a little boy
was born dead to me by my wife Catharina Wiererin born Obervördner. Thereupon
we went to the Annunciation of Our Beloved Virgin and praised her with an offering

born into the Christian community and that only through this was there any prospect for the resurrection of the dead and entrance into the majesty of God. On the other hand, it should not be forgotten that the church also taught that the younger these small baptized children were when they died in a state of complete innocence, the more certain was their acceptance into the divine host. Moreover, they would almost certainly intercede with God and the saints on behalf of those who survived them back on Earth, naturally first for their mother and father, brothers, sisters, and other relatives and family acquaintances.

As an illustration let's look at one of the tens of thousands of so-called votive tablets, some of them still hanging today, one after the other, on the walls of pilgrimage churches (see fig. 25). Most of them were dedicated in a moment of great need on the believer's part to a particular saint or to the Mother of God, hoping that a danger would be averted by means of their powerful intercession with God. The occasion for many of the dedications in these images is clearly visible. The tablet reproduced in this case comes from the parish church of Abfaltersbach in the Pustertal of eastern Tyrol, located close to the Italian border about twenty kilometers southwest of Lienz. It refers to an event in the year 1680. Before a picture of the Annunciation of the Virgin a dead child in swaddling clothes lies on the altar. On the steps eight men and six women are gathered in fervent prayer. As can be read from the inscription on the bottom of the painting, the appeal to the Virgin Mary was successful. The son of Martin and Catharina Wiererin, stillborn on May 14, 1680, returned to life briefly after an appeal to the Mother of God. His cheeks became rosy (a reflection of the burning candles?), and beads of sweat appeared. While alive the child was able to receive an

---

and a Holy Mass so that the child gave signs of life and this first time changed its color. The second time it perspired, and two times the midwife wiped [the perspiration] off and then the midwife baptized it." On children's life signs see Klaus Anderegg, *Durch der Heiligen Gnad und Hilf: Wallfahrt, Wallfahrtskapellen, und Exvotos in den Oberwalliser Bezirken Goms und Östlich-Raron* (Basel: Krebs, 1979); and for the French-speaking regions, Jacques Gélis, "Miracle et médecien aux siècles classiques: Le corps médical et le retour temporaire à vie des mort-nés," *Réflections Historiques* 9 (1982): 85–101. I am thankful to Dr. Klaus Anderegg, Freiburg, Switzerland, for providing additional picture material, and Jacques Gélis of the University Paris–Vincennes for his constant readiness to discuss. This votive tablet was originally called to my attention by Lenz Kriß-Rettenbach, *Das Votivbild* (Munich: Hermann Rinn, 1958), figure 73, p. 66.

Inn Justu der Gottlichen Mutter
und mihr Zeitod geborne Kinder
Alhier lebentig, und getauffet worden
Da einle 1747 Den 9len May ein Jöhn
Ein andere ein Tochter 17 51 bezeuge
Beat Lauli Keüsser Zug.

26. Life signs for two children on a votive tablet from the parish church of the Ascension of the Virgin in the Swiss village of Schattdorf, 1747–51. *Source:* this votive tablet is still to be found in this location, but it is no longer accessible to the public. I am grateful to Pastor Hans Loretz, Schattdorf, for permission to make a new photographic reproduction in the fall of 1982. See, in this regard, Hans Loretz et al., *250 Jahre Pfarrkirche Schattdorf 1733–1983* (Schattdorf: Pfarramt, 1983), 48.

Since stillbirths in the same family were not unusual in this period, parents sometimes used a single votive tablet to make a double dedication for the children's life signs. In the picture, a stillborn boy (1747) and girl (1751) are lying bundled up peacefully on the left and right sides of the altar and waiting for the Virgin Mary's intercession to take effect with the Holy Trinity.

A text from another votive tablet in the same church in Schattdorf suggests that even very young stillborns could make a child's life sign, in this case a fetus who had emergency baptism from the midwife present, and then, when he died soon thereafter, he was buried in the consecrated ground of the cemetery. The proper sequence of events was therefore restored, and, according to contemporary belief, the child was transformed into "a lovely angel in heaven."

It would be misleading to think that this picture and text involve an exceptional case or a fleeting manifestation of passionate religious feeling from the baroque era. Two hundred years later a similar tablet appeared in Riffian near Meran in South Tyrol, where pilgrimages had taken place to Our Lady of Sorrows since the fourteenth century. Here parents kneel in their despair before a small corpse and plead in their need to the Mother of God. The text under the image reads: "A memorial in thanks to Mary, Mother of God, for her intercession on behalf of a stillborn baby who lay four days in the grave and whose face turned a beautiful pink and the lips the color of blood, the surest signs of life, in order that he be baptized and buried.—The grateful parents."[5]

Since stillbirths were not an infrequent occurrence in this age, parents tried by misfortune occasionally simplified things by making two dedications at the same time and absolving themselves with a single votive tablet. Figure 26 de-

---

died at only twelve weeks. The passage reads: "Listen Christians to what I have to say. A great miracle has taken place. There was a woman who was very sick and who brought a child into the world after only twelve weeks. In this my need I thereupon took refuge here in the sunshine to the merciful Mother: Through her prayer I then received a great miracle in this form: because this child gave a sign from itself: so that he could be given Holy Baptism."

Occasional entries in the miracle books are even more detailed than these often extensive accompanying texts on the votive tablets. An example is the entry from 1649 above the baptism of a child who had "given a sign of life" at the pilgrimage shrine to Our Beloved Lady of Einsiedeln, in central Switzerland: "Anno 1649, April 11, Anna Martina von Anstaetten bore her husband Georg Fuchs a child / indeed, it was more a body without a soul since this same fruit of the body turned whiter than a [page of a] book within three-quarters of an hour and no mark of life remained. The grieving mother on account of the stillbirth was very worried / turned in her hope to Einsiedeln / and commended the dead child to the Mother of Life. At this the child then reached out its right arm and foot / and received life / and then Holy Baptism." *Source:* Conrad Hunger, *Kurtze Chronica . . . mit mehr als 200 schoenen juengsthin beschehenen Wunderwercken gemehrt* (Lucerne: David Hautt, 1653), part 3, section 16, pp. 188–89. I am thankful to archivist P. Joachim Salzgeber, Einsiedeln, for his help in the research and in this same matter P. Dr. Daniel Schönbächler of the Benedictine monastery of Disentis.

picts one such case around the middle of the eighteenth century in the parish
church of the Ascension of the Virgin in the Swiss village of Schattdorf. The
text in this case is brief and to the point: "Through the intercession of the
Holy Mother two stillborn babies were brought back to life and baptized. The
first, a son, on May 4, 1747. The second, a daughter, in 1751. Witnessed by
Beat Paul Keysser, Zug." The two of them are lying peacefully on the altar,
one on the right and the other on the left. The Virgin Mary floats above the
clouds as an intercessor with the Holy Trinity, who relents and takes pity on
both of them. The two bodies were then briefly resurrected so that they could
be baptized and buried, and the souls then entered divine bliss.

All of these cases over the centuries involved the same thing: despairing
parents bringing to a pilgrimage shrine their stillborn babies or children who
died before baptism and pleading that they be brought back to life briefly in
order that they be baptized and buried in consecrated soil. Only in this way
could they avoid wandering around for all of eternity as unsaved souls. Only
thus could they join the heavenly host and their bodies avoid being dumped
somewhere like dead animals.

The custom of "children's life signs" has been well known for quite some
time. Before the Reformation it was widely practiced in many parts of Europe, and since that time it has been especially known in those parts of Germany, Switzerland, and Austria that remained Catholic, as well as in Italy,
Belgium, and France. In German-speaking regions the expression "children's
life sign" (*Kinderzeichnen*) refers literally to what happened: dead children
"gave a signal," that is, they showed brief signs of life. The eyes or lips moved,
they sweated, the color of their faces or bodies changed, blood flowed, or
they breathed through the nose or mouth so that a feather placed there was
blown away. In French the expression *sanctuaires à répit* is more common.
Literally translated, it means a "sacred place" where death is briefly postponed.

Children's life signs are also known to the historian, since the spiritual
and secular authorities responded in a divided and ambiguous way to these
resurrections from the dead. (How can they be called anything else?) These
reactions are found in written disputes, synodal resolutions, pastoral letters,
decrees, and counterdecrees all the way to the removal of local priests from
office. At times the proceedings surrounding children's life signs were toler-
ated. At other times they were suppressed, while sometimes the parents were
even encouraged to bring in their unbaptized children. Rarely did simple
religious reasons play the main role in the reactions of the religious or secular

authorities. Instead tangible economic interests often came to the fore. Pilgrimage sites were hardly stagnant backwaters, even when located in isolated areas. The farther out their power radiated and the more believers streamed to them, the more such sites grew as a lucrative source of income.

After the Reformation, Catholics in Europe clung to the necessity of baptism for eternal salvation. After a temporary lull in the sixteenth century, and especially in connection with the propagation of the cult of the Virgin, the practice of looking for children's life signs renewed its growth in Catholic regions. Rome simply found it impossible to remain silent. The specific inducement for papal intervention came with the explosive increase in pilgrimages to the oldest German Premonstratensian monastery in Swabia: Ursberg on the Mindel River, thirty-five kilometers southwest of Augsburg and only fifteen kilometers southwest of the village of Gabelbach. Although the shrine at Ursberg can be dated back to the twelfth century and had enjoyed great popularity since that time, the practice of making pilgrimages there for the specific purpose of baptizing stillborn infants dates back only to 1686. In that year a peasant brought the body of his infant there, where it was then baptized after showing signs of life. After this and between 1686 and 1720 alone, over twenty-four thousand dead children, some from far-off regions like Austria and Bohemia, were said to have been baptized after being temporarily resurrected. In the light of such large numbers, Rome had to act.

On April 27, 1729, the order went out from the Congregation of the Holy Office to the Bishop of Augsburg to stop the "abuse of baptizing dead children." The monastery, however, refused to have anything to do with banning the baptisms. On the contrary, in 1733 it formulated its own views on the problem and sent them to Rome, a step that only led to a renewal of the prohibition in 1737. Only then did Ursberg submit and discontinue the baptisms. The flood of people to the monastery, however, did not cease; the baptisms, while smaller in number, were now taken over by laymen. Rome's dilemma therefore continued. It could hardly be eliminated once and for all, since the church could never rule out completely the chance of a miracle.[6]

The Reformed church, however, had fewer scruples in dealing with the problem. Sacred statues and tablets were torn down along with everything else in a storm of iconoclasm. On February 28, 1528, shortly after the introduction of the Reformation in Bern, the city council sent the emissary Anton Noll to the most famous pilgrimage site for baptizing dead children in all of Switzerland at the time: Oberbüren, located on the Aare River between

Solothurn and Biel. Noll abruptly removed the miraculous image of the Virgin from the church and burned it before everyone's eyes. When this was to no avail and the elders failed to keep people from making the pilgrimage despite publicly denouncing pilgrimages, sacred images, and children's life signs as the unmitigated superstition of simple people, the council on July 6, 1530, adopted an apparently radical course and arranged to have the church pulled down. What little understanding these "gracious gentlemen" had of the spiritual needs of their subjects! How little they cared about them! But in 1534 fathers and mothers were still coming to Oberbüren. There on the rock where the altar with the sacred image had stood earlier they lay the bodies of their stillborn infants and children who died before being baptized.[7]

Who would not agree with the Dutch folklorist Meertens, cited in chapter 2, at the end of his study on "pre-Reformation survivals in the Protestant Netherlands": "The Reformed faith failed to understand that it could not eliminate values from traditional folk life without replacing them with new values. Because it missed this opportunity, it had to undertake a battle both unnecessary and hopeless and from which it carried away only a partial victory." In the region around Bern, too, it was obviously not enough to fill the resulting vacuum with high-sounding synodal resolutions that pointed out that the Holy Scripture, now the only source of authority, had nothing to say about the fate of children who died without baptism. According to such decrees, it was absurd to wonder where dead and unbaptized children went, whether there was a kind of antechamber to hell, where this place was located, how many rooms it had, and so on. It is therefore hardly surprising that popular beliefs about the eternal misfortune of unbaptized children, passed down for generations and still alive, are easy to document three hundred years later.

Earlier I invited readers to look with me at sixteenth- and seventeenth-century Dutch and French paintings, and I added my own commentary. In a similar way I want to include a short segment from chapters 14 and 15 in part 2 of Jeremias Gotthelf's novel *The Sorrows and Joys of a Schoolteacher.*[8] The work, which appeared in two volumes in 1838 and 1839, was set in Gotthelf's own time. The schoolteacher, Peter Käser, works in Gytiwyl, a place not found on any map but which certainly was located in the lower Emmental. He was therefore perhaps ten, twenty, or at the most thirty kilometers from Oberbüren. Käser reviews his life up to this time and then, in these two chapters, speaks about the death of his second child, a girl. The schoolteacher explains:

She was a beautiful, a wonderful child. She had large, deep blue eyes and an indescribable look in them. On the third day she became restless and even made anxious and whimpering noises. Convulsive shakes soon ran over her little body. An alien force seemed to cover her and seemed to want to overpower the barely conscious life with powerful pressure. The poor child's lips turned blue and then foamed. She convulsed one more time and then became still. Her little eyes stayed closed forever.

At dawn women came to us who had heard that our child was dying. "The child is better off this way," one of the women said. "Yes," another one said, making a doubtful face, "if only she had been baptized. I didn't want to say anything, but I pity the child being unbaptized because no one knows now what will happen to her." "Yes, you are right," said the first one, "I didn't even think about that. I too have lost four children, praise God, but none of them before they were baptized. I think I would have gone mad. I do not mind God taking her, but certainly not the Devil. They say that she wouldn't go to the deepest part of Hell, but it's hot enough at the top. Poor thing!"

This weighed heavily on my heart. I was familiar with the still widespread old Catholic belief that every child who dies unbaptized is damned, but I had never thought about it. I trembled at the thought that such a sweet little being might fall into the Devil's hands. People simply assumed this, and one simply does not ask for reasons about assumptions like that. I wrapped a black scarf around my neck and walked over to see the pastor. "Oh woe," I said, "I would be able to accept it if only she had been baptized. What's to be done then if she is not saved?" "Do you believe that too?" the pastor asked. Then he said, "Teacher, here's how it is. The old belief that the unbaptized belong to the Devil was not only widespread among the people but was also the teaching of the church, even though it clearly has no basis in Scripture. *So, for example, in the town of Büren there was an image of the Mother of God. It was believed that all of the dead and unbaptized children would be brought back to life in her arms long enough to receive the sacrament of baptism. One can imagine how many children were brought to her and how many parents cried when it was burned down during the Reformation. Yet though the image was burned the old belief persisted.*[9]

"If one were to study people's beliefs, the beliefs that really influence their lives, one would find amazing things. One would discover that the Bible plays little part in them. The actual beliefs that circulate among people change over the course of time, but only slowly, and when they coincide with biblical beliefs then that's fine, but we are unfortunately not yet there. Such a belief is really nonsense."

This writer speaks to the historian from his soul! And it is done in a way that makes it difficult to find the voice of the historian again. What a profound understanding of life! What a deep psychological probing beneath the surface of events! What a wonderful source for the history of everyday life and the mentality of rural people in the first half of the nineteenth century— their ideas, their feelings, their everyday cares and worries, and how they tried to come to terms with problems in their own way. Only slowly does its meaning sink in, but then it is as if a veil is lifted from before one's eyes!

This is only one side of the story, however. Just as above, when we had to consider the structure, form, and color of sixteenth- and seventeenth-century paintings in order to appreciate them, it would be shortsighted of us in the case of this novel to read it purely for the enjoyment of the writer's powers of observation and expression or as a fascinating document in cultural history. Gotthelf, too, was conditioned by his time and place. He not only intended in this case to write an educational novel, and this in the homeland of Pestalozzi and his tradition, but he meant to do more. His real name was not Jeremias Gotthelf but Albert Bitzius (1797–1854), and in his official capacity as the minister of the area's Reformed congregation in Lützelflüh he took a passionate position in contemporary disputes in Bern involving educational and school reform. It is Bitzius himself who speaks with the voice of the pastor of Gytiwyl. Gotthelf's early works overflowed with educational zeal to enlighten the "ignorant" peasant in the countryside. He repeatedly used references to the customs of their grandfathers and grandmothers as an opportunity to make fun of them. He attacked their resistance against "reasonable" innovations and pilloried their mixture of blindness and stubbornness. In my opinion, entire sections of his work are filled with unseemly contempt for the "good old days."

I want to avoid the impression, however, of claiming with this criticism to be better informed than he was. What historian has sharper psychohistorical insights or a better ability to express them than Gotthelf? Even if the historian greatly admires his literary work, however, he should not be hindered in developing his own point of view about a subject first opened up by the writer and to draw conclusions different from Pastor Bitzius's own. Above all, my main objection would be against his harsh judgment concerning "current popular beliefs" among the peasants as "real nonsense." "The people are full of contradictions, and where do they come from? It comes from the fact that they are ruled by superstition and not faith, that they believe everything instead of only that which comes from God," he argues in the same chapter.

I completely agree with him "that the Bible has little to do with these beliefs," an observation that, to be sure, is the main reason why he (but not I) was offended. As a historian, and not a pastor, I find it difficult to see contradictions or gaps in our peasant ancestors' understanding. These ideas made up an entirely coherent whole. They were conditioned by and adapted to *their* world, however, to their needs and not to those of the intellectuals, the secular and spiritual authorities in the towns and the pastors and school-teachers in the countryside. These people participated in a different "enlightened" or "high" culture, a culture that has ultimately shaped our own attitudes and outlook by virtue of its dominant and superior power. The transformation that has taken place makes it extremely difficult for us today to understand the world of our ancestors, to grasp their different worldview as a coherent system and to approach it as such. And because for so long it has been so thoroughly denounced and discredited as "strange ideas," "superstition," "fantasy," and "a bundle of contradictions," we have to try hard to understand it and treat it with dignity as a reasonable and appropriate response to life.

This statement applies not only to our ancestors' world and worldview, but obviously also to that of a number of our contemporaries. If Gotthelf came across the persistent anxiety and fear of parents worried about the uncertain fate of children who died unbaptized and the survival of children's life signs in the collective memory a good three hundred years after they were "abolished" by the Reformation, then we cannot exclude the possibility that they are still alive in our own time. How can we find out? Problems in research arise not only from the fact that stillbirths and infant deaths have become relatively infrequent, but mainly because the affected mothers and fathers feel no need to open up to a curious stranger and provide him with information.

In the face of this dilemma, I finally arrived at the following solution. In the winter of 1982–83 I sent a letter to the chief physicians and head nurses from the obstetrics department of fifty-one selected hospitals, mostly in Catholic Bavaria. After a brief description of the customs surrounding children's life signs came a firm request that I reprint here verbatim: "In the modern period it is extremely difficult to detect the persistence of these kinds of cares and worries on the part of parents, yet I still want to know more about them. I am turning to you, since in your practice you are probably among the first to be confronted with these spiritual concerns of mothers and fathers. My specific question is therefore this: Have you ever encountered parents who, in the case of a difficult childbirth, urged the immediate baptism of a baby who was in danger, or cases in which they even tried later to baptize a stillborn baby or one who died before baptism?"

Eighteen responses came back. In the light of the delicate and nonmedical nature of the question, I was completely satisfied with the results. In many cases the respondents expressed open astonishment at how unmodern my research supposedly was. Often there was also a certain (Bavarian) suspicion of the "Professor from Berlin" evident in their replies. Perhaps he only wanted to make fun of the backwardness of the Bavarians? Since as a rule chief physicians, not nurses, responded, a certain distance or even barrier was evident between "knowledgeable" medical professionals and the laypeople who believed in such "strange stuff." We have already mentioned above that this attitude is an obstacle to a fair understanding of these old attitudes and views, or even of those of our fellow human beings. Pediatric nurses and midwives, on the other hand, would have listened to people more closely. They would have heard things more directly and would be drawn into people's confidence more readily. Occasionally they would even be asked to make a donation for the baptism.

Despite all this, six responses clearly indicated the persistence of these ancient fears of mothers and fathers, and they should be shared with the reader. In their own way each of them is a unique witness to the tenacity of traditional ideas. As always, whenever one stumbles across beliefs like these that have endured so long, their historical poignancy is thought-provoking.

A specialist in obstetrics and gynecology at a district hospital wrote: "It is only natural in our hospital that severely crippled children, or even stillborns whose time of death is not known with certainty, immediately receive an emergency baptism." From the chief physician of a children's clinic and infants' home: "The emergency baptism is usually performed when a newborn assigned to the clinic shows no more signs of life." The specialist in women's health and gynecology: "A questioning of pediatric nurses and midwives—

especially midwives who have served for twenty-five years and who have also been present at home births—resulted indeed in confirmation of your suspicion. Stillborn babies and children who are born and show no vital signs of life were and still are immediately given an emergency baptism." The director of the children's clinic of a university hospital: "Regarding your letter, I have gathered information from various nurses and colleagues of our clinic who are close to these serious cases. All seriously ill newborns are baptized in our clinic, the emergency baptism being the same for Protestants and Catholics. A question about baptizing newborns who were already dead was answered in rich detail and very ambiguously: often one does not know whether a child is already dead or not. I remember that the procedure, including the baptism of children who were already dead, was also carried out at Clinic X [in Bavaria] where I was employed in the early 1960s. Also in The Y Children's Clinic [in Northwest Germany], where I later worked for ten years, dying and probably also newborns who were dead were baptized." The chief physician of the obstetrics and gynecology department of another district hospital: "I wrote to our oldest living midwife and sent her a photocopy of your letter, and she wrote, 'Children who appeared to be dead were baptized with the words, "If you are still alive I baptize you." I still remember very well that children who died unbaptized were buried in the cemetery before dawn in the corner of the family plot.'" Finally, the chief physician of another obstetrics and gynecology division of a clinic mentioned: "After a stillbirth the question is always asked, Where do these children go?"

Even after sifting through these awkward oral and written questionnaires, what shines through is the whole range of ancient cares and worries: What happens to children who die unbaptized? They are buried in consecrated ground, even if it has to be done before sunrise and without an officiating minister. Over and over again these cases revolve around baptism, whether through the express wishes of the parents or a sense of duty on the part of midwives and nurses.

Naturally I am not the first person to note the gulf between an increasingly scientific and "enlightened" world and an older, more emotional, faith-oriented world. Nor am I the first to face this with a sense of unease. Two quotes from more competent authorities, ones who have struggled with this question their entire lives, may illuminate what I mean. They both get to the heart of the problem in their own way and open up a new perspective that can then be developed later. In the course of a lecture he was giving in Munich in 1919, the German sociologist Max Weber (1864–1920) coined the phrase "the disenchantment of the world": "The increasing intellectual-ization and rationalization do *not,* therefore, indicate an increased and gen-eral knowledge of the conditions under which one lives. It means something else, namely, the knowledge or belief that if one but wished one *could* learn it at any time. Hence, it means that principally there are no mysterious incal-culable forces that come into play, but rather that one can, in principle, mas-ter all things by calculation. This means that the world is disenchanted."[10]

In his last work, "Approaching the Unconscious," which first appeared in English, the Swiss psychoanalyst Carl Gustav Jung (1875–1961) wrote: "As scientific understanding has grown, so our world has become dehumanized. Man feels himself isolated in the cosmos, because he is no longer involved in nature and has lost his emotional 'unconscious identity' with natural phe-nomena. These have slowly lost their symbolic implications. Thunder is no longer the voice of an angry god, nor is lightning his avenging missile. No river contains a spirit, no tree is the life principle of a man, no snake the embodiment of wisdom, no mountain cave the home of a great demon. No voices now speak to man from stones, plants, and animals, nor does he speak to them believing they can hear. His contact with nature has gone, and with it has gone the profound emotional energy that this symbolic connection supplied."[11]

Knowledge is not the same as wisdom. It is one-dimensional. We sit here today with all of our specialized knowledge, holding it in our hands like fragments of something that is broken. We have lost the tie that binds, or, to put it in the words of Martin Buber (1878–1965), a philosopher of religion, "Our relationship with the world has deteriorated into ways of looking at things that no longer provide any unity. In the end, the new 'worldview' consists in the fact that we no longer have any view of the world."[12]

What interests us, however, is neither the disenchantment of the world nor the decline of a worldview nor the loss of the tie that binds nor man's isolation in the cosmos. Indeed this chapter is about its opposite, "The Search for Stability." Our ancestors may have sought stability in a world and an age that was definitely uncertain, but it was not yet disenchanted, and it still had a unifying thread. One need only think back on the Grimm's fairy tales discussed earlier or the children's life signs that have been described.

At this point I want to return one more time to Johannes Hooss. How might this thread of life and his own worldview have looked? Hooss lived in an age in which no regular evening entertainment existed in the form of newspapers, radio, and television. He lived in an age before electricity, when twilight, night, and dawn were still experienced as the onset of darkness, the pitch black of the night, and the coming of a new day. But it was also a time when stargazing during the evening, night, and morning was easier, since people lived in remote areas and no sea of city lights obstructed their view. In that age the curiosity of our peasant ancestors was not yet distracted by hundreds of little things, and they may have been freer to think about the Sun, Moon, and stars in the heavens above. Even if they didn't see very far on the ground—only to the next hill and the edge of the nearby forest— they often looked higher into the sky than we do, since we learn about the universe, the stars, and the moving planets, if at all, mainly through television, horoscopes, and shows in a planetarium. By contrast we rarely look at the stars in the evening sky at all.

Of course it is far easier for us today to understand more about physics and the natural sciences than did Johannes Hooss or most of our ancestors two or three hundred years ago, such as the peasants of the Schwalm region. This is true despite the fact that the first observatory in Europe was set up in 1560 by the prince of this land, Landgrave Wilhelm IV, "the Wise" (1532– 92), at his court in Kassel and was regularly staffed with superb scholars.[13] And yet, strange as this may sound, few of us can compare with our ancestors in this area.

In what follows, what interests me is not the spread of astronomical knowledge or contemporary philosophical, theological, medical, and astro- logical ideas and arguments. In an earlier chapter, the positions and teachings of the Catholic, Lutheran, and Calvinist churches did not concern us either. Rather, we were interested to know what ideas our ancestors might have gained from them, how they adapted them to their daily worldview and used them to manage *their own* lives. In the same way, we want to try to find out what mattered to them in this area as well. Let's not deceive ourselves about how difficult this undertaking is. Even in the eyes of contemporaries, "current popular belief" easily shaded over into "superstition" and "non- sense," as it did with Gotthelf. How can we really understand "current popu- lar belief" or even judge it? Do *we* believe, for example—and this is related to the question—that the Sun governs *Sunday* and the Moon *Monday,* or that everything in the heavens corresponds with something on Earth, and vice versa? Do we really believe—without thinking about it, perhaps—the phrase "on earth as it is in heaven" when it is frequently repeated in our prayers? Prayers, proverbs, and symbols may clearly be handed down from this period or another, and it may be shown that a certain part of the popula-

tion uses them, but this is a long way from saying that people actually believed in them and are guided or influenced in their behavior by them. Every
age has its empty words and meaningless formulas.[14]

With all due caution, it is difficult to imagine people more closely and
intensely involved with nature and the cosmos than our peasant forebears.
Didn't all of them experience firsthand good and bad harvests, abundance
(seldom) and starvation (more often), heavy floods and drought, lightning
and hail, hunger and cold, sickness and disease, death at every age, and live
births and stillbirths among humans and animals alike? How could these
people not have felt themselves a part of nature when it encompassed everything and their whole existence depended so totally and directly on it? How
was it possible for them to see themselves as all alone in the cosmos?

Among the everyday experiences people have had since time immemorial
are the natural rhythms of time, whether the daily rhythm of morning, noon,
evening, and night or the yearly rhythm of spring, summer, autumn, and
winter. Year in and year out the Sun rises every morning, climbs to its zenith
in the middle of the day, and sinks below the horizon in the evening. But
each day it does so a little differently. Anyone can easily observe the fact that
the point where the Sun rises and sets moves across the horizon. The Sun
does not rise above the same tree every day or set over the same bush every
evening. The shorter and the cooler the days, the farther to the south the
points are; the longer and the warmer the days, on the other hand, the farther
they are to the north.

If people in the past turned their gaze from the horizon toward the heavens—which would be the appropriate thing to do given the nature of the
Sun—the daily changes in sunrise and sunset are easy to follow and locate
in the morning and evening skies. Instead of trees and bushes on the horizon,
the annual points of reference are composed of unusually bright stars and
readily visible constellations. We can assume that the twelve most important
of these constellations traversed by the Sun during the year—looked at from
the point of view of an observer on Earth—were generally known at the
time (see fig. 27, p. 144). Many of them looked like animals, whose names they
have carried for a long time: Aries (ram), Taurus (bull), Cancer (crab), Leo
(lion), Scorpio (scorpion), Capricorn (goat), and Pisces (fish). Even though
there were also Gemini, Virgo, Libra, Sagittarius, and Aquarius, one still refers
today in German to the "twelve animal constellations of the zodiac."

When over four thousand years ago the first high cultures of Babylon and

Egypt began regular observations and records of these yearly rhythms, it was soon discovered that day and night lasted the same length of time each new year when the Sun first rose in the sign of Aries. In any given year this occurred on March 21 (see fig. 27, top). This day was called the beginning of spring. About a month later the Sun went into the sign of Taurus, and a month after that into the sign of Gemini. Its northernmost point was reached in any given year on June 22 in the constellation of Cancer, the day of summer solstice. Then it moved through the constellations of Leo, Virgo, and Libra. When it had reached Libra on September 23, day and night were once again the same length. Then came Scorpio, Sagittarius, and then, with sunrise at the southernmost point on December 22, the constellation of Capricorn. From here the Sun returned through the signs of Aquarius and Pisces to its beginning point, Aries.

Some readers may wonder why I am explaining all of this at this point. Are these not the same constellations and dates familiar to us today? Were the dates not simply taken from horoscopes in modern newspapers and magazines—Aries, March 21–April 19; Taurus, April 20–May 20; Gemini, May 21–June 21, and so on for the rest of the year? This is not the case, however, and here it seems to me that Johannes Hooss had an advantage over us simply because he derived his knowledge from his own observations and not from newspapers and magazines. Were we too to trace the area of the sky where the Sun rises and sets, we could immediately discover that the Sun does not rise between March 21 and April 19 in the sign of Aries, or between April 20 and May 20 in Taurus, or between May 21 and June 21 in Gemini, and that the modern start of spring on March 21 has little to do with the first sunrise in Aries. This is due not simply to the fact that the constellations vary enormously in size and that the Sun stays in them a different number of days. Today the Sun actually rises in Aries between April 15 and May 13, in Taurus between May 13 and June 18, and in Gemini between June 18 and July 18. Spring now begins for us when the Sun is in the sign of Pisces (from March 14 to April 15) (see fig. 28, p. 146, bottom).

The confusion here—*our* confusion—is due to the fact that spring begins each year about twenty minutes earlier than it did the previous year. This makes a difference of only twenty-four hours in any human lifetime (or every seventy-two years) and will therefore hardly be noticed by someone on a daily basis.[15] These twenty minutes are enough, however, for the beginning of spring (or summer, autumn, and winter) to cycle through all of the

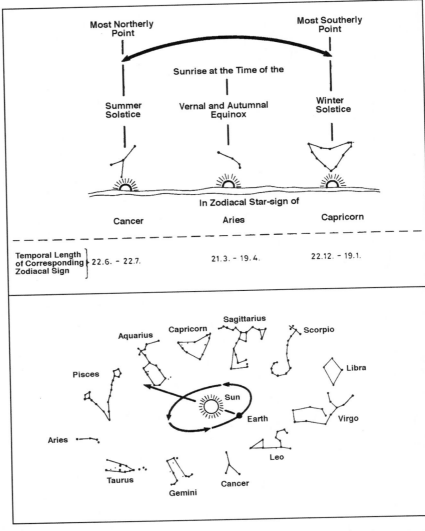

	Most Northerly Point		Most Southerly Point
	Summer Solstice	Sunrise at the Time of the Vernal and Autumnal Equinox	Winter Solstice
	In Zodiacal Star-sign of		
	Cancer	Aries	Capricorn
Temporal Length of Corresponding Zodiacal Sign	22.6. - 22.7.	21.3. - 19.4.	22.12. - 19.1.

27.   Hundreds of years of human observation and experience: annual movements of the Sun at sunrise and sunset. Even today many of us can identify the tree or house on the horizon behind which the Sun rises or sets at any given time of the year. Looking up into the sky at twilight, one can also observe the rising and setting taking place within unusually prominent constellations of stars. Depending on the season, the Sun rises in one of twelve different constellations. Since in our imagination many of them resemble the figures of animals, for ages they have been called the twelve signs of the zodiac. [In German the signs of the zodiac are called *Tierkreis-Sternbilder,* which, when translated literally, means "animal circle star-pictures."—Trans.]

constellations of the zodiac over the course of 25,800 years and for the Sun to rise on March 21 in a different constellation every 2,150 years. As the Babylonians and Egyptians correctly established for the first time, this occurred in the constellation of Aries up to around the time of the birth of Christ. Since that time and right up to the present, and therefore including the time of Johannes Hooss, it has been in the sign of Pisces, and it will remain there for another century. Then it will be in the sign of Aquarius for two thousand years.

In our horoscopes, however, or in anything else today where the signs of the zodiac appear, we act as if nothing has changed in four thousand years. March 21 and the beginning of Aries are still thought to coincide with each other just as they did among the ancient Babylonians and Egyptians. And the same goes for the beginning of Taurus on April 20, Gemini on May 21, and so on. All of the modern *signs of the zodiac,* along with their dates, have the same number of days since each encompassed a thirty-degree section of the zodiac. But this is an entirely different thing from the rising and setting of the Sun in the visible *constellations of the zodiac.* The *signs* of the zodiac, in other words, should not be confused with the *constellations* of the zodiac. The former have fixed dates, the latter movable dates.

Even though they never read newspapers and magazines, Johannes Hooss and his rural neighbors three to five hundred years ago did not see the signs of the zodiac only in the sky. They saw the symbols of the zodiac everywhere. One often has the impression that they even learned them formally. Since few of them could read, signs and symbols had a much greater meaning than they do today. Those who thought they had something to say or argue used the language of symbols. This simple method of understanding among illiterate people is largely forgotten today, and we concentrate more

---

Top: Four thousand years ago, when regular observations of sunrise and sunset began in Babylonia and Egypt, it was found that day and night were the same length when the Sun first rose in the constellation of Aries on March 21 (and again a half year later in the constellation of Libra on September 23). One therefore marked the beginning of "spring" and "fall" from these dates. The Sun reached its northern and southern zeniths a quarter of a year later when it rose for the first time in the sign of Cancer (summer solstice on June 22) and Capricorn (winter solstice on December 22), respectively. *Bottom:* When viewed by an observer on Earth, the rising and the setting of the Sun moves through the twelve different constellations of the zodiac once every year.

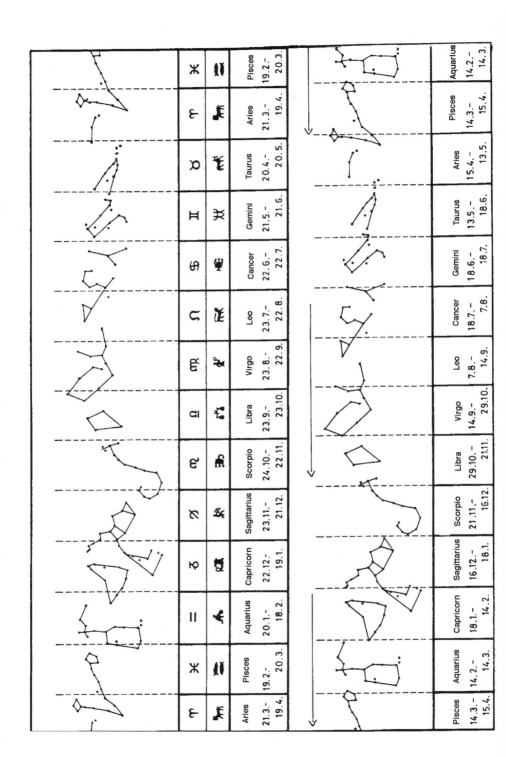

♓	♊︎	Pisces	19.2.-	20.3.
♈	🐏	Aries	21.3.-	19.4.
♉	🐂	Taurus	20.4.-	20.5.
♊	👫	Gemini	21.5.-	21.6.
♋	🦞	Cancer	22.6.-	22.7.
♌	🦁	Leo	23.7.-	22.8.
♍	👧	Virgo	23.8.-	22.9.
♎	⚖	Libra	23.9.-	23.10.
♏	🦂	Scorpio	24.10.-	22.11.
♐	🏹	Sagittarius	23.11.-	21.12.
♑	🐐	Capricorn	22.12.-	19.1.
♒	🌊	Aquarius	20.1.-	18.2.
♓	♊︎	Pisces	19.2.-	20.3.
♈	🐏	Aries	21.3.-	19.4.

Aquarius	14.2.- 14.3.
Pisces	14.3.- 15.4.
Aries	15.4.- 13.5.
Taurus	13.5.- 18.6.
Gemini	18.6.- 18.7.
Cancer	18.7.- 7.8.
Leo	7.8.- 14.9.
Virgo	14.9.- 29.10.
Libra	29.10.- 21.11.
Scorpio	21.11.- 16.12.
Sagittarius	16.12.- 18.1.
Capricorn	18.1.- 14.2.
Aquarius	14.2.- 14.3.
Pisces	14.3.- 15.4.

on the much more awkward evidence offered by books of "traditional advice."

Long before the time of Johannes Hooss, the medieval church incorporated into its worldview the Babylonian, Egyptian, and Greek symbols of the zodiac. With their help, the church addressed nonliterate people in picture-book fashion. On the portals of many Romanesque churches, for example—places easily seen by everyone—Christ, portrayed as ruler and judge of the world, was enthroned in the middle of an arc animated with *pagan* symbols arranged next to each other: the signs of the zodiac (fig. 29, p. 148, top). Even though the major theme in this example is the sending out of the apostles—an image readily understandable to everyone—the meaning of the arc and the planets surrounding it and the related monthly agricultural activities was clearly intelligible. Christ was ruler of heaven, earth, and the heavenly bodies and stars. He was Lord of mankind and nature and of all the activities and seasons of the year, governor of time and eternity.

In 1593—about half a millennium after the building of this middle portal on the Burgundian abbey church at Vézelay (around 1130)—an impressive clock dial was erected in the Friars' Church in Brunswick (see fig. 29, bot-

28.   Time discrepancies between the signs of the zodiac and the annual movement of the Sun through the constellations of the zodiac. At the beginning of regular observations by the Babylonians and Egyptians about four thousand years ago, these dates corresponded with each other. Today the signs of the zodiac may carry the same names as the constellations, but they are now two different things. The difference originates in the fact that spring begins twenty minutes earlier each year than the last. Over the course of a single human life (of exactly 72 years) that makes a difference of only 24 hours (72 times 20 minutes). This is sufficient, however, to make the Sun rise and set on the same day in a different constellation every 2,150 years (on March 21, for example). What was true for the ancient Babylonians and Egyptians—that is, the beginning of spring corresponded with both the sign and the constellation of Aries—occurred up to about time of the birth of Christ. Since that time and for about another hundred years, it will occur in the constellation of Pisces, followed then for the next two thousand years by the constellation of Aquarius. It takes a total of 25,800 years for the starting dates of spring, summer, fall, and winter to cycle through the entire zodiac.

All of the time periods are roughly the same length among the signs of the zodiac, since each of them encompasses thirty degrees of the visible path of the Sun in its annual movement across the zodiac. In reality, however, the constellations differ in size so that the Sun rises and sets for different lengths of time in each. (For the times that are valid today see the dates at the bottom of the figure.)

tom). Here too it was not placed in an obscure location but in a place easily seen by everyone on the rood screen. The wheel of time was made up of a combination of the numbers representing the hours and the twelve signs of the zodiac. For anyone looking at it who still doubted that the master of time was not man, that death and mortality were more powerful, three other images around the face of the clock hammered the point home: Death, who rang the hours; the hourglass with its sand running out; and the unmistakable symbolism of the skull. Who needed this explained in writing? Who had to have it spelled out to get the point?

The art of printing also used this visual method of instruction as it rapidly developed at the end of the fifteenth century and the beginning of the sixteenth. Through a kind of a pictorial language—familiar to us today in comic strips—a significantly larger reading audience could be reached than through simple printed texts. Annual *Calendars for the Simple Man* were printed in especially large numbers of editions. Most of them were only a few pages. Each month had its own column, and within the column each day had its own line. Next to the name of the saint for that day there were usually several signs that were supposed to make it easier to choose the right day for a particular activity. There were, for example, different types of crosses or clover leaves, scissors that opened upward or downward, or a finger pointing to the right or the left. These symbols indicated whether or not a given day was favorable for a particular activity—sowing grain, for example, or planting beets, but also cutting wood or hair, bleeding someone, or weaning an infant, and much, much more.

29.   Signs of the zodiac as symbols of the cosmos and of time in the Western Christian church. *Top:* Christ as Lord of the cosmos and Lord of time, seated in the middle of an animated arch of twelve sequentially arranged signs of the zodiac and depictions of the months with the customary agricultural activities associated with them. This cosmic aspect of Christ as ruler and judge of the world is a theme frequently treated on Romanesque portals in particular. The illustration shows the middle portal of the interior entrance hall of the Abbey Sainte-Madeleine in Vézelay, Burgundy. See Ingeborg Tetzlaff, *Romanische Portale in Frankreich,* 3d ed. (Cologne: Dumont, 1982), figure 84. *Source:* © 1995 Artists Rights Society (ARS), New York/SPADEM, Paris. *Bottom:* next to the great clock face on the rood screen in the former Friars' Church in Brunswick (built 1592/94), Death assumes the role of ruler over the passing of time. See Jürgen Diestelmann, *Die Brüderkirche in Braunschweig* (Königstein im Taunus, 1982), 9. *Source:* The clock from the rood screen in the Friars' Church is located today in the Städtisches Museum Braunschweig.

Martius.　Wertzmaen.

September.　Herustmaen.

A

B

C

D

E

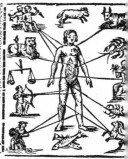

The signs of the zodiac also played a significant role in these printings of calendar symbols. There was not a single page on which they were not reproduced several times. Following the name of each month, for example, there came the sign of the zodiac and the primary agricultural work that was to be done in that particular month (see figs. 30a and b). In this way, for example, Aries "governed" the month of March and Libra the month of September. Everything was supposed to occur at the *proper* time: trees had

30.   Signs of the zodiac and the human body. The signs of the zodiac did not simply influence nature and the seasons so that all agricultural activities were to take place at the right time. They also exercised a decisive influence on people and the organs of the body. *A and B:* a season for all things! Two monthly symbols from the *Shepherd's Calendar* of 1523. Aries "governed" March, Libra September. In the sign of Aries trees were to be pruned and new shoots grafted; in the sign of Libra fall sowing took place. *C:* ever since the development of printing, impressive editions of almanacs appeared every year for simple people. Even those who could not read were supposed to be able to understand the content of pamphlets, which were often only a few pages in length. Just as the connection between the signs of the zodiac and the activities performed under their influence were to be easily understandable without reading knowledge, as illustrated in *A* and *B,* so the association with the organs of the body were also to be understood without difficulty. Aries "governed" the head and face; Capricorn the neck and throat; Gemini the shoulders, arms, and hands; and so on right down to the feet, which were governed by Pisces. Anyone with a little reading ability could often find this knowledge confirmed right and left on the page. From the same *Shepherd's Calendar. D and E:* the ideas evident in *A, B,* and *C,* and illustrated with an almanac from the early years of printing (the year 1523), were still valid generations later and reprinted unaltered at the time of our Johannes Hooss (1670–1755), shown here with an almanac from the youth of Hooss (the *Writing Almanac* from Goslar for the year 1680) and one from his adulthood (the *Christian and Planet Calendar* for 1727 from Hamburg).

Sources: all of the partial illustrations come from the collections of the Herzog August-Bibliothek in Wolfenbüttel. *A, B,* and *C: The Shepherd's Calendar* (Rostock: L. Dyetz, 1523), sig. 36, Astronomica; *D: Großer alt- und neuer Schreib-Calender, beschrieben durch Michaelum Crügenerum* (Goslar: Duncker, 1680), sig. Ne 376; *E: Hamburgisch verbesserter Christ- und Planeten-Calender, beschrieben von Johann Henrich Voigt* (Hamburg: Conrad König, 1727), sig. Ne Box 4 (18). For introductory literature the following are recommended: Hartmut Sührig, "Die Entwicklung der niedersächsischen Kalender im 17. Jahrhundert," *Archiv für Geschichte des Buchwesens* 20 (1979), cols. 329–794; and Geneviève Bollème, *Les almanachs populaires aux XVIIe et XVIIIe siècles: Essai d'histoire sociale* (Paris: Mouton, 1969). I am grateful to Ursula Zachert and Dr. Werner Arnold of the Herzog August-Bibliothek in Wolfenbüttel for advice and help in my research.

to be cut under the sign of Aries in March; the fall sowing came in September under the sign of Libra; sheep were shorn in June under the sign of Cancer; the harvesting of hay and grain took place in the signs of Leo and Virgo in July and August, respectively; and the wine harvest occurred in October under Scorpio.

The stars or the "twelve signs of the zodiac" influenced not only the growth of plants, trees, bushes, and animals. They also exercised their influence on people and all of the organs of the body (figs. 30c, d, and e). To follow the list, Aries "governed" the head and face; Taurus the neck and throat; Gemini the shoulders, arms, and hands; Cancer the breast, lungs, spleen, and stomach; Leo the heart, liver, and back; Virgo the upper stomach and entrails; Libra the lower stomach; Scorpio the sexual organs; Sagittarius the hips and upper thighs; Capricorn the knee; Aquarius the shins and calves; and, finally, Pisces the feet.

All of this appeared within the first decades of the development of printing, since they followed ancient ideas (see fig. 30c, *The Shepherd's Calendar* [1523]). And it was still the same at the beginning and end of Johannes Hooss's life (1670–1755) (fig. 30d, *The Writing Almanac* [1680], and fig. 30e, *The Christian and Planet Calendar* [1727]).

Even if these cheap calendar books were not in every peasant house, there was still no shortage of visual material about the signs of the zodiac from at least one year or another. One of the neighbors or, at the very least, the nearby barber-surgeon or the barber had one. The midwife or one of the other "cunning people" also almost always had a recent or well-thumbed copy on hand. Finally, it was difficult to miss the symbols on the entrance of the church or during a visit to the market in town.

At this point the historian could easily succumb to the temptation to speak more broadly and try to explain the broader history of these signs. Our ancestors' ideas and reflections about the association or close relationship between the little world of man, the microcosm, and the larger external world, the macrocosm, goes back a long way back into the past. These ideas can be shown among the oldest civilized peoples.[16] What persisted was the conviction that the microcosm and the macrocosm formed a meaningful whole and that each and every thing in the bigger world had its correspondence in the small one: "on earth as it is in heaven."

In the Christian West, even at the time of Johannes Hooss, ideas like those of the German abbess Hildegard of Bingen (1098–1179) from the High Middle Ages were likely to have been common knowledge. She presented these powerfully in schoolbook form in her work *The World and Man* (see the "Cosmic Man" from this book in fig. 31, p. 154). The small man (but disproportionately large when compared with the rest of creation) is on the sphere of the world, surrounded by the other spheres of air, water, the winds, the stars, and the planets. As the most important creation, man was at the center of the world, a world that, in its turn, rested in the outstretched arms of God. This type of idea naturally made no place for a view of man as alone and dependent only on his own resources. Better yet, the entire world and all of nature was oriented around man, and, even though he had fallen, God had not turned away from him. Instead he had left him in the center of creation. There was nothing beyond man that was not already contained within him. On the last day of creation God created man out of the same material out of which he had already fashioned the elements, the earth, heavens, stars, planets, plants, and animals. Everything had the same divine origins, so the same laws were at work between the corresponding parts of heaven and earth, both in the macrocosm and in the human microcosm. Everywhere there were analogies and correspondences.

This basic principle involving correspondences between the larger and smaller worlds, or vice versa, operated in turn like a law in which influences were completely reciprocal. The above ideas—in which a certain constellation exercised influence on a corresponding organ of the body or a particular season or day of the month—flowed freely from this, as did dozens of further rules of everyday behavior. These too were in the almanacs. Activities that aimed at making something increase, such as sowing, planting, and grafting, were to be carried out under a waxing moon. On the other hand, it was possible according to these views to create rain by pouring out water.

Embedded in the same set of ideas were notions about the presumed effects associated with the power of similarities, correspondences, analogies, and sympathies. Discredited today as "prescientific," "irrational," or, to put it bluntly, "magical," they were especially useful in keeping people and animals healthy or in curing them. The following names are reminiscent of their former uses: the liverlike leaves of the crowfoot leaf helped with liver ailments, saxifrage with bladder stones, and eyebright with eye diseases. Yellow saffron was appropriate for treating hepatitis, while bleeding could be stopped with the red buds of St. John's wort or with any red wine on hand.

However fascinating it would be to delve into this foreign worldview, resurrecting its spirit and its functions over the centuries, a brief sketch will have to suffice. First of all, I am not really interested in describing an ancient

and now archaic system of ideas. The degree to which our ancestors were familiar with it I really do not know. Realistically speaking, one cannot assume that Johannes Hooss had read Hildegard of Bingen's text on the cosmos, much less the Greek texts of Aristotle. Already in Aristotle's work, many of the assumptions about the microcosm and the macrocosm and the teachings about correspondences are to be found. It was not even likely that he knew the works of Paracelsus (1493–1541), the Swabian naturalist, physician, and philosopher, who was much closer to him in time and whose teachings reinvigorated them in German thought (among the learned and those who could read, of course!).

The second reason will, I hope, not sound ridiculous. I want to protect Johannes Hooss and many of our peasant ancestors from overly arrogant and condescending judgments, whether from their own "educated" contemporaries or from modern rational and enlightened people—or those who at least appear to be so. No one likes to see himself described as stupid. The living can defend themselves, but Johannes Hooss cannot. Let me give an example.

Naturally one cannot assume that Johannes Hooss knew the laws of astronomical progression described above, even though Hipparchus of Nicea, one of the most important ancient astronomers (ca. 190–125 B.C.), had already discovered and described them. Hooss would therefore hardly have been able to explain the discrepancy in dates between the signs of the zodiac and the actual movements of the constellations (look once again at figs. 27 and 28). Even modern people have difficulty understanding it, even though every imaginable reference book is available. While by our frequent observations of sunrise and sunset *in nature* we might have long since detected the discrepancy, most of us are not only not aware of it, we read astrological dates in newspapers and magazines and never consider whether they coincide with

31.   "Cosmic Man" from Hildegard of Bingen's *World and Man*. The little world of man (the microcosm) and the larger world of water, air, wind and light, the stars and planets (the macrocosm) form an orderly whole and are elevated in the outstretched arms of the Trinity. A worldview such as this did not represent a person as alone and left only to his own devices. *Source:* Hildegard of Bingen, *Welt und Mensch: Das Buch "De operatione Dei": Aus dem Genter Kodex übersetzt und erläutert von Heinrich Schipperges* (Salzburg: Otto Müller, 1965), figure 4, between pp. 48 and 49. For a commentary see the chapter "Vom Bau der Welt," pp. 35–60, and the additional comments of the translator on pp. 321–36.

the actual position of the Sun. The reader can decide who the ignorant one in all of this is. In this regard I myself do not feel particularly clever.

I would naturally not object to the idea that Johannes Hooss had a whole set of views in common with the almanacs of his day. He may also have acted on them, behaving "superstitiously" in everyday life, employing "magical" practices and believing in their effects. One can after all hardly expect Johannes Hooss to have understood the human body, its organs, and their functions very well in an age when the medical sciences of the day did not understand them either; that is, they did not understand what caused a liver ailment or the suffering occasioned by bladder or kidney stones. The advice about "how to cut hair" that appeared repeatedly over the generations in the almanac books of advice probably did not seem nonsensical to him. It would not have been alien to his way of thinking. Alluding to principles already familiar to us concerning sowing, planting, and grafting, one of them says: "To cut hair so that it grows back quickly and well it should be done when the moon is waxing. If it is to grow back slowly it should be done when the moon is waning." How could Johannes Hooss deny that the Sun, Moon, and stars influenced natural events here on Earth and in his own body? How could it be denied when year in and year out close personal observation showed the closest connections between what happened in the heavens and the progress of the seasons and the rhythms of nature, plants, and animals? For his own good and that of the Vältes Farm, he freely submitted himself to these rhythms.

These alert observations, on the other hand, protected him from everything printed in the almanacs as "wisdom" and pushed off on the "simple man in the countryside" as the absolute truth. Johannes Hooss knew better than this even when it was printed in black and white. He was not fooled even when the community barber-surgeon or barber, who could read a little and had a big reputation among "ignorant peasants," babbled on for a while and then triumphantly pointed to the commentary next to the sign of the month:

> In March one should know
> that the sun into Aries goes.

or for September:

> In September you should know
> that the sun into Libra goes.[17]

In contrast to the information from the almanac, he *knew* that the sun *did not* rise in Aries in March or in Libra in September. How could he then believe the rest of the wisdom in the almanac or the barber-surgeon's sayings about how a particular sign of the zodiac "governed" a certain day of the month? Hooss would never have been fooled to this extent, even though a number of "learned" contemporaries and modern people would like to think so. People say these things and are unaware of their own arrogance, or they even feel that they have "superior knowledge." And this too can be unfounded.

In order to demonstrate this further, let me provide the reader with two more illustrations. Figure 32 (p. 158) depicts a model of the planetary system that was in use from antiquity well into the sixteenth century. Circling the earth in the center were the six "older" planets: the Moon, Mercury, Venus, the Sun, Mars, Jupiter, and Saturn. (The three "newer" planets were only discovered later: Uranus in 1781, Neptune in 1846, and Pluto in 1930.) The entire system was then enclosed in the last sphere, that of the fixed heavens. The irregular speed in the movements of Mercury, Venus, Mars, Jupiter, and Saturn, easily observable by anyone at the time, was explained by means of small circular movements (epicycles) around an imaginary central point (a referent). Although this worldview essentially went back to the Greek philosopher Aristotle (382–322 B.C.) and an astronomer from Egypt, Claudius Ptolemy (ca. 100–160 A.D.), the church had taken it over in the course of the Middle Ages and incorporated it, so to speak, into its own thought. According to Western Christian ideas, as already illustrated by the work of Hildegard of Bingen from the eleventh century (see fig. 31), this entire world system, including the earth, spheres, and fixed heavens, was encompassed and supported by Almighty God.

The Polish astronomer Nicolaus Copernicus (1473–1543) expressed the first serious concerns about this so-called geocentric worldview. In his main work, *On the Revolutions of the Heavenly Spheres* (1543), which appeared only shortly before his death, he offered his heliocentric system as an alternative to the earth-centered system of Aristotle and Ptolemy. In this way he introduced the "Copernican Revolution," and over the next two centuries scholars debated whether to accept it or not. Its proponents gradually gained the upper hand, since their work in the physical, experimental, and empirical sciences made the heliocentric system a more likely probability. For a long time resistance came from the Catholic Church, which held dogmatically to Aristotelian physics. The new planetary laws, basically formulated by the

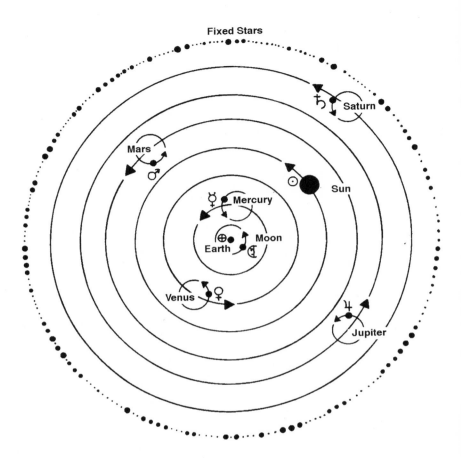

Fixed Stars

Saturn

Mars

Sun

Mercury

Earth Moon

Venus

Jupiter

32.   Geocentric universe of Johannes Hooss (the Aristotelian-Ptolemaic model), with the seven "ancient" planets (Earth, the Moon, Mercury, Venus, the Sun, Mars, Jupiter, and Saturn) and the fixed stars in the firmament around it. Mercury, Venus, Mars, Jupiter, and Saturn did not simply traverse their orbits around Earth, they also carried out small circular movements (epicycles). Therefore they sometimes moved across the heavens faster, and then slowed again or even temporarily moved backwards. Nicolaus Copernicus (1473–1543) may have lived two hundred years before Johannes Hooss (1670–1755), but it is doubtful that Hooss experienced the "Copernican Revolution" or was even aware of it. According to this, a heliocentric system replaced the earth-centered model. The Aristotelian-Ptolemaic system, which had remained valid for about fifteen hundred years, had the advantage of making daily observations and experiences comprehensible and completely satisfied the demands of common sense.

German astronomer Johannes Kepler (1571–1630), gradually experienced a decisive breakthrough in the first third of the eighteenth century through the more broadly recognized mechanical laws worked out by the English mathematician, physicist, and astronomer Isaac Newton (1643–1727).

We can comfortably assume that the Aristotelian-Ptolemaic worldview with Earth as the center of the universe was Johannes Hooss's worldview and that of his forebears for centuries. Even if some scholars had called the model into question with Copernican ideas and no longer considered man and Earth as the center of the divine creation, for Johannes Hooss the Sun *rose* in the heavens, *moved* across the sky during the day, and *sank* below the horizon in the evening. From our modern point of view, of course, Johannes Hooss believed in a false worldview. But it had the advantage of making sense out of his everyday observations and sense experiences, and it therefore satisfied his "common sense." The conclusions of a geocentric system were virtually irrefutable, even if they had long since rested on false assumptions. Who can guarantee *us* that *our own* ideas are ultimately the correct ones, even if they conform with the most recent state of scientific knowledge? It may not even take two hundred years before our own descendants make fun of their ancestors' ideas from the last quarter of the twentieth century.

With this idea we return to the idea at the heart of the chapter, the search for stability. I would be careful about arrogantly denouncing Johannes Hooss's "false" worldview as "wrong." For him it was *right* and it formed a coherent whole. It offered him understandable explanations of the world insofar as he needed them in his everyday life. His perceptions, values, and ways of doing things were therefore in harmony with each other. They were not "wrong." His worldview was stable and offered him some of the stability he was looking for.

With the final illustration for this chapter (fig. 33, p. 160) I would like to think about what was happening in the long term and was already beginning to be apparent everywhere around Johannes Hooss. This involved the world slipping gradually from the hand of God, where it had rested for centuries (fig. 33, top left), and man's growing attempt to master it. That this inevitably led to a spiritual and religious dilemma for a number of our ancestors is easily understandable. Already in the time of Johannes Hooss there were a number of people who felt this way, so that the *Christian and Planet Calendar* could depict precisely this *Man in Discord* on its title page in its 1727 edition (fig. 33, bottom), that is, when Johannes Hooss was in middle age. At the left the man is still kneeling on the earth created by God and prays to his heavenly

Christum lieb haben/
ist besser denn alles
wissen.

Die Himmel erzehlen
die Ehre GOttes.

Father in the clouds: "To love Christ is better than all knowledge." On the right and symbolically separated from his *alter ego* by the tree of knowledge, he is standing and trying to discover the secrets of the stars and planets with instruments he has designed himself. In his dilemma he naturally comforts himself with the thought that he does not want to establish anything other than how "the heavens declare the glory of God." The ancient and all-encompassing worldview was beginning to fade. And the stability associated with it for generations was crumbling.

33.   From the world in the hands of God (upper left) to the world in the hands of man (upper right). This plunged many of our ancestors into spiritual and religious conflict (bottom). *Sources:* upper left: Meister von Frankfurt (b. ca. 1460), *The Holy Family*. Middle picture from the altar at the Dominican Church, tempura on oak. Historisches Museum Frankfurt am Main. Upper right: Jan Vermeer van Delft (1632–75), *The Astronomer*, 1669. Städelsches Kunstinstitut Frankfurt am Main. Bottom: title page from *Hamburgisch verbesserter Christ- und Planetenkalender, beschrieben von Johann Henrich Voigt* (Hamburg: Conrad König, 1727). Herzog August Bibliothek Wolfenbüttel, sig. Ne box 4 (18).

CHAPTER 5

Why Life Is So
Hard Today

HROUGHOUT THIS BOOK we have discussed the difficult conditions under which our ancestors had to live. With this background in mind, one could consider it a real pleasure to be alive *today,* or so one might think.

Far be it from me to deny the fact that more people are materially better off today than at any other time, that society's safety net today is more comprehensive than ever before, or that more men and even more women have a longer life expectancy these days than at any previous time. All of this is doubtless true, and these achievements deserve our respect and grateful acknowledgment. Look at how often our ancestors in their helplessness had to plead repeatedly, "Protect us, oh Lord, from plague, famine, and war!" This does not even take into account many of the "less important" unpleasantries, such as freezing in houses without central heating, enduring pain in a world without pills and pharmacies, hauling drinking water from springs, carting away sewage, dealing with nearsightedness and failing eyesight without eyeglasses, and relying upon one's memory, since reading and writing were not yet widespread.

We often casually assume that all of these problems, the three scourges especially, have long since been overcome or that they are as good as taken care of. The plague? The last epidemic of plague occurred in Europe in the early 1720s, and even then it was restricted to Marseilles and the surrounding area. Since then we hear no more reports of it. Famine? The post–World War II generation has at most heard of it, what it was like and what it was capable of driving people to do. War? Never have so many people been living in Europe at one time who have never experienced war firsthand.

This is all true, and yet again, not quite the whole truth. One need only

162

listen to the daily news on the radio about small wars repeatedly breaking out somewhere in the world in order to doubt whether we have actually brought the scourge of war permanently under control. The balance of nuclear terror has certainly guaranteed Europe several decades of peace, but this is no guarantee that it will continue. In previous chapters I have already mentioned how these conditions, which hardly inspire confidence, create and perpetuate a climate of constant and general anxiety for many of us.

With regard to the problem of hunger, some people, after having a nice meal, might salve their bad consciences by making a donation to world famine relief. Afterward the old Malthusian question might come up. Won't the earth's faster-growing population still outstrip the world's production of food? A famine of catastrophic proportions would therefore seem virtually inevitable with or without a war. It therefore appears that we have by no means brought famine under control, especially not on a worldwide scale. One does not have to invoke any anxiety-arousing visions about the future in order to show that modern conditions are in many ways comparable to those in the past. Further, if one were to define hunger as a life-threatening condition caused by improper nutrition, then the consequences of famine in the past and overeating today are in the end the same. Being overweight constitutes one of the primary risk factors for death for a number of people today. Continuous overeating and improper nutrition are just as harmful to health as when the body continuously receives an inadequate and imbalanced diet. Those who overeat kill themselves slowly. Hunger does the same thing, only faster and more cruelly. In both cases years of life are lost.

The most serious doubts come to mind when one begins to think about the plague. In a strictly biological and medical sense plague is, on the one hand, what we call a highly infectious disease, a fatal illness, discovered in 1894 by Alexander Yersin as caused by the plague bacillus. In its most dangerous form as pneumatic plague, it is communicated directly from person to person, inflicting mortality rates of up to 100 percent. What Arnold Böcklin looking back at this horror depicted in 1898, that is, more than a century and a half after the disease had died out on the European continent, was something else. Here the "plague" is portrayed as the Grim Reaper on a senseless rage, slashing away, terrorizing the population and slaughtering without pity every life in his path (see once again fig. 15 above).

A third, and still different, meaning was what the public authorities at different levels, from village elders and town fathers all the way up to government officials, meant by the word "plague." They meant a disease that invaded from the outside and which was particularly dangerous because within a short time it could kill a lot of people in the population from all social classes in a small area. They saw it as preventable through rigorous precautionary measures, especially quarantines. In contrast to smallpox, for example, which was restricted to infants and small children, or the so-called "diseases of the hungry" that overwhelmingly visited the poorest and hungriest social classes, plague struck the whole population. During a serious epidemic it could strike right at the foundations and the stability of an entire society. It was precisely this danger that had to be warded off. A fourth and final meaning of the word was what common men, women, and children on the street associated with "plague." It was a swift death from almost any kind of vicious disease: a "pestilence" that struck everyone, whether rich or poor, and quickly snatched away their lives.

What we have brought under control is not at all insignificant; ultimately, however, it is only the "plague" narrowly defined in its medical and biological sense as a fatal disease. No one in Europe must fear it any longer. In every other regard, however, what strikes me as far more important are the trade-offs we have made involving the "plague." Whether one is a painter, a magistrate, or a simple person, "plague" was always thought of as only one of many possible ways of dying. The elimination of the "plague" as a disease and as an important cause of death naturally did not mean that death and dying were eliminated from human experience. Other diseases and causes of death immediately took its place. Those who were spared the plague would still die sooner or later from either intestinal typhoid or spotted fever or perhaps from childhood smallpox. Was this really a good "trade-off" in each case?

Since this point can advance my main point quite a bit, let me use two illustrations to explain what may otherwise be a surprising notion for many readers. Both graphs originated within the context of a study of about forty thousand deaths in the Berlin parish of Dorotheenstadt between 1715 and 1875.

The computer-generated picture in figure 34 gives us a three-dimensional representation of the annual distribution of the absolute numbers of these deaths according to age. What immediately leaps out is the huge black wall in the background. It shows the enormous infant and child mortality rates of that time. From among a total of 39,251 deaths, no less than 12,193, that is, almost one-third (31.1%), were infants under one year old. By adding in small children up to eight years old, we can account for roughly one-half of

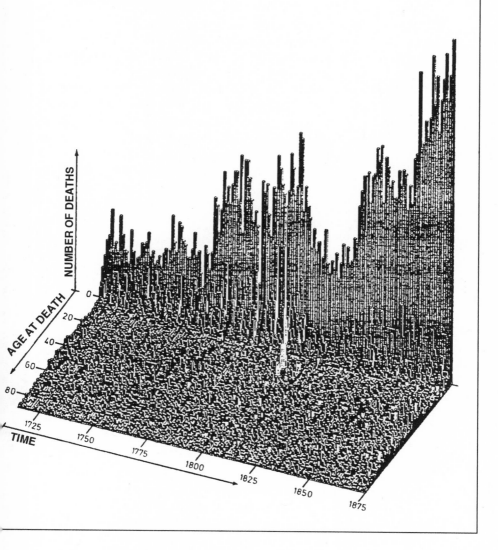

DOROTHEENSTADT

DISTRIBUTION OF AGE GROUPS
FROM 1715 - 1875
YEAR BY YEAR

NUMBER OF DEATHS

AGE AT DEATH

0
20
40
60
80

TIME

1725 · 1750 · 1775 · 1800 · 1825 · 1850 · 1875

34. Number of deaths by age in the parish of Dorotheenstadt in Berlin, 1715–1875. Total number of deaths: 39,251 (100%). Age 0–1: 12,193 (31.1%); age 1–8; 7,664 (19.5%); age 0–8: 19,857 (50.6%). *Source:* ongoing study using the death registers of the parish of Dorotheenstadt in Berlin, Evangelisches Zentralarchiv, Berlin (West), and the databank in the Friedrich-Meinecke-Institut of the Free University Berlin.

all mortalities (50.6%). The remainder are distributed relatively evenly across all of the other ages between nine and ninety years.

There was no comparable concentration of deaths, or anything approaching it, for any other time later in life. One person lived for twenty years, another for forty, a third for sixty or eighty, and here and there someone lived to be ninety or more. All of these deaths are equally distributed across the flat black carpet in the foreground of the picture.

Had the computer depicted the next one hundred years in a similar way, our view would change completely so that today the pattern would no longer be recognizable. The whole black wall has moved from the back of the image up to the front. People no longer die as infants or small children today. Only in exceptional cases do people die as adults in the prime of life—from an accident, for example. The back wall has been removed, the carpet thinned out. Today we die at the standard age of sixty-five, seventy, or eighty years. In former times the wall was behind us. Each living person had already outlived one out of every two children who were born and therefore belonged to the group of fortunate survivors. Today the wall stands before us, and, while all of us are approaching it, we simply ignore it as long as possible. In the end, however, death will still take each and every one of us.

Death and dying today are therefore no longer the same thing that Böcklin saw in his vision. For most age groups the Grim Reaper's scythe has been dulled. His harvest of children, youths, and young adults has become a meager and thin one today. At the very most, death can still terrorize people who are advanced in age, those who are perhaps sixty-five or seventy or older. Even in this regard, however, a decisive transformation has taken place. Death once struck not only people of all ages, it also occurred in the streets or out in the open for all to see. Mothers and fathers died in the presence of their children. Farmhands and servant girls died right before the eyes of the peasants who hired them. Journeymen and apprentices saw their masters and mistresses die. When no epidemics were raging and one therefore had more time to die, when one could prepare for death with more peace, one took one's leave, in keeping with the contemporary rite of dying, from those who had been closest throughout life: children, husband, wife, friends, relatives, neighbors. This was simply how it was done.

Today almost all of us have time—a lot of time, in fact—to make such farewells. This occurs at an advanced age when death keeps one waiting a long time—days, weeks, months, even years—and relief comes frequently only "after a long and difficult illness," as it says in many obituaries. Yet while we have postponed death and dying to an increasingly later age, we have simultaneously pushed it out of public sight. In West Berlin in 1978 no fewer than 27,413 out of a total of 36,060 deaths occurred in hospitals. That represents over three-fourths (76%) of all deaths. Yet it is not enough for us that members of our society die behind the familiar brick walls of hospitals, retirement homes, and nursing homes for the chronically ill. Even inside of them people are transferred behind another wall shortly before passing away. They are brought into a special room for the dying. It goes without saying that this process of continuously pushing death and dying away, removing it from the public behind double walls of secrecy, corresponds with the repression of death and dying from our conscious minds and our everyday lives. Indeed it may be predicated upon it.

When death and dying are concentrated so heavily in these older groups, then they no longer threaten the community. For those who are in the fullness of their years, death and dying are no longer able to elicit fear as did the massive mortalities from the plague in former times. Even though death is concentrated within a single but marginal age group, it is still just as certain for the elderly today as it once was for infants and small children. In both cases it involves age groups that have the lowest status, the least amount of influence, the ones who have no powerful pressure groups or effective lobby. Then, as well as now, where was a "surplus" of people in these groups, so they were not cared for very much.

In looking at figure 34 one instinctively wonders whether more than a century and a half ago no one really saw that, on average, one out of every two deaths every year was of an infant or a small child. Why didn't our ancestors do more to prevent this? Apparently enough people survived even after this halving of the population. Only at the end of the nineteenth century and the beginning of the twentieth, when the birthrates dropped rapidly and dramatically, was there more investment in the children who came into the world. Today, when there is no more talk about a surplus of infants and children, when one can read, on the contrary, anxious headlines like "Are the Germans Dying Out?" hardly any children are allowed to die. Pediatricians concern themselves with every little cold and prescribe careful treatment and bed rest. Over the course of only a couple of generations, what a massive change in attitudes when compared with our ancestors!

To be sure, we treat the age group at the other end of the scale in the opposite way. These are the ones who exist as a "surplus" and who die in large numbers: people around sixty-five and older. One consequence of this

modern trend should have been an increase in the number of doctors special-
izing in the diseases of old age, since the most cases and the most important
interventions were here. As everybody knows, however, this has not been
the case at all. To ascertain this one only has to look through the yellow pages
of any telephone directory and see that there are rarely, if ever, specialists in
geriatrics listed. Admittedly, modern doctors are no different from anyone
else. Up to now old age has yet to be "discovered" as a problem. It is certainly true that a day hardly passes without some discussion in the mass media
of some of the problems of the elderly. Their sheer numbers, however, make
it difficult to ignore any longer. But rarely do we dedicate ourselves more
than halfheartedly to answering the questions they raise.

Death and dying alone do not disturb a society. What disturbs a society is
the death or loss of people who are important for its functioning and stability.
Neither the large number of children in the past nor the elderly today are
important to society in this way, even when they remind us of the fact by
becoming activists like the Grey Panthers. Rarely can they ever be certain
of more than a pained but superficial interest in their plight. In any case,
they wait in vain for our intervention to prevent their deaths even when
everyone is affected, as in the time of plague or the cholera epidemics.

What we have completely overlooked and forgotten is that the wait for
death and dying, while theirs today, will be ours tomorrow. All of us without
exception still have that black wall in front of us, and when we reach it we
will find as little comfort and help there as they do today: it is an anxious
feeling that we continually repress.

Returning to figure 34, one can find one more point worth thinking
about. An astonishing change in the wall in the background is evident
around 1800. At that time infant mortality rates dropped dramatically by
about one-half. For a number of years they remained at this unusually low
level, but then a generation later they shot back up to their old high rates.
The explanation for this is easy to find, and figure 35 (p. 170) serves to
illustrate its significance. What we see in this case is nothing less than the
replacement of one important cause of death by another.

Shortly after 1800, beginning in England, inoculation against smallpox
spread rapidly across the entire European continent. It was introduced in
Berlin in 1801. The death rates from this infant disease abruptly declined.
Naturally immortality was not conferred to infants and small children
through the inoculation. The only consequence was that those who were

inoculated may have survived smallpox only to fall victim several weeks or months later to another childhood disease, especially to gastrointestinal diseases. Figure 35 shows us how the mortality rates from these gastrointestinal diseases actually experienced a boom right after smallpox disappeared. They replaced the old disease as the new child killers.

We can no longer ask the infants affected at the time what they thought about this trade-off. Nor can we ask their parents whether they preferred to have their children survive smallpox and die later from, say, a serious case of diarrhea. Perhaps we can now understand the reports of a number of doctors from the first half of the nineteenth century about parents refusing to allow their children to be immunized. And they refused even though it could not have escaped their attention that those who received immunizations really did survive this particular disease.

This example raises the general question about what it means to replace one cause of death with another, and the reason for doing so. What does it mean to suppress one particular disease, only to make room, usually unwittingly, for another? At the beginning of the nineteenth century it was smallpox that disappeared. Later in the nineteenth century and on into the twentieth, all of the traditional infectious diseases and causes of death were gradually suppressed. Today up to two-thirds of us die from heart and circulatory diseases and cancer. But the question remains: Is this really a good trade-off? The old diseases generally killed people swiftly. They did not allow their victims to suffer for months or years and make them dependent upon other people. The new ones, in contrast, are often chronic in nature. They represent an irreversible loss of health that one must deal with not only physically but also psychologically, and to which one is forced to succumb since the disease has the upper hand in the end. A fair exchange? It may be seriously doubted. We can't say that we really have these modern diseases under control.

Another question, moreover, arises with regard to the future. What will happen when these diseases are conquered and others replace them? What will occur when the billions of dollars invested across the world in research on heart and circulatory diseases and cancer succeed, and in two to four generations no one is victimized by these diseases any longer? Our grandchildren and great-grandchildren will certainly not become immortal as a result. They too will have to die in the future, perhaps at a somewhat more advanced age than we do today. But what will they die of? The best outcome

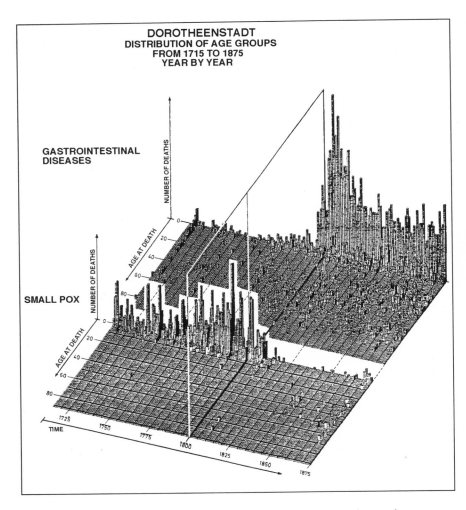

DOROTHEENSTADT
DISTRIBUTION OF AGE GROUPS
FROM 1715 TO 1875
YEAR BY YEAR

GASTROINTESTINAL
DISEASES

NUMBER OF DEATHS

AGE AT DEATH

0
20
40
60
80

SMALL POX

NUMBER OF DEATHS

AGE AT DEATH

0
20
40
60
80

TIME

1725
1750
1775
1800
1825
1850
1875

35. Deaths from smallpox and gastrointestinal disease in Dorotheenstadt, 1715–
1875. Replacement of one source of death by another—in this case, the disappearance of small pox following the introduction of smallpox vaccination at the
beginning of the nineteenth century and its replacement by a larger number of deaths
from gastrointestinal, that is, stomach and intestinal, diseases in the Berlin parish of
Dorotheenstadt. The general term *gastrointestinal* encompasses the extremely un-
differentiated diagnosis of constipation, diarrhea, stomach cramps, and so on. From
among a total of 2,014 deaths from "gastrointestinal" illness (out of a total of 2,443
deaths), 1,356 alone (55.5%) were "cramps." An additional 370 (15.1%) were from
"diarrhea" and 288 (11.8%) from "inflammations of the abdomen." These therefore
account for more than four-fifths (82.4%) of all deaths from "gastrointestinal" illnesses. *Source:* as for figure 34.

one could imagine is a "new way of dying," one that combines the advantages of old and new ways of dying. On the one hand, death would once again come swiftly. On the other hand, it would come at an advanced age but without someone painfully and slowly wasting away, only then to have final relief from all of the modern burdens of old age.

The above discussion of plague, famine, and war may well be enough to dampen any overbearing pride we may have in our apparent mastery over these ancient threats to life. Indeed it may show that our pride may be completely without foundation. Yet this is still not enough to explain why we make it so difficult for ourselves today in so many ways. Up to this point only one side of the issue has actually been discussed. All of the earlier chapters aimed at showing not only the manner and the extent of the threats to life confronting our ancestors; they also described what counterstrategies they developed to survive in spite of their helplessness, what success they had with them, and the almost incredible stability they achieved. They didn't so much engage these scourges in a direct and, what was for them at the time, hopeless battle as they attempted to outwit them, if one can put it this way. Today we attack them on a broad front, and our goal is to exterminate them. Up to now this has been only modestly successful, as we have seen. Let me develop a few thoughts about this using figure 36 (p. 172).

Two developments make up the background of this graph. The first involves the transformation of death from occurring at any age in the past to the mostly standard experience of death late in life today. The second involves one of the most profound consequences of the simultaneous de-Christianization of our concepts of life and the afterlife: the widespread loss of belief in eternity and eternal life. We often look with condescension at the short life expectancies of people in the past—twenty-five, thirty, or thirty-five years—and proudly compare them with the doubling and tripling of life expectancies over the course of the last few generations. In doing this, and because we are so shortsighted, we completely overlook the fact that in this same period we have shortened life tremendously. What does it mean to double or triple the life expectancy of one's physical existence when eternity has been lost? That still amounts to nothing.

With this background in mind, I have compared in the graph five hypothetical earlier life courses to five modern ones. Earlier, life was made up of an earthly part, more or less short and, at any rate, rather unimportant, and an otherworldly or eternal part that was longer and infinitely more important. Since that time we have completely eliminated the otherworldly

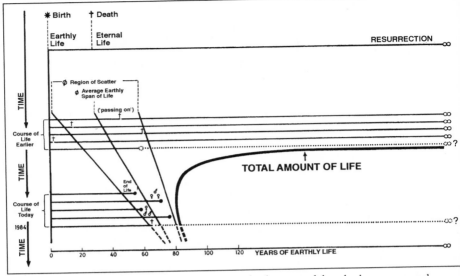

36. Development of life expectancy over the last several hundred years: several more years on Earth—but the loss of eternity. Strongly emphasized is the dramatic shortening of overall life expectancy by reducing life only to its earthly phase. The incomparably larger dimension of eternal life has been lost to us. Compared to this the lengthening of the average span of physical life (at birth) from approximately thirty years earlier to about seventy years today seems like nothing.

part, secularizing it out of existence. The only segment of life that remains for us is the earthly part, and, for better or worse, it has had to assume the role of the only important one.

Even in the nominally Christian era it is difficult to know, and naturally even more difficult to prove with statistics or graphs, how many of our ancestors believed in the resurrection of the dead and the life everlasting as it was promised and taught to them by the church. I therefore suggest sketching in a line that leads "into all of eternity" for four of the five "earlier" life courses and indicate possible doubts that one of them may have had about it with a question mark. The situation seems to me to be reversed with regard to contemporary life courses. Only one in five believes in life continuing on after death, and even then there are doubts about it.

When people still believed in the resurrection and eternal life, death and dying represented only a passage between life in this world and life in the hereafter. Dying as such was comparable to the other important transitions in human life that were marked by the traditional rituals: baptism, first communion, confirmation, and marriage. In the previous chapters we have seen what a prominent role baptism played within this sequence of events, for only through it did a newborn become a member of the Christian community. Only from this moment on did one have a justifiable prospect for resurrection from the dead and an eternal and blissful view of the countenance of God. Parents of stillborn children or of children who died before baptism therefore did everything in their power to bring about this one correct sequence of events, if need be with the aid of children's life signs, that is, temporarily waking children from the dead expressly to make it possible for them to be baptized (see fig. 26 above once more).

With this background in mind, their "indifference" toward life on Earth appears in a new light. We have mentioned this attitude repeatedly and always with some amazement (return to fig. 19 and the comments about indifference toward dilapidated bridges). As long as the afterlife was more important, life on Earth after baptism, however long or short, naturally assumed a subordinate role, regardless of whether it was ten, thirty, fifty, or even eighty years. The years were accepted however they came. This certainly did not mean that one neglected to provide for stability during the earthly portion of life. In his temporary role as peasant of the Vältes Farm, each respective individual named Johannes Hooss must have found it easier, as old age gradually came, to bow to the guiding principle that endured over the generations: the undiminished prestige of the farm was to be placed once again ahead of one's own life. In a similar way, it may have been easier to anticipate eternal glory in the afterlife, to take leave of one's earthly existence and enter the last passage of life, regardless of how old one was when that happened.

Death came *more easily* in contrast to today, when leaving the world is more difficult for us. In no way do I wish to give the impression that fear and anguish about death and dying did not also plague our ancestors. That death came "easier" to them does not mean that it was "easy." In spite of the strong religious injunctions of the time—the belief in the resurrection and in the life everlasting—the swiftness of death during epidemics, or, in times free of plague, the peaceful and public farewells in a circle of trusted friends, the humblest of people may have faced their last hours with quiet calmness, enduring them with complete detachment, almost as if they were observing themselves in a detached way.

A unique type of source allows us to shed some light on this delicate issue:

the so-called "funeral sermons." They are available in large numbers and as a rich source only in German-speaking areas, primarily from the sixteenth, seventeenth, and eighteenth centuries. As smaller or larger printed works they are housed in German archives and libraries across the country, and from 1500 to 1800 they number about two hundred thousand. Up to this point scholars have hardly noticed them. Most of them contain not simply the eulogy, the text of the sermon, and the words of consolation offered at the graveside or in the church. They also almost always contain a virtually complete life history, beginning with the family line and going on to education, professional development, family and social life, and then describe the final illness and the course of the death in its physical, mental, and spiritual aspects.

Naturally one must take these sources, as with any other historical documents, as expressions of the time and circumstances of their origin. Despite the large number of them, they were hardly distributed evenly across the entire population at the time. The expenses associated with their publication were so high that only the wealthy from the middle and upper classes could afford to leave behind this kind of "paper monument" to deceased members of their families. They were also primarily restricted to Protestant circles that created this form of memorial as a substitute for funeral celebrations abandoned after the Reformation. In this way the memory of the deceased could be properly honored. It is therefore no wonder that there is hardly anything negative to read about the deceased in a funeral sermon. Since they were addressed to the survivors and the descendants of the deceased, one finds only what was edifying and exemplary. In addition, they often used formulas that recur over this entire period. For our purposes it is important to recognize such formulas in passages that described how someone had taken his leave of the world in a proper way and had "died well." In reading this material one must therefore be careful. Still, many insights can be gained from studying these funeral sermons.

Fortunately, for a number of years a University of Marburg research group has studied and worked on this unique source material in an interdisciplinary fashion. Using an ingenious coding process, the group recorded a large number of texts on computer tapes so that now, using several dozen key words individually or in different combinations, the data can be called up and placed at the disposal of interested researchers in the form of a computer printout. Looking at the hundreds of such printouts under code number

1550, for example, "the course of death physically and spiritually," one is immediately impressed with how frequently the expression "gentle and blissful death" recurs.[1] Thus seventy-two-year-old Sigmundt von Götze "passed away gently and blissfully" on December 15, 1650, in Berlin (Marburg Funeral Sermon Computer Data Bank no. 1001). On February 12, 1657, in Zella, sixty-two-year-old Thomas von Grote "passed away in the Lord gently and blissfully without a quiver in his body" (no. 998). On January 4, 1665, in Braunschweig, eighty-three-year-old Johannes Grotejan "gave up his spirit gently and blissfully without a quiver or painful expression" (no. 128), while on May 11, 1701, a fifty-six-year-old man from Kassel, Johannes Hackenius, "gently and blissfully passed away in his Savior and Redeemer Jesus Christ" (no. 206).

Considering how often these expressions were repeated, one might assume that death was a "tame" affair for our predecessors in the seventeenth and eighteenth centuries. But this was almost certainly not the case for the people who often used these stereotypical formulae at the time, because on their own they frequently considered it necessary to point out the absence of any fear of death. This probably points to the opposite, at least as a suppressed presence. Thus fifty-five-year-old Stephanus Reimer, for example, died on March 27, 1641, in Goslar, "gently and blissfully without any sign of anxiety about death" (no. 758). Sixty-three-year-old Friedrich Wilhelm Gans passed away in Wolfenbüttel on February 11, 1648, "with his complete faculties and without a single sign of worry about death or pain in his expression" (no. 131).

Not all of those dying had completely mastered the high "art and skill of the good death," not even those described in the texts of the model funeral sermons. For many it was instead an ideal, a goal that was never reached. This is plainly evident in the data assembled under code number 1490: "Dates, Duration, and Descriptions of Illnesses." What interests us here are remarks concerning the final illnesses terminating in death. With regard to Friedrich Wilhelm Gans mentioned above, the entry reads: "A number of years ago several difficult ailments often sorely afflicted him, as when he got stones and the like. They let up, but then at times were harder than others. On the third Sunday in Advent he could not get out of bed, and everywhere was wracked with great pain from stones and other awful afflictions, especially the great anxiety that overcame him. And he realized that death had him in its grip" (no. 131). Fifty-three-year-old Hieronymus von Grapendorff from Celle was overcome with "great anxiety" in the course of his last illness (no. 1490) before he then "blissfully fell asleep in Jesus Christ without moving," on March 28, 1671 (no. 71).

One other recurring expression should be mentioned for our consideration. It is largely to be found under no. 1570: "The Course of Death: Metaphors of Death." Looking back to the simplicity of the funeral sermon about Friedrich Wilhelm Gans of Wolfenbüttel, one reads about him, as about many others, that he "was transported through a gentle death from this temporal life into the life everlasting" (no. 131).

All of the examples mentioned here under these three headings—a gentle and blissful death, a fear of death and dying that is not completely suppressed, and the continuation of life into eternity—can be multiplied at leisure using the Marburg data bank. It is an inexhaustible quarry where the rocks are fortunately already cut to manageable size and are lying about ready for our use.

Regarding the source of the passages in the texts we have studied, it is irrelevant whether the deceased himself composed them as a form of personal obituary or whether they were written by his relatives, by friends, or by the minister. What is important is that they were repeated. It is also important that the formulaic expression "gentle and blissful death" was used without alteration over generations, repeated decade after decade by those who were dying and by the people who were with them. The more frequently they were used, spoken, heard, repeated, printed, read, and thought about, the longer these recurring expressions endured, creating a framework, a norm providing support that was rooted in the collective unconscious. In the end they became a generally accepted, self-evident guide for a proper death. A person was supposed to die "gently and blissfully." The formula, the person who was dying, and those who were present saw to this even when one may have been painfully racked deep inside by the fear of death.

In this way our forebears were once again striving for an enduring and sustaining stability that stretched across the generations and which we discussed earlier with regard to worldly affairs. In this case, however, the attention was focused on the deepest problems in life. Here a norm helped the individual and the community alike. It helped both the dying individual and those closest to him to cope better, to get through this final and difficult passage in life without feeling that the whole world was collapsing.

In the meantime we have not only done away with the principle of a gentle and blissful death but, more importantly, we have not replaced it with anything else. No one today, neither those who are dying nor those around them, can offer any guidance in how to die properly. The people around the dying "solve" the problems in their own way by simply avoiding them, acting as if death no longer existed. Meanwhile the dying go on dying, even though the community does not notice them, closed off in rooms behind the hospital doors, beyond the sight and sound of the living. There they are largely left to the art of dying under medical supervision, and, in the end, to their own devices. Who would not be anxious today thinking about the final hours of life in these circumstances? Is anyone surprised that leaving this life is so difficult for us today or that we repress every thought of it whenever possible?

A review of the evidence from the funeral sermons could be summed up for our purposes in three points: First, a gentle and blissful death was the generally desired goal in the art of correctly and properly dying current at the time. Second, there was an active belief in death as the transition from the temporal to the eternal life. Third, both of these ideas helped temper or even reduce latent anxieties and fears about death and dying. Despite ritualization and a belief in the resurrection and the eternal life, however, fears obviously persisted.

In earlier chapters we gradually learned to handle sources from the past cautiously, regardless of whether they were of a statistical, literary, or artistic nature, and not to take them at face value. With this in mind I would like to introduce one more painting from the sixteenth century so that I can demonstrate, as dramatically and visually as possible, the fundamental transformation in death and dying: from death with an afterlife to death with no further life at all.

Figure 37 (p. 178) portrays the most important cemetery in Paris in the middle of the sixteenth century. The Cemetery of the Innocents, an unusually large cemetery (about 120 by 60 meters), spreads out before the Church of the Innocents in the heart of the city. Since the other parish churches in the central part of the city had little room for graves, the dead from about two dozen other parishes were also buried here. Bordering the rows of houses in the painting at the back are the modern-day Rue de la Ferronnerie at the right of the painting and the Rue Berger on the left. Considering the time when the painting was made and the purposes of such paintings, it is possible that the artist, an unknown painter of Flemish origin, in no way intended to depict the cemetery exactly. He may have been more concerned with summoning people to devote themselves to the seven temporal works

of Christian charity: feeding the hungry, succoring those in need, housing the homeless, clothing the naked, caring for the sick, visiting prisoners, and burying the dead. Moreover, it is conceivable that the painting was meant to be understood within the context of an artistic rendering of the legend of a saint. Apart from such questions as what religious theme may have inspired the painting or concerned its artist, however, I think we can still draw a number of conclusions from the minutely depicted details of the painting and consider them in our own context.

Ever since the tenth century, as we well know from other sources, generations of Parisians and foreigners who died in the city were buried in this cemetery: the young and the old, men and women, rich and poor, those who died in childbirth or through accidents, patients from hospitals, dead prisoners, aristocrats and commoners, the prominent and the obscure. In 1785, however, it was decided that burials like this in the middle of the city were no longer tolerable for reasons of hygiene and health. Those who had developed, as a result of the civilizing process, a more sensitive sense of smell

---

37.   Cemetery and Church of the Innocents in Paris around the middle of the six-teenth century. Flemish school (Jakob Grimer?, 1526–89), *Le cimetière et l'église des Saints-Innocents*. 60 × 50 cm on wood, painted around the middle of the sixteenth century. Musée Carnavalet, Paris. About this picture see *Paris au XVIe siècle et sous le règne d'Henri IV*, Bulletin du Musée Carnavalet 32, nos. 1–2 (1979), especially pp. 8–9. Tens of thousands of Parisians were buried in this cemetery from the tenth century to 1785, and, in order to make room for still new generations of people, their bones were exhumed after decomposition and then stored around the cemetery in public bone galleries and skull repositories. "In the middle of life / we are surrounded by death" was the natural backdrop for all kinds of everyday activities, such as trading, peddling, exchanging novelties, begging, burying, exhuming, letting dogs do their business, going for walks, seeing and being seen. The living and the dead were united. Two additional paintings in the same Musée Carnavalet in Paris show the destruction of this church in 1787 and the condition of the plaza after its transformation into a vegetable market (until 1860; since then it has been known as the Square of the Innocents): Pierre-Antoine de Machy (1723–1807), *Démolition de l'église des Saints-Innocents, rue Saint-Denis, en 1787* (in Room 63), and Thomas-Charles Naudet (1773–1810), *Le marché des Innocents*. Watercolor, 51.5 × 82 cm; not on continuous display. On the multiple functions of this great Parisian cemetery in the late Middle Ages and in the early modern period see Jacques Heers, *Fêtes des fous et Carnavals* (Paris: Fayard, 1983), chapter 1.4, "Le cimetière: champs des morts, carrefour de la vie sociale," esp. 49–51; and Jacques Hillairet, *Les 200 Cimetières du Vieux Paris* (Paris: Editions du Minuit, 1958), 23–28.

took particular offense at the putrid stench of the full and open mass graves at the time. So the revered cemetery was then closed, while the Church of the Innocents, at the same time, was pulled down and the entire area leveled.

In 1785, then, about two hundred years ago, the progressive removal of death and dying from the visual field and the public space of the living got under way in a tangible and carefully documented way. This is a development familiar to us. The first step was the removal of the graves and the dead from the heart of the city to its outer edges or even beyond the town walls of the time. The dying were then banished from the houses of the living to special establishments where they spent their final months, weeks, days, and hours. Finally, our thoughts about death and dying were then repressed from our conscious thoughts.

In the age before this, between the tenth century and the end of the eighteenth century, the living and the dead shared the same space in the Cemetery of the Innocents. Neither group had contested the right of the other to the space or pushed the other out. At the most this happened when peddlers and traders jostled among themselves as they spread out around the arcades in front of the painting of the Dance of Death at the rear of the plaza. Undisturbed, some of them opened their shops and stalls for business on top of the graves: stocking weavers, peddlers of ironwares, old clothes dealers, booksellers, painters. All of them were small craftsmen from the surrounding streets that still bear their names today: Rue de la Ferronnerie, Rue de la Lingerie, Rue de la Verrerie. Water carriers transported their buckets across the plaza. Snacks were sold and eaten. Peddlers came and went. Young men and women of loose morals sold their services for pleasure.

The whole cemetery looked much more like an open and public square than the enclosed place of today. People came here, as is evident from the picture, in order to see and be seen, to meet friends and acquaintances, to hear news and to pass it on, to tell and listen to stories, to play with other children, to beg or to offer alms out of Christian charity, to walk dogs, to brawl and scuffle, or simply to saunter about and promenade. People also delighted in the paintings of the Dance of Death. Wasn't Death leading away the king, the archbishop, the princes, the monks, and the fine ladies all in the same way? Many people may also have looked at the square as an extension of the northwest boundary of the central market, the Halles. At the same time, a few burials continued to take place. Corpses wrapped up in simple sheets—they weren't usually put in coffins at the time—were laid in open pits. Here and there gravediggers dug up the bones of decomposed bodies in order to make room for the next generation of the dead to decay. Ever since the fourteenth century, the remaining bones and bleached skulls were piled up into large heaps on the roofs above the peddler's arcades. This was an excellent place in which to memorialize them, lest the common fate that awaited all the living be forgotten: "Ponder your own death, oh man!"

The Church of the Innocents was the only building that towered toward the heavens, and, as if for emphasis, at the back right of the picture was the tower of the neighboring church of Sainte-Opportune. Both of them were visible reminders that the piles of skulls and the charnel houses were not ultimate resting places. These buildings towering above guaranteed one last stage in life: the resurrection of the dead and the life everlasting in heaven.

Could one imagine a more compact and, at the same time, more powerful reminder of everything that we have been discussing? Wasn't the cemetery a sign of the unity of the living and the dead? Wasn't it a reminder of death and the grave simply as a transition from this life to the eternal life in the hereafter, the continuity of the mundane and short life here below—filled with all kinds of trivial and important, serious and foolish activities—with the never-ending life in the undisturbed glory of God? No dead person, no matter how little he may have been esteemed in his earthly life, simply disappeared here without a trace. Just as his corpse was buried and rested in the midst of the living and their busy activities, so his fleshless bones were welcomed into the huge collective heap of all of his ancestors. He himself took his place among other Christians who would someday be resurrected and enter into eternal blessedness.

What was left of this vivid world and its view of the afterlife after 1785? The worldly activities that earlier represented an integral part of life, for one, simply continued. The area was leveled and became a simple marketplace for fruits and vegetables until, in the aftermath of the great reconstruction of the Halles in 1860, it gave way to the new layout of the square today. No visual evidence of death and the afterlife, or meanings associated with it, remained after that time. They were removed and thoroughly repressed in every way. Absolutely nothing would remind one of the old tradition, forty generations in the making; nothing reminded one of the intimate community of the living and the dead. In the late 1780s the remains of about two million bodies that had been buried and piled up there were interred for months in the catacombs in the southern part of the city. There they were left to disappear into old quarries below the ground. The only step that would have been more radical would have been to burn them, much as we cremate the remains left in our way today.

Today the piles of bones and skulls can be viewed or stared at in the dark passageways a few times a month, depending on the season. (The catacomb entrance lies near the Denfert-Rocherau Metro Station.) They have become macabre museum objects that attract attention by making the flesh crawl, turning one's stomach, or making one lose his appetite. Most visitors are glad to get back to the light of day after a short visit. One would prefer not to have anything more to do with the endless heaps of skulls and bones. Today the living mingle freely only with each other and no longer with the dead.

Returning to figure 36, let us now pick up one additional point that has not yet been considered. Once the life cycle was secularized, the earthly portion of life became much more important than in earlier times, since it was all that remained. As a result, the body and everything associated with it assumed much greater significance: from diet and clothing to fitness fads, health cures, cosmetics, and the inflated claims of medicine. Good health, a perfectly functioning body, became the sole guarantee of life, indeed of one's entire life. When our bodies decline today our lives automatically wither away as well. The more the body is kept from declining, the younger, more vibrant, more unspent and free of wrinkles it is—that is, the more it corresponds with our public and personal ideals—the more it is made into a fetish and elevated as idol. We are prepared to invest, individually and collectively, huge sums of money in the body and its smooth functioning, and, as a result, the costs of health care have skyrocketed. We let medical experts supervise our physical well-being and restore it from the least impairment through necessary, and sometimes not so necessary, medical interventions and medicines. We feed our bodies granola and the highest quality foods and stuff them with extra vitamins as a precaution so that they lack nothing. They are clothed in velvet and silk, washed daily in bubble baths, perfumed and deodorized, and allowed to work in air-conditioned rooms. Our bodies are protected from injury through protective equipment and laws of every type. We lay them down to sleep on special mattresses in hygienic beds. We go jogging and join antismoking campaigns and indulge our bodies with leisure time as well as summer and winter vacations. In between we tan our bodies under the noonday sun, probably hoping for a permanent tan and an improved immune system.

All of this has enabled us to extend the "best" years of life physically by a substantial amount. It is possible for us today, as never before in history, to stop irreparable damage to health or even to prevent a "premature" death. Death at age forty is no longer taken for granted as it was for centuries. It strikes us instead as a kind of tragic accident. Because it seldom happens, it not only attracts attention but also creates dismay and resentment. "Why?" the obituary notices now ask reproachfully.

I often suspect that the result of this undeniable success has not been simply to postpone our physical decline and death. Subconsciously we have long since begun to confuse illusion with reality—indeed, to the same extent that we have successfully covered up, glossed over, or played down the frailties of our own bodies—and started to consider ourselves virtually immortal, at least during our best years. By rigidly distancing ourselves from death and dying in our everyday lives, by removing the dying as much as possible from our visual surroundings, we have further encouraged this trend. Without a doubt our best years are incomparably more secure than a few generations ago. Simple biological existence is virtually guaranteed to last many more years than before. A long life expectancy has become a standard, virtually a common expectation; it is a life span available to each and every person, and not simply for the privileged few or for those who have been otherwise spared from plague, famine, and war.

But all of this has not made us immortal. Despite it all, a rude awakening awaits us, at the very latest when we are repeatedly forced to attend funerals. Then the fragile myth of immortality bursts like a bubble. We are not satisfied with the fact that death and dying are no longer a part of our lives, however, and that death no longer marks a brief interruption, a passage, in the whole course of life as it did in the past. Death and dying seem to take place in a vacuum today. During the best of our years, when the myth of our own immortality has its strongest appeal, death is simply dissociated from the rest of life in a way not unlike our rationalizing away the afterlife. But when the good years are behind us, our lives end somewhere in a no-man's-land. People are written off when their physical deterioration can no longer be masked or when they have suffered an irreversible loss of health and are warned of their decline, when they have slipped beyond medical help and their biological existence can no longer be guaranteed. The people who inhabit such bodies become a caste of untouchables or, at the minimum, social and physical incompetents. Death begins then in piecemeal fashion: first professionally; then within the family and the community; and then, at the end and long overdue, the biological end finally comes. It now usually slips in silently when one is all alone in a room for the dying in some establishment for the dying. At this point the end comes to a life that in many ways has long since been over. It is hardly an encouraging prospect for the future, since no one can be certain that his case will be any different. Is it any wonder that we have such a difficult time coming to terms with life when it ends up slipping away unnoticed and forgotten?

Despite these unpleasant prospects, I do not believe we should try to turn back the wheel of time in order to rehabilitate a "good old-fashioned death" and restore the lost faith in the eternal. Every historical period is unique. Each age, once it has passed, can never be brought back. Earlier chapters should have made it clear, moreover, that a "good old-fashioned death" never existed in the way that many people nostalgically seem to assume today. Even though there were no rooms in hospitals and nursing homes where every man and woman died as they do today, a closer examination has shown that the "peaceful death in the beloved circle of one's family" was a myth. First, about a quarter of all deaths involved infants less than a year old, and they could hardly have been aware of "the intimacy of family life." Second, many adults died during epidemics, that is, they died quickly from infectious diseases and were hardly allowed time to take their leave of life peacefully. Often there may well have been no one to say good-bye to, since the rest of the family, friends, and relatives had died from the disease a few days before. Besides, the danger of infection was hardly an incentive to treat the dying with any particular kindness. Finally, we should not forget the miserable burials that frequently took place under these wretched circumstances. Given the fact that so many people died within such a short period, one could never exclude the possibility that one might be thrown into a mass grave along with a number of other bodies. There may not even have been enough time to bury someone before decomposition had set in! Was this a "good old-fashioned death"? Only a few people were ever granted it!

However difficult current conditions may be, however, one need not be a historian to know that this situation cannot last forever. Everybody knows this from experience.

Looking into the future, I believe that two tasks await us. Both involve compensating for the twofold loss we suffered when death was twice disassociated from our lives. The first task is for us to remain human right to the end of life, even at an advanced age, by making the last stage of life once again an integral part of the whole life cycle. There is the prospect that a solution could be found to this in the not-too-distant future. If what we said above is true, namely, that today's piecemeal death is closely connected with the decline of the body, its deterioration beyond the point of medical recovery, and the marked dependency on others associated with this decline, then a decisive breakthrough would occur if the two leading causes of death today, heart and circulatory diseases and cancer, were not simply brought under control but were also not immediately replaced by other diseases as in the past.

The result could be a swift and natural death in old age without a long and lingering illness, dying slowly and longing for the end. A series of studies point explicitly in this direction.[2] The fact that this task is in no way a strictly medical, biological, or genetic one must be emphasized. It is a problem that scientists working in their ivory towers cannot solve alone. Instead it must be solved jointly with other students of the "human sciences"—from psychologists to theologians—as well as with the people most directly affected, the aging and the elderly themselves. The solution cannot simply be to add more years to life. The primary goal must be more than that: to fill the final years with so much life that they acquire value equal to the "best" years of life, that is, that they all be good years, that the life cycle remain full of *life* right to the end.

The second task is much more difficult. Even if our wish were to come true and we enjoyed good health right to the very end of life in our seventies or eighties, the fact still remains that for most of us death still marks the absolute end. The aging process, even if it takes place in good health, brings us unavoidably to this terminus and leads to an inescapable fate. It seems possible that fear and anxiety about death and dying will increase in those who no longer chronically suffer and no longer long for death as a release from "the burdens of age."

Let us grant that the historian, based on his specialized knowledge and experience, can generally pass judgment about ages that are past. The key theme of this book then has been that our forebears did not do so badly in their efforts to survive a difficult world constantly threatened by plague, hunger, and war. They created kinds of stability that lasted for generations, norms that remained valid for centuries. These frameworks that supported life not only astonish us and demand our respect, they also give us pause to reflect. To put it briefly, one could say that they had it worse than we did with the not-so-difficult things in life—above all, when it came to securing a physical existence—but that the really difficult things in life, death and dying especially, were not as difficult for them. The main reason for this lay in the fact that their worldview reached further than simply the end of life on this earth. The everyday worlds of our ancestors may have been smaller in terms of space and shorter in time, their horizons narrower than our own. Their lives could end at any moment. But these physical limits—the next hill and the edge of a great and dense forest, as well as death and dying— weren't the same as *real* boundaries and *the end of life*. In terms of space and time their worlds reached much further than this. For they did not always have to keep their eyes on the ground or their gaze on the next mountain or the edge of the forest. They could also turn their gaze boldly (or perhaps anxiously) upward to the Sun and the Moon, the stars and the planets, the rain clouds and storms that were approaching. For present life in a peasant world, all of this was certainly of greater importance than the question of who lived on the other side of the next mountain or forest. Likewise, death and dying were accepted as a natural and understandable break, as a passage, but this in no way distracted the view of what was to come: continuation of life everlasting.

This worldview offered enough room for the macrocosm as well as the microcosm of our forebears and allowed for an unhindered and continuous interplay between them. Within this context there was a time for everything: a time for sowing and one for reaping, a time for work and one for rest, a time for marriage and love and another in which one denied the desires of the flesh.[3] But it also included a time for death and dying: room for one's own death as well as for the deaths of others, whether close or far away, for the enormous infant mortality as well as for the massive die-offs during epidemics. The only thing that was feared was the unexpected death, the sudden death while in a state of sin, and, among children, death before baptism. But even here an aide had been created. Back then infants who were stillborn or who died before the baptism could often return to life for a few moments and be baptized in this state. In this way the door to eternity was kept open.

Fear was certainly present everywhere at that time: daily, nightly, hourly. It was a fear of concrete things: plague, hunger, war, bad harvests, lightning, cattle disease, robbery on the way to the market in the city, souls who were not yet saved and spirits who returned from the dead, curses and the magical sayings of evil-minded people. But there was no room within this worldview to suffer from a general anxiety. The worldview was all-inclusive, and there- fore everything within it was provided for.

It is exactly this that we have lost and this that explains why we have so much more difficulty with the most difficult issues in life than our ancestors did. We no longer have a coherent worldview, let alone one that includes and makes provisions for death and dying. Physically speaking we see much farther than our ancestors did. We peer from taller buildings into the distance or look out from airplanes across whole stretches of land, across hills and valleys; we also see farther simply because every shortsighted person has glasses. By means of television we can look into the most distant corners of the earth, and with telescopes or by means of satellites we gaze right to the end of the universe. And, vice versa, with electron microscopes we gaze at the smallest parts of our microcosm.

But all of this television watching, gazing through telescopes, or peering through microscopes doesn't create a worldview. And we are equally unlikely to get one from more detailed or more colorful pictures from yet more distant satellites. Despite all of these instruments and technical aides, we don't see as far as our forbears did, and what we do see cannot be fitted into a larger and more meaningful context. We look around the world in hundreds of ways, but we don't see *the world*. With great clarity we see thousands of colorful and tiny parts of a mosaic, but we don't see the picture of which they form the smallest part and for which they actually exist. Despite our busyness, or even because of it, we scurry around in a confusing way, letting red, yellow, and green lights direct us in the stop-and-go traffic of life. And in the end we drive off with no purpose at all.

Sometimes we become dimly aware of the dangerous situation we have maneuvered ourselves into through the loss of a sustaining and integrated worldview. This could easily usher in an age of false prophets. Against this background my point once again is not to long for a return to that lost world and its worldview. They are irretrievably gone. Even if we wanted to we could no longer live that way. Our world *has* microscopes and satellites. It consists of atoms, genes, and cells. It can be observed and supervised from the outside, and, for the first time, it is completely destructible. It *has* cathedrals of learning, with all of the books that belong to them, instead of cathedrals of faith with their bell towers that ring out the time. And even though we are not all intellectuals, we are still so intellectualized that we always want to know the *reasons* for things. As long as the world and the fate of people lay in God's hands, as our ancestors believed, he was both beginning and end, the origin and the goal. Why did anyone need to ask for more "explanations"? Today we *have* these explanations, but for all of that we can no longer find a beginning or an end.

Notes

1 The Little World of Johannes Hooss

1. See the references to the sources in figure 2. A number of details have been taken from the prefaces to the genealogical books of the Schwalm by Gottfried Ruetz, the pastor familiar with the locality; from the annual journal about the Schwalm region; and from the family correspondence of the Hooss family.

2. See Bernhard Martin, "Die Mundarten," in *Geschichtlicher Atlas von Hessen* (Marburg: Landesamt für geschichtliche Landeskunde, 1960–78), 43.

3. This inheritance contract of November 29, 1724, is published in *Familienbrief der Sippe Hoos, Hooss usw.* 3, no. 7 (June 1939): 32.

4. For the details see the local genealogical books of Gabelbach and Hesel: Franz Hauf, *Ortssippenbuch Gabelbach, Landkreis Augsburg in Schwaben* (Frankfurt am Main: Zentralstelle für Personen- und Familiengeschichte, 1975); and Ludwig Janssen and Hans Rudolf Manger, *Die Familien der Kirchengemeinde Hesel (1643–1900)*, Ostfrieslands Ortssippenbücher, vol. 8 (Zurich: Verlag Ostfriesische Landschaft, 1974).

2 A Multitude of Little Worlds

1. At the moment the collection is available in two solid and inexpensive paperback editions. One is published with a preface by the Hessian folklorist Ingeborg Weber-Kellermann as Insel-Taschenbücher, nos. 112–14, 5th ed. (1981); the other is edited by the German literary historian and folklorist Heinz Rölleke in Reclams Universal-Bibliothek, nos. 3191–93 (Stuttgart, 1980).

2. A number of translations of Perrault's fairy tales are available in English. See, for example, Charles Perrault, *The Fairy Tales of Charles Perrault,* trans. Angela Carter (London: Gollancz, 1977).

3. Edith Ennen and Günter Wiegelmann, eds., *Festschrift Matthias Zender* (Bonn, 1972), I, 395–96.

4. A good introduction to this problem is the study by the Geneva historian Alfred Perrenoud, "Malthusianisme et protestantisme: 'Un modèle démographique weberien,'" *Annales: E.S.C.* 29 (1974): 975–88.

3 Dangers

1. Günther Franz, *Der Dreißigjährige Krieg und das deutsche Volk,* 4th ed. (Stuttgart: Gustav Fischer, 1979), 8; and for the higher losses in Württemberg, 52–55 and figure 14.

2. Franz Xaver Mezler, *Versuch einer medizinischen Topographie von Sigmaringen* (Freiburg, 1822), 154–61.

3. Assembled from the medical topographies of P. J. Horsch on the region of Würzburg, *Versuch einer Topographie der Stadt Würzburg, in Beziehung auf den allgemeinen*

Gesundheitszustand und die dahin zielenden Anstalten (Arnstadt: Langbein & Klüger, 1805), 43; J. Schneider on the region of Ettlingen (1818), 133; F. Pauli on the region around Landau, *Medicinische Statistik der Stadt und Bundesfestung Landau in Rheinbayern* (Landau: Geiger, 1831), 63; and by A. Martin on the district of Au near Munich, *Topographie und Statistik des Königlichen Bayerischen Landgerichts Au bei Münchien* (Munich: Franz, 1837), 80–81.

4. For an accessible and unabridged translation of this classic see Hans Jackob Christoffel von Grimmelshausen, *An Unabridged Translation of Simplicius Simplicissimus* Lanham, Md.: University Press of America, 1986).

5. Bernard of Clairvaux, "Apologia ad Guillelmum Abbatem," in *Sancti Bernardi Opera* 3: 29.14–25. With reference to the translation by Diether Rudloff in *Das Basler Münster* (Basel: Münsterbaukommision, 1982), 149.

6. Take note of two recent French works that are concerned with these kinds of questions, each of them examining a small region. Alain Lottin, *Chavatte, ouvrier lillois: Un contemporain de Louis XIV* (Paris: Flammarion, 1979). Pierre Ignace Chavatte (1633–93) was a weaver in the northern French city of Lille. He left behind an extensive diary from the years 1657–93 ("Livre de raison") that served Lottin as his main source. Elisabeth Claverie and Pierre Lamaison, *L'impossible mariage: Violence et parenté en Gévaudan, XVIIe, XVIIIe et XIXe siècles* (Paris: Hachette, 1982). In contrast to the historian Lottin, Claverie and Lamaison are ethnologists. The region of Gévaudan in the south of France, modern-day Lozère, is their area of study, and their main object of study is the so-called "Ousta," that is, the family property, the farm. In order to keep it intact and improve its standing, the inhabitants used every means available, from well-devised marriage strategies all the way to slander and violence against competitors who stood in the way. Here "violence" became a structural component that had a thoroughly positive value.

4   *The Search for Stability*

1. Gottfried Ruetz, *Deutsches Geschlechterbuch,* vol. 176, Hessisches Geschlechterbuch, vol. 21 (Limburg an der Lahn: Verlag Starke, 1977), 67.

2. From a text of a funeral sermon given in 1612 for Jan von Döberitz, the former cellar master at the court of Elector Johann Georg of Brandenburg. Source: Datenbank der Marburger Forschungsstelle für Personalschriften, Leichenpredigt no. 1011, code no. 1055 (= Subjects). Kindly provided by the director of the research center, Dr. Rudolf Lenz.

3. I am thankful to the folklorist Professor Dr. Matthias Zender, Bonn, for this written and verbal information and especially for unpublished materials and citations from the *Atlas für Deutsche Volkskunde.*

4. See Alain Croix, *La Bretagne aux 16e et 17e siècles: La vie—la mort—la foi* (Paris: Maloine, 1981), 1085. The provocative thesis about the supposed absence of maternal instincts before the romantic discovery of maternal and paternal love is primarily found in Elisabeth Badinter, *Mother Love: Myth and Reality: Motherhood in Modern History* (New York: Macmillan, 1981).

5. Illustrated and explained in Arthur Imhof, ed., *Der Mensch und sein Körper: Von der Antike bis heute* (Munich: C. H. Beck, 1983), 27.

6. The details about children's life signs in Ursberg are in Georg Rückert, "Brauchtum und Diözesanrituale im Aufklärungszeitalter" and "Zur Taufe toter Kinder," in *Volk und Volkstum: Jahrbuch für Volkskunde* 2 (1937): 297–305, 343–46.

7. For details see Oskar Vasella, "Über die Taufe totgeborener Kinder in der Schweiz," *Zeitschrift für Schweizerische Kirchengeschichte* 60 (1966): 1–75. I am grateful to Dr. Christine Burckhardt-Seebass and Dr. Theo Gantner of the Schweizerisches Museum für Volkskunde in Basel for additional information and references.

8. Walter Muschg, ed., *Jeremias Gotthelfs Werke in zwanzig Bänden,* vols. 1 and 2: *Leiden und Freuden eines Schulmeisters* (Basel: Birkhäuser Verlag, 1948) (originally published in 1838–39). Chapters 14 and 16 are in vol. 3, pp. 158–80. Concerning this novel see the introduction by the editor in vol. 2, vii–xxvi. [The passages in strong Bernese German have been translated into standard English. Other passages from the original have been left out or shortened without further note.—Trans.]

9. The emphasis is my own. Is this not a grand summing up of the state of affairs involving children's life signs from Oberbüren, the consequences of its prohibition, and its survival in the collective memory? Gotthelf needs three complete pages for it!

10. Max Weber, "Science as a Vocation," in H. H. Gerth and C. Wright Mills, eds., *From Max Weber: Essays in Sociology* (New York: Oxford University Press, 1946), 139.

11. Carl G. Jung, "Approaching the Unconscious," in his *Man and His Symbols* (New York: Doubleday, 1964), 95.

12. Martin Buber, "Der Mensch und sein Gebilde," *Die Neue Rundschau* 66 (1955): 6.

13. The section on astronomy and physics in the Hessisches Landesmuseum in Kassel is worth seeing if one has the opportunity. See Ludolf von Mackensen, *Die erste Sternwarte Europas mit ihren Instrumenten und Uhren: 400 Jahre Jost Bürgi in Kassel,* 2d ed. (Munich: Callwey Verlag, 1982).

14. Anyone wanting to become familiar with this problem can begin with one of the numerous exhibition catalogues that repeatedly take up and depict the theme of the medieval and early modern worldview becuse it is so fundamentally alien to modern viewers. Among the newer catalogues one could name: Staatliche Museen Preußischer Kulturbesitz Berlin, *Katalog zur Ausstellung "Christus und Maria: Menschensohn und Gottesmutter" analäßlich des 86. Deutschen Katholikentages 1980 im Zusammenhang mit der Ausstellung "Bilder vom Menschen in der Kunst des Abendlandes"* (1980) (especially Herbert Schade, "Der 'Himmlische Mensch': Zur anthropologischen Struktur des biblischen Menschenbildes in der Kunst," 19–58); Bibliothèque Nationale Paris, *Katalog zur Aussstellung: "La médecine médiévale à travers les manuscrits de la Bibliothèque National"* (1982); Herzog August Bibliothek Wolfenbüttel, *Katalog zur Ausstellung "Pharmazie und der gemeine Mann: Hausarznei und Apotheke in deutschen Schriften der frühen Neuzeit"* (1983) (especially Irmgard Müller, "Arzneien für den 'gemeinen Mann': Zur Vorstellung materieller und immaterieller Wirkungen stofflicher Substrate in der Medizin des 16. und 17. Jahrhunderts," 27–34; and Wolf-Dieter Müller-Jahncke, "Medizin und Pharmazie in Almanachen und Kalendern der frühen Neuzeit," 35–42). In addition, see the authoritative overview of Karl Ed. Rothschuh, *Konzepte der Medizin in Vergangenheit und Gegenwart* (Stuttgart: Hippok-

rates Verlag, 1978) (see especially chapters 2–9 on iatro-demology, iatro-theology, astromedical-iatro-astrology, iatro-magic, humoral pathology, iatro-phyics, and iatro-chemisty, 21–290). Very stimulating in this regard is A. J. Gurevich, *Categories of Medieval Culture,* trans. G. L. Campbell (London: Routledge & Kegan Paul, 1985); and Paul Sébillot, *Le folklore de France: Le ciel, la nuit et les esprits de l'air,* 2d ed. (Paris: Imago, 1982).

15. 20 minutes times 72 equals 1,440 minutes, or 24 hours. In technical language this phenomenon is called precession (Latin = advance).

16. For those who are interested, the slim volume by Bernard Lovell is a suitable introduction, *In the Center of Immensities* (London: Hutchinson, 1979). More thorough and accompanied by a number of figures and illustrations is the book of Edward R. Harrison, also historically oriented, *Cosmology: The Science of the Universe* (Cambridge: Cambridge University Press, 1981). This work is by far the best "popular scientific" work on cosmology at present and goes back to lectures for an audience from all the disciplines at the University of Massachusetts. It assumes only an elementary knowledge of physics, but challenges one to constant thought and reflection. This is not easy reading, but it is richly rewarding.

17. In this case according to *The Shepherd's Calendar* from Rostock for 1523. Source: Herzog August Bibliothek Wolfenbüttel, *Der Schapherders Kalender* (sig. 36 Astronomica).

5   *Why Life Is So Hard Today*

1. I would like to thank the director of the Marburg Forschungsstelle für Personalschriften, Dr. Rudolf Lenz, for his obliging preparation of these computer printouts and other information. For an introduction to the work of this research institution and the various research possibilities using the funeral sermons, see a number of the collected works of Rudolf Lenz, especially *Leichenpredigten als Quelle historischer Wissenschaften,* vol. 1 (Cologne: Böhlau, 1975); vol. 2 (Marburg: Schwarz, 1979), and the series *Marburger Personalschriften-Forschungen* (Marburg: Schwarz, 1978).

2. See, for example, J. F. Fries and L. M. Crapo, *Vitality and Aging: Implications of the Rectangular Curve* (San Francisco: Freeman, 1981).

3. See the first volume in the triology by Jean-Louis Flandrin, *Un temps pour embrasser: Aux origines de la morale sexuelle occidentale (VIe-XI siècle)* (Paris: Seuil, 1983), which is thoroughly influenced by the idea of the rhythm of time.

Guide to Further Reading

ANY GUIDE to reading about everyday life in early modern Europe is selective and reflects only one of many possible approaches to a rich and complex literature. The books below are recommended for the general reader. In addition to a few books of a general nature, they focus on three subjects particularly important in this book: the family and life cycle, the world of the village, and popular mentalities or culture. Most are also gateways to further reading, with bibliographies on specialized topics.

One of the best places to begin is the first volume of Fernand Braudel's magisterial study of civilization and capitalism in Europe, *The Structures of Everyday Life: The Limits of the Possible,* vol. 1 of *Civilization and Capitalism, 15th–18th Centuries,* trans. Siân Reynolds (Berkeley: Univ. of California Press, 1992). Braudel describes the material culture underpinning everyday life, the slow pace of change, and the limits facing premodern people. Drawing on a generation or more of scholarship in social history, Henry Kamen identifies the major trends that contributed to uncertainty and conflict in everyday life in his book *European Society, 1500–1700* (London: Hutchinson, 1984). For an introduction to popular culture in this period one should start with Peter Burke's broad-ranging book *Popular Culture in Early Modern Europe* (New York: Harper Torchbooks, 1978). For a general portrait of the climate of fear in the early modern world one should read Jean Delumeau's *Sin and Fear: The Emergence of a Western Guilt Culture, 13th–18th Centuries,* trans. Eric Nicholson (New York: St. Martin's Press, 1990).

Concerning the history of the family and the life cycle, the most readable introduction is still Peter Laslett's pioneering study *The World We Have Lost: England before the Industrial Age* (London: Scribner, 1965), updated and revised in *The World We Have Lost: Further Explored* (New York: Scribner, 1984). Even though it first appeared thirty years ago, when the historical study of the family and the household had only just begun, Laslett's book retains its freshness and insightfulness. To find one's way through the vast literature on the family and household today one needs a good guide, and two are recommended: Andrejs Plakans, *Kinship in the Past: An Anthropology of European Family Life, 1500–1900* (Oxford: B. Blackwell, 1984); and Beatrice

Gottlieb, *The Family in the Western World from the Black Death to the Industrial Age* (Oxford: Oxford Univ. Press, 1993).

For readers wanting to strike out into the field of population history and the life cycle, the best survey is still Michael Flinn's remarkably concise little book *The European Demographic System, 1500–1820* (Baltimore: Johns Hopkins Univ. Press, 1981), even though it is now dated in some respects. For vivid accounts of death and dying, two books come to mind: Philip Ziegler's story of the plague, *The Black Death* (New York, John Day, 1969); and the breathtaking vista by Phillipe Ariès, *The Hour of Our Death,* trans. Helen Weaver (New York: Oxford Univ. Press, 1991).

Most Europeans lived out their lives within the world of a village, and one therefore cannot go far in learning about everyday life without exploring these microcosms of the early modern world. A veritable forest of books has grown up around this subject, but, happily, several books can lead one down the main paths and introduce life in a small, face-to-face community. The following two books depict life in modern villages, but they do so with such vividness and clarity, even poignancy, that they can serve as starting points for understanding. Robert Blythe's description of life in an English village, *Akenfield: Portrait of an English Village* (New York: Pantheon Books, 1969), has a timelessness and poetic quality. One can learn about the precariousness of life and the delicate balance between land, humans, and animals in the village from Robert M. Netting's study of a Swiss alpine village, *Balancing on an Alp: Ecological Change and Continuity in a Swiss Mountain Community* (Cambridge: Cambridge Univ. Press, 1981).

Turning to the early modern period, studies of the French village stand out as the most imaginative and groundbreaking over the last thirty years. Emmanuel Le Roy Ladurie and Pierre Goubert, grand masters of the historian's craft, lay out the broad patterns of change in two books: *The French Peasantry, 1450–1660,* trans. Alan Sheridan (Berkeley: Univ. of California Press, 1987), and *The French Peasantry in the Seventeenth Century,* trans. Ian Patterson (Cambridge: Cambridge Univ. Press, 1986). One can savor the richly complex tale of one peasant and his village in Natalie Zemon Davis, *The Return of Martin Guerre* (Cambridge: Harvard Univ. Press, 1983). For a panoramic view of the rise and decline of the peasantry from the Middle Ages to the present day we now have Werner Rösener's survey in English, *The Peasantry in Europe,* trans. Thomas M. Barker (Oxford: Oxford Univ. Press, 1993).

The most difficult subjects to study are the cultural, spiritual, and intellectual worlds of everyday people. In addition to reading Peter Burke's book, one might reflect on the idea of collective mentalities—those ideas, emotions, fantasies, and fears shared by many people in a culture at any given time. Robert Mandrou introduces the concept nicely in his *Introduction to Modern France, 1500–1640: An Essay in Historical Psychology,* trans. R. E. Hallmark (London: Edward Arnold, 1975). Broader still, and interesting for the way they sketch out archaic worldviews and vast associative ways of thinking, are the two books by Aaron I. Gurevich, *Categories of Medieval Culture,* trans. G. L. Campbell (London: Routledge & Kegan Paul, 1985); and *Historical Anthropology of the Middle Ages,* trans. Jana Howlett (Chicago: Univ. of Chicago Press, 1992). Naturally one cannot explore this topic without discovering that early Europeans thought differently about magic, science, and religion. Keith Thomas's *Religion and the Decline of Magic* (New York: Scribner, 1971) remains the most important book on this subject.

Readers wishing to explore specific regions of Europe may wish to approach this task by pairing a general survey with a case study. For Germany, for example, one might acquire a general picture from R. Po-Chia Hsia's *Social Discipline in the Reformation: Central Europe, 1550–1750* (London: Routledge, 1989), and then turn to Michael Kunze's *Highroad to the Stake: A Tale of Witchcraft,* trans. William E. Yuill (Chicago: Univ. of Chicago Press, 1987), a gripping and fascinating story of one peasant family accused of witchcraft. A similar approach comes to mind for France: Robert Muchembled's essay on France, *Popular Culture and Elite Culture in France, 1400–1750,* trans. Lydia Cochrane (Baton Rouge: Louisiana State Univ. Press, 1985); and Natalie Zemon Davis's lively reflections about popular writings, rituals, and beliefs in *Society and Culture in Early Modern France* (Stanford: Stanford Univ. Press, 1974). Carlo Ginzburg has written an intriguing story about one peasant and his world in *The Cheese and the Worms: The Cosmos of a Sixteenth-Century Miller,* trans. John and Anne Tedeschi (Baltimore: Johns Hopkins Univ. Press, 1980).

Index

Page numbers in italics refer to illustrations.

197